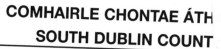

TWIN TRACKS

THE AUTOBIOGRAPHY

ROGER BANNISTER

TWIN TRACKS

The Robson Press

First published in Great Britain in 2014
This edition published in 2015 by
The Robson Press (an imprint of Biteback Publishing Ltd)
Westminster Tower
3 Albert Embankment
London SE1 7SP

ISBN 978-1-84954-836-6

10 9 8 7 6 5 4 3 2 1

A CIP catalogue record for this book is available from the British Library.

Set in Baskerville

Printed and bound in Great Britain by
CPI Group (UK) Ltd, Croydon CR0 4YY

*To my beloved family and all those good
friends who have so enriched our lives.*

Contents

Preface

I remember vividly a moment as a child when I stood barefoot on firm dry sand by the sea.

The air had a special quality. The sound of breakers on the shore shut out all others. I looked up at the clouds, like great white-sailed galleons, chasing proudly inland. I looked down at the regular ripples on the sand and could not absorb so much beauty. I was taken aback – each of the myriad particles of sand was perfect in its way. I looked more closely, hoping perhaps that my eyes might detect some flaw. But for once there was nothing to detract from this feeling of closeness to nature.

In this supreme moment I leapt in sheer joy and started to run. I was startled and frightened by the tremendous excitement that so few steps could create. I glanced round uneasily to see if anyone was watching. A few more steps – self-consciously now and firmly gripping the original excitement. I was running now, and a fresh rhythm entered my body. I was no longer conscious of my movement. I discovered a new unity with nature. I had found a new source of power – a source I never dreamt existed.

Chapter 1

Growing Up in Harrow

I struggled into the world on 23 March 1929. Unlike most babies then, I was not born at home, but in a midwife's house in the road where we lived, which had been converted into a small nursing home. Our road was lined with redbrick Edwardian terraced houses. Each had two floors and tiny front and back gardens. The speculative builder had embellished the roof corners with some fancy shaped tiles and the upper section of each front door had an elaborate stained-glass panel with a stylised picture of mountains and a rainbow. Except that one day, aged about three, I found myself in my pram outside the front door, restrained by much-chewed leather straps, frustrated by boredom and demanding attention. I must have been provoked beyond fury, for I hurled a Marmite jar, apparently then my favourite toy, through this fancy glass panel. Some might have predicted for me a future as a shot-putter, not a runner. To this day, the coloured panel has never been restored to its full glory and remains dull, frosted glass.

Discipline was paramount in many homes then; eating and sleeping were closely regulated. Truby King, the then guru on childcare, warned mothers against picking up their crying babies, lest the baby became a spoilt child. Another strange myth persisted that, if encouraged to walk too much before the age of three, children's legs might be overstrained. My mother had no truck with such myths. 'It's nonsense,' she said. 'Your legs will only get stronger the more you use them.' How sad that some pampered children were prammed around until they were almost three. Even the photographs of royal children show them being wheeled about in Kensington Gardens in the Rolls-Royce of perambulators, the Silver Cross. Rickets, which caused children's bones to become weak and bowed, was known several years before my birth to be due to a lack of vitamin D. My mother said, 'Yes you do have to swallow this halibut-liver oil. I've made it nice for you on a lump of sugar.' Ugh – that never did disguise the horrible taste.

Even on hot summer nights an early bedtime was enforced. As I lay sleepless, looking at the cracks in the ceiling, I imagined monsters and grotesque shapes coming to life. Neurologists have yet to understand why our long-distant memory is threaded through with such strong emotion, in my case born of frustration. I can still remember as a child a vivid feeling that there must be more to life than this, but I had not the slightest idea where that magic place might be found.

Years later, when my wife Moyra and I had our own children, Chris Brasher's mother, a most kind and maternal woman, was our neighbour. She recalled her own anguish in the 1920s when she paced up and down outside her sons' rooms, hearing them cry bitterly, but not daring to go in and comfort them. Our own generation, partly under the benign influence of Dr Spock, reacted strongly against this, so Moyra always picked up and comforted a crying child, as indeed Mrs Brasher did when she became a grandmother. Our mothers can hardly be blamed for adhering to the bleak and misguided view of childcare. Every generation of parents clings to its nostrums in the hope that they will succeed where their own parents failed.

When they learn that I was born in Harrow, most people think of the great public school founded in the sixteenth century and attended by Winston Churchill. But my family had no connection with the school, except for the first road we lived in being called Butler Road after a famous headmaster. Presumably the local council, when searching for street names, had exhausted their lists of English authors and Crimean victories and so turned closer to home.

Harrow for us was a part of Betjeman's Metroland, houses built to absorb London's expansion during the years of Edwardian prosperity; then followed a second building boom between the wars. For some, the area embodied an escape from the inner London slum clearance; for us it was a formulaic group of streets, radiating from the railway station, with a Victorian primary school, perhaps a recreation ground with swings, a boating pond, some tennis courts, and also, if you were very lucky, a public library.

My father had bought the house in Butler Road for £700 in 1925. It was then customary to secure a house before marriage. Given his horror of indebtedness, he bought it outright from his savings, accrued from fifteen years' work as a clerical officer at the Board of Trade in London. His caution was balanced by generosity and, when my sister and I came to buy our own houses, he gave us substantial help. By then, in the 1950s, every sensible person was advised to buy a house and take on any mortgage they could afford, later selling in a rising market, and so move up the housing ladder. But in the 1920s, with the slump approaching, there was no certainty that house prices would rise.

It may seem strange to people today for a man to buy his own house, to bring his newlywed down from Lancashire, to be able to sustain them both and their children, and all in order that his bride could become a full-time wife and mother. It will puzzle them as to how the middle classes then considered this pattern of life fulfilling. My daughter once exploded with incomprehension that it should have been so. Freedom gives a mother time to read, to think, to exercise, to go to classes, to fulfil her educational gifts. It can only be achieved when women are liberated from the grind of juggling home and full-time work, a dilemma that is with us still. Then, the fear of indebtedness haunted those who had seen the boom and bust of the cotton industry, and my father was no exception. He must have been a proud man to bring his bride from the north to a home free of mortgage.

When we were buying our first house in 1963, my father said, 'This is a mistake. In my day in our family it was a point of honour to save enough money to buy *without a mortgage* and bring one's bride only when the transaction was completed. *Autres temps, autre mœurs.*' We blithely plunged on, buying the house of our dreams with a mortgage. Looking back, my father was half right. We were in the midst of the terrible financial turmoil of the 1970s monetary crisis, with a grotesquely high tax rate of 87 per cent and a stock market fall from 900 to 200. There was an equally grotesque rate of inflation. Then we had a serious car accident, stopping me working, and so we were forced to downsize so we could make ends meet. It was, to borrow a phrase from our own Queen, an *annus horribilus*. I said to Moyra, 'Darling, there is no alternative. We'll have to move. The school fees have rocketed. Unless the children go to the local comprehensive there's no way we can stay in this house.'

However, back in 1935, when I was five and just starting at

the elementary school, we were moving up in the world, to 89 Whitmore Road, a semi-detached house with a garage. It had been built ten years before, on a wider road which was half a mile from our old house and adjoined the Harrow School cricket ground and fields with cows that provided the daily milk for the metropolis. It had larger front and back gardens and the road was lined by grass verges with small trees. The house cost £1,500 freehold.

My father particularly enjoyed gardening and growing vegetables, apples and pears, which supplemented food rationing during the war. I never liked gardening. For a start, I found the whole activity stunningly boring, perhaps lacking the patience to wait for the seasons to pass before reaping the benefits of such mundane labour.

A visit to relatives in Lancashire gave me the dream of acquiring untold riches. They kept chickens and sold both the birds and their eggs for profit, as did many families during the war. It would have been a delight to have fresh eggs instead of the wartime dried egg powder, but any idea of a chicken run in our back garden was quashed by my father.

While the Butler Road house had been dark and cramped, the house in Whitmore Road was definitely a notch up. I could gaze from my bedroom windows across the Harrow School playing fields. My father could delight in a fair-sized back garden.

One evening I heard my father in serious tones talking to my mother: 'I'm transferring from the Board of Trade to the Exchequer and Audit Department. Where I am, the men who served in France are being promoted over my head and my service in Ireland doesn't seem to count. That's why I am changing to a department that seems to be expanding, though by moving I shall have to start again at the bottom.' From this superior dwelling

I had my first lesson in class distinctions. Between Butler Road
and the new house there lay a pre-war council housing estate.
This was built for families who were moved out of the London
slums and so the children were, in my parents' words, 'rough'.
My sister and I were warned not to stray too near this estate
and I suppose this stirred my first fears of danger and violence,
from which, if I broke their injunction, my parents could not
protect me.

In 1935, my father duly made his transfer to the Exchequer and
Audit Department. This came with one exciting reward: he was
appointed the junior member of a team to inspect the accounts
of the Canadian government, which, as a dominion at the time,
submitted itself periodically to British audit. He travelled across
the Atlantic on the *Queen Mary*, in cabin (second) class, as a mark
of respect for the British civil service. To be properly attired,
he had to purchase his first dinner jacket, which the family all
admired. He sent back the menus, filling us with wonder at the
plethora of extravagant dishes.

At home in Harrow the food was simple but must have been
nutritious. Otherwise, despite fifteen years of food rationing
starting in 1939, I would hardly have grown to more than six
foot one inch, five inches taller than my father. Looking at the
photograph of Chris Brasher, Chris Chataway and me at the end
of the four-minute mile, it is noticeable that I am taller than
either of the Chrises, both of whom, one might feel, had the
supposed advantage of being at a prep school and a boarding
public school. From 1940, food rationing was strict, but my
mother cycled into Harrow every day with shopping bags on
her handlebars to buy fresh vegetables to supplement our diet,
especially the well-remembered spam and dried eggs. Our food,
except for bread, was all cooked or baked at home. We had no

refrigerator, only a walk-in larder with marble shelves. We never went to restaurants and so, when we went into London to visit the museums, frequently the Museum of Natural History, we always took our own sandwiches.

On rare occasions, as a treat, we bought muffins from a muffin man who would come down the road singing his street cry, balancing a tray on a curious flat-topped hat and ringing a hand bell. On Shrove Tuesday we had pancakes and I soon learnt how to toss them out of the pan to turn them without their hitting the ceiling. Christmas we usually celebrated with pork, home-made stuffing and apple sauce, rather than the traditional turkey, followed by mince pies and Christmas pudding.

In the week after Christmas we would go to a pantomime or a children's play such as *Peter Pan*, and it was when travelling on the London Underground that I was first shocked by the sight of helplessly drunk men and beggars. My first visit to the Harrow Cinema was to see *Treasure Island* when I was eight. My sister and I were enthralled to see a performance of the play *Charlie's Aunt* put on by the Harrow Boys' County School. Coming home from school one day, my sister Joyce ran towards me, her face all eagerness. 'This Christmas we've got tickets for a performance at the Harrow School Speech Room,' she said. This was the large auditorium where Winston Churchill returned to sing school songs, weeping with emotion. When my father got home he said, 'Yes, it's true, we're going to the *Messiah*.' Such treats were few and far between but gave us all the more delight when they came. It is hard to conceive now how great was our excitement over these trips to the cinema and rare live performances, which we talked about for days in anticipation.

On our birthdays our parents were good at giving children's parties in return for our having been invited to our friends' homes for their birthdays. My father presided over a Victorian magic lantern, which showed cartoons of animals and clowns. Decades later we experienced our grandchildren's ever so sophisticated parties in New York with a live Punch and Judy show. Moyra murmured to me, 'This is some contrast to our children's parties in which the games were "Sardines" and egg-and-spoon races and the going-home present was a balloon and a block of chocolate.' No musical chairs for them, or hunting for marbles round the house in such pristine, designer-furnished apartments. It would have been unthinkable for chocolatey fingers to leave their mark on the decor.

Imagine the elation of my first bicycle when I was aged seven. This opened up a whole new world of freedom and exploration. Until then, my energies were used for zipping along at speed on a ramshackle trolley, constructed from a wooden draining board and wheels from a tricycle, which my long-suffering father had watched me assemble with nails, not screws as he would have preferred. But it worked! As for many a boy, the allure of speed inspired me, though pushing myself along at up to ten miles an hour made me a menace to pedestrians.

All over England the middle classes forced their children to learn music almost as a rite of passage. It was my lot to be put to the piano, though from the very start I had the dread feeling I would never be any good at it. The climax came when my gaunt, lantern-jawed teacher had inveigled my eight-year-old self into playing at her end-of-term concert. Climbing the platform, sitting on the piano stool, I looked down at the keys as they danced before my uncomprehending eyes. On which note should I start? To my shame, the teacher eventually climbed the steps, placed my fingers where they should have been, and I stumbled through my piece. Even she had realised that we should part company.

Later, in Bath, I came 'under the baton' of an elderly spinster music teacher. She had thick, knitted woollen stockings and knitted skirts and blouse to match – boys notice these things. In her orchestra I was consigned to the back row of the second violins, where I could cause least damage, scratching away at some dull, repetitive dirge. I was next to the violas and a boy who, rather pretentiously, I thought, made endless comments to me about mistakes in the way the music was being conducted, whispering that the adagio was 'too slow' and so on. I should have known better – this viola player later became Professor of Music at Cambridge. I just knew that I would never excel with the instrument. It is a very great regret that I know so little about music, and I deeply envy our friends whose lives are so enriched by their musical knowledge. It has been a sad gap in my life, but on some occasions our friends invited us to the opera, in which we took much delight.

When I was seven, miracle of miracles, my father said, 'I've bought a car.' A box on wheels though it was, my father drove it back from Coventry after the briefest instructions – no driving test was necessary then. The next weekend we were off to admire Burnham Beeches in Hertfordshire, with sandwiches, cakes, lemonade, and tea in a thermos. There followed many jaunts which gave us children unfettered glee. My father's obsessive checking of the tyre pressure and level of water in the radiator seemed to take forever when we were so eager for the off. To his credit, he never had an accident or even a slight scratch on this treasured vehicle. How deeply shocked he must have been at my cavalier approach to its upkeep when, many years later, after I had left Oxford, I bought the car in the hope that he would stop worrying about it. I used it to zip my girlfriends about the countryside. Moyra remembers her first outing in it: we drove to St Mary's country convalescent home near Henley, singing all the way.

These days, an injured child would be taken to hospital at the drop of a hat. When I fell out of an elm tree, frightened of being caught trespassing by an irate farmer, I gashed my hand on barbed wire. Today it would have been sewn up after a tetanus injection at the A&E department; then, stoicism and home remedies were the order of the day. Many of my generation wince at the memory of iodine being poured on an open wound, causing sharp pain. I still have the scars. Many owe their health to the assiduous nursing of their mothers. There was often no other remedy than maternal attention through all those childhood illnesses which are virtually unknown today thanks to enormous medical advances in inoculation.

In those days, the terrors of poliomyelitis and tuberculosis (TB) were the most menacing. Every summer brought the threat of a polio epidemic. Victims who had respiratory weakness usually died, until iron lungs were invented. Deaths of both women and babies during childbirth and of school-age children, extremely rare today, were then an accepted part of life. In Whitmore Road, a pretty girl, a friend of mine with blonde curly hair, died within a week of contracting meningitis. Another girl caught rheumatic fever and disappeared from home for many months' treatment in a sanatorium.

I must have been a tiresome brother, because my sister Joyce still shivers at certain memories today – and never more so than at the recollection of the whole family nearly drowning on the river Wye. It is still a mystery that a reluctant boatman's warnings about the waves and current went unheeded by my parents. How could they have given way to my insistent importuning? Like the apothecary in *Romeo and Juliet*, the boatman gave us due warning but then accepted our money. Not twenty yards from the river's edge, the boat was being swamped by waves. My father rowed as best he could and four frightened Bannisters reached safety, wet and chastened. My love affair with boats and water resurfaced many years later when I owned a sailing cruiser. I learnt respect for the sea after some dire episodes.

In vivid contrast to our staid, heads-down and homework-encompassed lives, come the summer, for two weeks our whole lives changed. In 1942 we were told we were going back to Lynmouth, which we had visited before. On the great day of departure we were instructed, 'Anything you forget is your own fault and we are not coming back for it!' Joyce and I would be both nearly choking with excitement. Would the car get up Porlock Hill, a few miles from Lynmouth, which had given us trouble two years earlier? Porlock Hill had a 1 in 4 gradient, the steepest road in the country. The car with four of us might be so overloaded with luggage that we would have to get out and walk, as we had done before. Joyce and I almost burst with impatience as at last we crested the hill and could see ahead the town of Lynmouth. On the journey we were told the story of how Coleridge was interrupted from his dream about Kubla Khan by a stranger from Porlock, and how his vision could never be recalled.

The Holiday Fellowship centre at Lynmouth was a modest manor house. What a welcome they gave us: many old friends, the children we had met on previous holidays, and some new faces. Joyce and I rushed to scan the notice board for events over the next two weeks for children of our age. There were walks, table tennis competitions, musical evenings, dancing and acting – a whole world away from Harrow.

We never went to a hotel or boarding house. Each time, we

travelled to a Holiday Fellowship guesthouse in a different part
of the country, and a family centre was chosen where we would
meet other children. This was our first experience of the wider
social contact which was lacking at home. I still clearly recall
the various places around England where we holidayed: Marske,
Cromer, Hythe, Swanage and Lyme Regis, Teignmouth, the
Wye Valley and the Lake District. Our two favourite places were
Lynmouth in north Devon and Portinscale, close to Derwent
Water in the Lake District. The flavour of the holiday can be
judged from the blunt guidance note to 'guests' in a brochure,
which stated, 'the simpler you dress in the daytime and the
evenings the better'.

The Holiday Fellowship movement, for which my parents and
other members took out the maximum holding of a £1 'share',
had been founded as a kind of mutual society or cooperative in
Lancashire after the First World War. It was intended to give
those who worked in northern cities the chance to escape to the
countryside for a cheap, healthy, Christian-based holiday which
was strong on temperance.

My parents acted as 'host' and 'hostess' for between sixty
and a hundred paying 'guests' in this movement at each of
their Easter and summer holidays for more than thirty years.
Their duties earned them a free holiday because they organised
the social programme for the guests. After walking in the countryside all day, the evening included debates, music and acting, the
guests contributing according to their talents. My parents could
of course have afforded such holidays as guests (in the 1920s the
cost was a mere £10 a week for the whole family), but I think they
took pride in using skills that lay dormant in suburban Harrow
for the rest of the year. They acquired kudos in the movement,
both admired for their organisational skills and also popular.

Later, when I was seventeen, I myself acted as secretary to the Holiday Fellowship at Derwent Bank. The princely salary was £1 a week with free 'board'. For this I had to collect the guests' money and would feel rather bold walking to Keswick with some £500 in a bag, this being the weekly receipts. More importantly, I had the responsibility of taking the guests on vigorous countryside excursions; a guide to these was left for me by my predecessors as secretary. One day, I was taking a shortcut through a farm as there was no clear guidance of the route from my notes. A week later, I took the same shortcut again, rushing down the same hillside to the farm at the bottom. There, I was faced by the farmer, red-faced with anger, who stood on his gate holding a pitchfork in his right hand. 'You came trespassing last week and I didn't manage to catch you, but I've got you today and if you effing move a step forward I shall kill you with this pitchfork, I promise.' I knew he meant it, so, rather crestfallen, I turned to the thirty or so guests behind me and said to them, 'I am very sorry but there are some times in life that you have to admit you are beaten; this is one of them. I must ask you all to turn around and we shall climb back to the road at the top of the hill.' As this six-week post involved walking approximately ten miles a day, it must have helped to strengthen me for all my later running.

※

I was trained to respect authority, keep in line, work hard and do well. For me, even then, home was a place of serious activity. No comics were allowed in our home. I knew of other homes where comics were read, and I had an orgy of guilty reading when I visited them. In our own home most books were of the 'look and learn' variety; we had a complete set of Arthur Mee's *Children's Encyclopaedia*. When we got married my wife was astonished that I knew so few of the cheerful or dramatic children's books, such as *Just William*, *The Scarlet Pimpernel*, or *Beau Geste*, which my parents had deemed not to be 'Literature'. In other homes, in my mother's terms, time was wasted, and the children in them risked failing the eleven-plus examination, which was my avowed target.

My class in elementary school seldom had fewer than fifty pupils. We sat paired in desks, each with an iron base, a hinged wooden seat and a hinged top under which we kept our books. Classes were mixed. Each week we had some kind of test and, based on these results, children with higher marks were moved towards the back of the class, as they were trusted to work further away from the eye of the teacher. Only the first two or three in the top class, aged ten or eleven, would get to Harrow County School, the best state school in the district, which was fed by the cleverest children from a very wide catchment area of the new suburbs surrounding Harrow. Although it was called a 'county' school, its standards were those of a grammar school, but without the historic tradition. There were alternative secondary schools that had been recently built around the housing estates at Ruislip, Northwood and Pinner, where competition was less severe. By then I was usually in the top three, although I can remember a girl who always got higher marks in mathematics. At that stage I had throbbing headaches nearly every Friday night, culminating in severe vomiting. No doctor was ever consulted but, in retrospect, as a neurologist I can diagnose that I had a variant of migraine from which some children suffer, in my case a response to the stress and intensity of school and the weekly tests. I am glad to say that this migraine went away when I was thirteen and only recurred very occasionally with some visual disturbances in my sixties.

During my childhood I think I was naturally assertive and cheerful at home. At school, minor offences were punished by standing the child in front of the class or sending him to stand in a corridor. Corporal punishment was then still common in elementary schools, though I managed to avoid it myself. The instrument was chosen by the particular teacher administering the punishment and was usually a ruler or a rubber-soled shoe, applied to the palm of the hand.

A fear grew inside me that I might be set upon by a group of boys from the nearby estate. In my vivid imagination, I could see myself captured by these boisterous alien boys evacuated from London slums. Tales of other boys being captured by this gang, taken hostage and tortured cruelly, terrified me. On one occasion I took to my heels when my friend and I were caught by this gang as we walked past the estate. I escaped and ran away, pounding hard down the road until I got home, breathless and frightened. In some way I expected my father to come and settle with the gang. But for reasons I now well understand, he would do no such thing. He made me feel ashamed of myself by asking, 'Why didn't you fight them?' My first experience of the fight and flight emotion had crystallised into flight.

The 'fight' and 'flight' response is one of the most powerful and primitive biological responses. A fair fight such as a boxing match in the gym at school held no fears for me. What frightened me was the thought of being captured and outnumbered, when fighting would be useless. So, when trapped by the gang, the balance of my excitement was switched from 'fight' to 'flight'.

I asked my father to pass on his knowledge of boxing and for a while he did so, but it was not a very wholehearted or successful training, as I later found out at my secondary school. But by the age of nine I had already learnt that my best defence was to be so fleet of foot that bullies thought it too bothersome to pursue me. They hadn't the puff I had.

After marriage and the arrival of her two children, my mother, to use her own favourite phrase, was very much thrown on her 'inner resources'. At the time, middle-class women rarely went out to work. The frustration of leaving school early generated an unassuageable yearning for music, poetry and literature, as well as open-air exercise. Each day was planned so that she had her own kind of freedom. After lunch she had a short rest and then walked briskly, alone, over Harrow Hill, taking perhaps three-quarters of an hour.

My sister Joyce said recently, 'I never heard a cross word spoken between our parents.' My mother believed she had an easy life, presumably comparing her position to the struggles of her own mother, who had been widowed young and had brought up six children on her own. As a trained dressmaker, my mother made nearly all her own clothes except for her outside coat, and also our clothes until we were about eight. I minded having to wear cut-down, altered clothes.

Summarising life in Harrow, it seems that my parents, with the best intentions, may have mistaken the cultural shadow of life for its substance. They were both immersed in their music, reading and listening to the radio.

As I see it now, neither my father nor mother really needed or wanted close friendships. They had come from large families and these had been all the ties they valued or needed. They may even have recognised difficulties in their own families from which they were glad to have escaped. My mother spoke about the unpleasant teasing from younger brothers which, in her own serious way, she had found intolerable. My parents felt that if you did not accept invitations, you avoided commitments that might prove onerous later. They were very self-contained.

Chapter 2

Family Origins

It is a common experience that as the years pass we regret bitterly that we did not ask our parents more questions about their own lives. We want to know more about their hopes, fears, ambitions, perceptions of their own parents, and even everyday occurrences which possibly seemed mundane to them but are now so different from our own. In Pepys's diary it is not the great events of state that appeal so much as his sprightly accounts of people and day-to-day happenings.

The early Bannisters who left some record are distantly related; although we are likely to share few of their genes, some part of their make-up must still exist in us. As Oscar Wilde remarked, 'Debrett is one of the greatest works of fiction in the English language.' Full of cheerful fantasies though it is, it is only human to try to find some evidence of reasonable distinction in our ancestors, however remotely connected. It is believed that our family's origins can be traced all the way back to a Norman soldier named Robert de Banastre, who came over with William the Conqueror in 1066 and whose name is enrolled in Battle Abbey at Hastings. He might be one of the moustachioed figures depicted on the Bayeux Tapestry.

Nevertheless, Tennyson cautions us: 'Kind hearts are more than coronets, and simple faith than Norman blood.'

My headmaster uncle diligently worked out a family tree, a copy of which now hangs on our corridor wall. There were ups and downs in their fortunes. One Bannister in 1215 was beheaded on the field of battle after a rising against the Duke of Lancaster. Other signs of awkwardness included a prolonged legal battle over a church pew. Another refused a knighthood because it would have cost him an annual payment. When I became a knight a kindly friend said I would become the victim of a 'Sir charge'. As in all families there were some rogues as well as some saints. One aunt became a missionary nurse in Africa and died of yellow fever. There is a mixed thread of non-conformity, idealism and sometimes a rather quixotic sense of purpose that has remained with them through the centuries.

Among his record of the most interesting Bannisters prior to the eighteenth century, my uncle found nine knights, eight Members of Parliament and ten Mayors of Preston, the largest nearby Lancashire town. Bannisters married into various prominent families, among them the owners of Marsden, Darwin and Townley Halls, all grand houses in the vicinity. Around 1450, our own branch of the family's fortune declined and thereafter they settled down to modest farming at Park Hill, Barrowford.

Park Hill, a manor house, was, rather remarkably, the home of the Bannister family for 300 years. This is not a myth. It is now a heritage centre which includes a room devoted to the genealogy of the Bannister clan. Prince Charles, because of his interest in the architecture of the house, visited it and I was struck by his detailed knowledge of the structure and its large barn.

My father's isolated village of Trawden was thought of as being on a road to nowhere. In fact, a small road winds from

Trawden into Yorkshire over the Pennines, the 'backbone of England'. These hills are generally bleak and cold. Ten miles from Trawden, in Lancashire, is the village of Haworth, over the border in Yorkshire. The Brontës lived in the rectory there and the surrounding country is well portrayed in *Wuthering Heights*, in which Heathcliff and Cathy share a secret rock on the moor's windswept pinnacle. Some early biographers of the Brontës tended to portray their work as the outcome of spinsters' fevered imaginations. In fact, the reverse is true and more recent meticulous biographies show just how wild and primitive life was in this part of England.

My father was the youngest of eleven. That small boy, gazing out from the photograph, perhaps slightly apprehensive, but no doubt much loved. The family had a cohesion, shown by a round-robin letter that went from brother to brother or sister with friendly additions from each. It could take six months to circulate as some correspondents were laggardly. On receiving the letters, each sibling withdrew his own previous contribution and added a new one and the group of letters was posted on. The letters included descriptions of their interests and hobbies, showing a blend of eccentricity, scepticism and ingenuity. There would be advice on a plethora of tasks, such as mending cars, buying houses or choosing holidays, as well as family gossip and folk history. It helped keep the family close, despite the fact that many siblings had left Lancashire, finding no prospects there, and only returned at Christmas and other holidays. Despite the diaspora, the chain of interest and affection was linked by this letter for seventy years.

My father was not tall by today's standards, but was sturdy and eventually grew to five feet eight inches, then the average height. What is striking is that all the siblings in the family, as you see them in photographs, grew up healthy. For eleven children, a number unimaginable today, to have grown to adulthood without a single death in childhood was an unusual event and an immense tribute to the nurturing qualities of their quite remarkable parents. In those days before antibiotics or immunisation, some families, on average, lost as many as half the children that were born to them before they reached adult life.

My parents both had a memory of the terrible poverty in Lancashire with the collapse of the cotton trade when supplies were cut off in the American Civil War. It was so strong with my parents that they feared such times might easily recur and this contributed to their caution over money. My father and his parents would have put aside their savings in a bank or 'friendly society', to keep it out of temptation's way. My father told me that at no stage in his life did he ever spend more than half his salary. He never had a mortgage and, as I have said, he was reluctant for me to take one out when I was buying my first house, even though I was then aged thirty-four and had the security of a hospital consultancy in the National Health Service. It was a caution bred of a bitter family experience of past hardship, rather than any meanness on his part.

Over the last century, our branch of the Bannister family's fortunes had slowly declined, largely due to the collapse of the cotton industry, and my father, at fifteen, left Colne Secondary School in Lancashire to come to London. All my children and nearly all my grandchildren were born in London or the south of England, though I sometimes like to feel proud of the vigour given to me by my Lancashire blood.

Most children worked in the family mill when they left full-time school at the age of thirteen or fourteen. While children were still living at home, they had to 'tip up' to their parents eleven pence of every shilling they earned to pay for board and lodging. Many young men and women also had to do this. It meant coming home on a Friday night and putting almost their whole wages down on the kitchen table.

Fortunately, my father, like his three immediately older brothers, but unlike most Trawden boys, did not have to work in the mill. They passed examinations from the village school in Trawden admitting them to Colne County Secondary School. My uncle Fred went on to a teachers' training college, then took an external BSc at Liverpool University and became the headmaster of a local secondary school. His research on family history was published in a book entitled *The Annals of Trawden Forest* in 1930. The other brothers, including my father, passed open public examinations for the civil service and the Customs and Excise Department and one of them became a policeman.

In 1910, at the age of fifteen, my father came second out of many thousands of candidates in the general civil service examination for the clerical grade for school leavers. On the evidence of this alone, he must be rated both clever and determined. He then came down to London, where he first worked at the Board of Trade. He went home to Lancashire for all his holidays, thanks to his affection for his family and loneliness in London.

One of my strongest early memories is of a visit to Oxford with my parents and Joyce in 1938, when I was eight. During the day we saw some colleges and my cousin Edith's lodgings; she was my uncle Fred (the headmaster)'s younger daughter, the first member of our family to go to Oxford. As a result of this visit I subtly absorbed my parents' ambitions for me to follow in her footsteps. If London had been my father's escape from Lancashire, Oxford became my hoped-for escape from suburbia.

My parents were engaged for over two years, not then unusual, and did not marry until 1925, when my father was thirty and my mother was twenty-five. My mother's father, Robinson Duckworth, died prematurely from a cerebral haemorrhage at the age of forty-six, when my mother, the eldest of six children, was only fourteen. My only knowledge of him comes from the obituary in the local newspaper, which described him as a 'Unitarian Worthy'. The Unitarian movement had been founded in the sixteenth century and became quite strong in Lancashire. Its believers did not accept the deity of Christ, instead regarding him only as a supremely good human being.

When my father was ten his own father was sixty-one, so my uncle Gilbert acted rather as a second father to him and took a direct interest in his development. When my father reached his twenty-first year Gilbert handed him a list of the most desirable qualities to be looked for in a wife. These were, in order, that she should be:

> healthy, sensible, able to look after a home, intelligent, well-educated, good-tempered (nice-mannered and agreeable), a credit to you – i.e. no sense of shame or apology for her, inexpensive and willing to remain so, not belonging to a 'swanky' lot, but one who can work for her living and has done so, has similar tastes to you, is beautiful, of your own class – with ambitions but no pride, and moderate in all things – no crank.

Physical beauty appeared low down on the list, perhaps because he thought most men are unduly swayed by this. I might add that Gilbert seems to have been better at giving advice in this respect than taking it. Sadly, his own marriage ended in divorce, something that happened to no other member of the family. His wife was an outstanding beauty but evidently this was not matched by enough other qualities, on both sides, to enable the marriage to endure.

My mother was undoubtedly beautiful and as far as I can tell she possessed in good measure all the other qualities too. At the age of twenty-nine my father was, in Jane Austen's phrase, 'in want of a wife'. He had a steady income, a secure job and, through assiduous saving, enough money to buy a house. I suspect his heart remained in Lancashire. London for him consisted of work and survival, as well as attendance at evening classes. Perhaps romance only blossomed when he went home for his holidays. He relied on his niece Mavis, with whom he had a close friendship, who arranged a meeting with Alice, my mother.

Their honeymoon, spent in the Pyrenees, set the pattern for the rest of their holidays together with the Holiday Fellowship movement. At that time my father's main diversion was photography. He had a heavy, nine-inch-square mahogany reflex camera which used glass plates, six inches by six inches, of which he carried a gross (144) in his rucksack. Their clothing for the holiday must have been sparse, but I believe he took some fine photographs, in the pictorial style of the time. Some were successful in photographic competitions.

One such winning entry was a photograph of me failing to eat up my lunch, with sunshine crossing my face. The prize was a camera and for some reason the camera was given to my sister. Disappointment was not the word for it – it was just one of those situations in which all children cry out 'it's not fair!'

Chapter 3

School in Bath and Hampstead

One day in September 1939, as I was sailing my toy boat on the West Harrow recreation ground pond, the terrifying wail of the first air-raid siren I had ever heard pierced the suburban calm. In every garden there was an Anderson shelter with emergency food rations stored inside. We had all been issued gas masks. War had been declared a few days earlier and, since I couldn't know that this siren was a false alarm, I was fearful that violence might be unleashed immediately. I grabbed my boat and sprinted home. I was already feeling guilty because a few days before, when hearing that war might be declared, it had occurred to me that this might be an exciting prospect, as it may have done to some other children. A truly wicked thought. Now, at any moment, bombs might be falling on innocent people.

The government imagined London would suffer a huge number of casualties through gas attacks and bombing and so plans were rushed through to send as many government departments as possible to safer cities, like Cheltenham, Oxford and Bath. Within weeks of the outbreak of war my father moved to Bath, where the Admiralty had been relocated. At that point he was helping to audit Admiralty accounts. When I asked him what he was up to in his office, he replied that he was trying to stop the electrical companies from overcharging the government for work done on submarines.

The historic Bath Grammar School was full, because thousands of civil servants and their families had already descended on Bath. I had been offered a place at the state secondary school. At the end of the first day, catapulted on the same day into a new town, new home and new school, the form master asked me to stay behind. He spoke kindly to me and it was too much for me. I burst into tears. This same master a year later took me aside again after class, having watched the intensity with which I threw myself into everything. 'If you can't slow up, you'll be dead by the age of twenty-one.'

Before my mother and sister joined us, my father and I lived in a boarding house, where we had terrible food. I remember particularly the high teas with 'brawn', bits of pork in jelly. Rather touchingly, my father, presumably hoping to cheer me up in my mother's absence, took me to the cinema every Friday evening, despite not really approving of it. There we saw patriotic war films about spying. I remember in *The Spy in Black*: the main character, a German spy, flashes messages from headland cliffs to German submarines. These were propaganda films intended to instil wariness about spying. At the end we all stood for the national anthem to be played and left with a warm patriotic feeling.

Later in January my mother and sister joined us in Bath. It was almost impossible for the whole family to find accommodation and at first we lived in a cramped top-floor flat in one of the five-storey Georgian houses at the bottom of Lansdown Hill. I slept in a small cubbyhole between the bathroom and the kitchen. After eight months we found a flat in a three-storey

Georgian house and we moved there so we could all have proper bedrooms.

It had always been as easy for me to run as to walk and, since I had no bicycle and did not want to travel by bus to school, each morning I had to walk or run down Lansdown Hill on the east side of Bath, through the city past the Roman Baths, to the school on Combe Down, the hill on the west side. The final part of the route was up 150 feet of steps called Beechen Cliff. It was no trouble for me to sprint up these steps, recovering my breath at the top.

My school was split between the Bath-born boys and the newcomers, most of whom, like me, had been working towards the more competitive London eleven-plus examination and whose intrusion was resented. Jealousy over work standards led some of the Bath boys to bully the Londoners. One day I was roughly and deliberately pushed over by a particular Bath boy in the playground. I got up and started a scrap with him. This was seen by a supervising master, who happened to be the school PE teacher. The bully was well known as the class's bruiser and had taken boxing lessons. The master came up to us and told us to come to the gym after school, put on boxing gloves and, supposedly, settle our quarrel fairly. At the end of school that day, the whole class came to watch the unequal struggle. I was much lighter than the other boy and had almost no boxing training and so of course was no match for him. After a couple of rounds my face was bruised, my nose was bleeding and the fight was stopped. I went home feeling ashamed and hid the real cause of my injuries from my parents, claiming they were the result of a game of rugby. After that I did try to get my father to give me some more boxing lessons, but in my heart I knew that my fists were not my real weapons. Later that year I discovered the knack of winning cross-country races for the school and my house. I was never bullied again and was free to work as hard as I chose without being taunted for being a swot. Never underestimate the importance of sport in English school life.

The following year, aged eleven, although I was still one of the smaller boys in the school, I won the junior cross-country race over some two and a half miles. I realised for the first time that, in contrast to most other boys, I could run myself to total exhaustion, taking more out of myself than they were prepared or able to do, and then I gradually recovered over hours or days afterwards.

After winning this first race, I was presented with a large silver cup at assembly in front of the whole school the follow-ing morning. I won this cup two more years in succession and broke the school record before I turned fourteen and became ineligible to compete. There was a notion in my mind, supported by a school rumour, that any cup which was won three times was then owned outright by the winner. Our schoolteachers, hearing of my misconception and touchingly not wishing me to be disappointed, clubbed together to present me with a silver replica, about four inches high, of the larger trophy. This cup, now rather battered, is my most precious athletic trophy, and sits among the others in the glass case in the gallery of the main hall at Pembroke College, Oxford. In this cabinet there is a faded photograph from the *Bath Chronicle* showing me having won the school cross-country race, which my father kept with pride, as any father would. In the same cabinet there is a silver badge on a watch chain, which, after badgering him, he told me was given to him when he himself won the one-mile race at Colne County Secondary School. Was my athletic success the result of genes, nurture or hard work? This is still the subject of heated debate.

At thirteen I won several events at the school summer sports and was junior victor ludorem for sports, receiving my second most valued trophy. I treasure them not only because they were the first ones I received, but because they made such a difference to my school life and growing up. I felt I needed some success at that age and this seemed an easy way to acquire it and to overcome my lack of confidence; all my later trophies were in one sense just an extension or completion of this beginning which had so genuinely surprised me. My running ability seemed to have come to me as a gift – as if by magic.

In Bath I worked hard and I remember with gratitude a few masters who ignited in me a real interest in their subjects. In contrast to the drabness of suburban Harrow, I was delighted by the city of Bath itself, with its Georgian and Regency buildings, the Crescent, the Assembly Rooms and the Pump Room and relics of its rich history in the Roman Baths.

At thirteen, my parents bought me my first grown-up bicycle, a second-hand BSA Roadster, at least twenty years old, with a three-speed gear which had the disconcerting habit of either slipping or getting stuck in a high gear. But to me it represented freedom – a kind of freedom I had never enjoyed in London – and I made full use of it. There were wartime hazards of large military convoys, including American trucks. Almost all my cycling was done alone. One of my early expeditions was to ride the 100 miles from Bath to London in one day to stay with a friend. It seemed to me quite natural and completely thrilling to be allowed to do this. For this trip I carried a rucksack on my back with the clothes I would need. Every weekend I would plan a cycle tour, taking with me my Ordnance Survey map, sandwiches and a bottle of home-made lemonade. North of Bath I could cross the battlefields of the English Civil War and reach Castle Combe, one of England's most beautiful villages. Heading west would take me to Bristol and Avonmouth, then an important target of German air raids as shipping was diverted there after heavy bombing had devastated the Port of London. To the south-west lay Clevedon, Weston-super-Mare, Cheddar Gorge and the remarkable stalactite chambers of Wookey Hole. I also cycled to Longleat Park and along the Avon Valley to Farleigh Castle and Bradford-upon-Avon.

Hardly any of these trips would be feasible today for a thirteen-year-old riding alone, given the fast-moving and heavy road traffic everywhere. I greatly regret the restrictions that my own grandchildren have to tolerate. Even our own children enjoyed more freedom to roam in the countryside than the current generation. For example, (not without some prior discussions) we allowed our children to spend a week taking boats up the River Arun in Sussex and camp on the banks at night wherever they found themselves. My hope is that some of these earlier freedoms will return, if the government can create a network of cycle paths to criss-cross the country. A possible consequence of these early expeditions was our son Thurstan's later exploit of canoeing round New York Island, which is just possible if you catch the right tides, to promote cycle routes in the city. At one stage a police launch approached him, suspecting he might be a drug smuggler. On hearing his English accent, they presumed he was an eccentric and let him be.

My mother's religious roots, as a Unitarian, were stronger than my father's Wesleyan background. My parents' attitude to religion was eccentric and non-conformist. In Bath we regularly attended a Unitarian church and my parents played a part in its activities. The adult school we sometimes attended met in a wooden hut in a poor part of the city; it consisted of a few hymns accompanied by a piano and then study classes on morals, ethics and humanism. Then later we attended a Quaker meeting house for a time. I recall the embarrassment of sitting in silence waiting for someone to feel moved to speak and listening to some rather strange contributions. These visits fizzled out. Clearly, my parents were concerned that we should be exposed to some religious experience but shied away from close involvement with any particular church.

I made some great friends during my time in Bath. One was a boy who was at the top of the class with me as we moved towards the School Certificate. His mother was a pharmacist. He was bold and knew which chemicals were needed to make a 'bomb'. One afternoon when his mother was at work we packed the necessary ingredients together into a tin which we then buried in his back garden. We detonated the bomb from twenty yards away, by lowering a paving stone onto a gramophone needle held in place by a piece of wood. This then struck a starting pistol blank cartridge, which detonated the 'bomb'. The enormous and satisfying explosion brought a local policeman down the road on his bicycle, knocking at the front door. My friend answered the door while I cowered out of sight, and calmly but firmly lied with a conviction that would have done credit to an MI5 spy, and directed the policeman farther down the road. Together we also explored disused mine shafts on the top of Combe Down and, at a nearby quarry, engaged in exploits which I am ashamed now to admit were both illegal and dangerous. I suppose, like other adolescent boys, I was skirting around the edge of delinquency. My grandchildren are particularly fond of these stories.

Our lives in Bath were changed drastically when in 1942 there was a Baedeker raid on Bath, so called because they were raids on towns without much industrial significance but often with great cultural treasures (and so included in the famous Baedeker tour guide), and were intended simply to undermine civilian morale. In the case of Bath, the Germans were also aware that the Admiralty was stationed there. Around Bath there were aerodromes with fighter planes, but none were available to defend the city against the German onslaught. The surprise first night attack brought German Stuka dive bombers, which were designed to generate a terrifying whining, screaming sound as they swooped down, almost as bad as the sound of the bombs themselves. As we crouched in the basement, every window in our house was shattered by a near miss and the glass roof over the central staircase fell in. We hoped that the Germans might leave us alone after the incendiary bombs had wrecked the Assembly Rooms. However, they returned the following night, causing even more damage, and in total killed four hundred people and destroyed more than a thousand homes. This damage, of course, did not compare with that wreaked on central London and the Docklands, where many thousands of civilians were killed. But it was a surprise attack and the lack of defence made us feel particularly vulnerable.

The question then became: 'Will they return for a third night?' I put pressure on my parents to leave Bath so that we did not risk being bombed even more seriously. On the third afternoon we joined an exodus from the city. We walked some four miles towards Bradford-on-Avon and camped in the woods. But the Germans had by then done enough and decided to switch to other targets. The city spent the next few months clearing up the damage. The wreckage made a grave impression on me and I made a linocut, later reproduced in the school magazine, depicting the crooked beams and steaming rubble of half-burnt homes.

Like most secondary schools at the time, we had three separate training corps, for the army, navy and air force. The headmaster, who had himself fought in the First World War, assumed that all the senior boys would enter the services in due course, as, even if the war ended, conscription would continue afterwards. In 1942, an old boy returned to the school wearing his army major's uniform to address the morning assembly, which usually consisted of hymns, prayers and notices. He gave a blunt pep talk to the whole school which shocked me. He told us, 'It is your job to go through school quickly and get out there and kill Huns.'

I never joined any of the service corps while I was at school. It was perhaps my parents' influence that discouraged me from belonging to any organisations. My parents had verged on pacifism, a strong movement in Britain between the wars, organised by the Peace Pledge Union, of which Vera Brittain, Shirley Williams's mother, was a prominent member. I am sure that I would have found the spit-and-polish and drill highly irksome. However, twelve years later, in admittedly rather different circumstances as an officer and doctor in the Royal Army Medical Corps, I found my two years of service thoroughly interesting. The successor to my first headmaster was Thomas Taylor, who had come from teaching at Bradford Grammar School and was a Quaker and a pacifist. He was unable to abolish the service corps, but from then on there was no pressure on boys to belong to them, though they still survive in the majority of public schools.

My school was a good one of its kind, doubtless improved by the influx of boys from London. It survives today as a comprehensive, called Beechen Cliff, with high academic standards. My first headmaster ran it along public school lines, with a house system revolving largely around the playing of team games. I was involved in most school activities. I played the violin in the orchestra, as already described, and had more success playing the leading part of Kate in Shakespeare's *Taming of the Shrew*, to favourable local newspaper reviews, just before my voice broke at the age of fourteen. The masters taught me well and I got the highest grades in my School Certificate, which enabled me to win a direct grant place to University College School in Hampstead. Despite the bombing raids, my years at Bath had been extremely happy.

We returned to London in 1944, even though the city was being bombed again, this time by V1 and V2 rockets. The letter 'V' stood for 'Vengeance'. The V1s, or doodlebugs, were unmanned flying bombs. The sound of them held terror for the civilian population. You could hear their engines but then, just as they were about to reach their target, the engines cut out and they became silent. At that moment you could not tell where within a certain range they would fall. The more advanced V2s were rocket-propelled shells containing a ton of high explosive, which crossed the channel at 600 miles per hour and on landing caused widespread blast damage up to a radius of 200 metres. By the time they started falling we knew the Allies were finally winning, but it was still terrible to have to endure Hitler's battering. Any information about them was suppressed, as the authorities dreaded aiding the enemy by revealing where the secret weapons had fallen.

War's horror is unbounded. In the American Civil War, Lincoln, so different in every way from Hitler, gave an order for all-out war and the burning of every Southern town. Britain has been criticised for pursuing the same policy and specifically for the fire-bombing of large cities at the time of the Dresden bombing in February 1945. Younger historians perhaps do not take into account the difficulties with which these extreme decisions were made under intolerable pressures. In any case, the courage everyone showed then is almost inconceivable. Today, having been a doctor and, for a while, an army officer, I cannot express enough my admiration for and gratitude towards those scarcely older than I was who ensured that I could go to university, become a doctor, pursue research and raise a family, though the nuclear threat was present for many years.

It might strike the outside observer as strange for our family to return from Bath's relative safety to a still disrupted and chastened London being bombed by the V1s and V2s until March 1945. This perhaps illustrates, better than anything else, my parents' eagerness for us to obtain educational advantages, which took priority even over avoiding physical danger.

University College School had been established in 1830 with a pioneering and reforming ethos. It was much more secular than other schools of its day and held no quota restriction on the entry of non-Anglicans, whether Evangelicals, Methodists or Jews. It also forbade corporal punishment, in marked contrast to most other British boys' schools, in which beating by both teachers and prefects then remained a generally accepted but wretched practice.

In the autumn of 1944 I entered this liberal school in Hampstead, with elegant Edwardian Gilbert Scott-style buildings, a good library and able boys, mostly hard-working and competitive: a markedly different atmosphere from my school in Bath. It proved to be both a relief and a shock: a relief that we were expected to work, and a shock that, whereas at Bath I had excelled in both work and sport, at UCS, thrown in halfway through the term, I immediately recognised I had a mountain to climb.

Many of the young masters had been recruited into the army

and so there were gaps. It was my ill luck that my important botany and zoology courses were taught by an eccentric and committed Communist. The boys who were not urgently seeking to become doctors, as I was, could easily divert him from these subjects to expounding his political views. I realised I would have to work very hard on my own. What books could not be found at school could be made up by the Harrow public library. I found the mathematical elements of my chemistry course difficult to master. It seems that in mathematics the guidance of an interested and gifted teacher is of first importance and without such a grounding it is almost impossible to catch up.

My father, sensitive to the statistics that only 2 per cent of school leavers in 1946 reached university, was anxiously aware that without hard work Joyce and I would stand little chance of being admitted. He yearned for us to have the enrichment in our lives that he had so missed. I now understand the necessity for the austere scheme of work and study.

The sports we played three times a week at UCS were rugby, cricket and rowing. There was no athletics, and it was only when the ground proved too hard to play rugby that the school invented an impromptu sports day, and I won the half-mile race by some thirty yards. I had earlier won the only cross-country race held while I was there: a five-mile scramble around Hampstead Heath. The first summer found me briefly rowing in the second VIII, which helped strengthen me. In my last year I grew five inches to over six foot, but, at ten stone, was still skinny. My eventual running weight was 158 lb.

An event occurred at UCS which was ironic in the light of my subsequent career. To me it seemed the headmaster was giving undue importance to sport in the appointment of the head of school, monitors and heads of house. He was an autocrat and made these appointments himself. When a debate on the subject of school policy was held I attacked the headmaster forcibly on this bias. My underlying anger was purely and simply because I was unsuccessful at the major sports of rugby and cricket. Indeed, I was merely captain of the second school rugby team and we were beaten in every match with other schools. On one humiliating occasion the referee was a master at Haberdashers' Aske's School, in which our second XV was matched against their third XV. At half-time, when the score was about 40–nil against us, the referee came over to us as we sucked our lemons and asked who the captain was. I sheepishly admitted the truth, whereupon he said, 'Just have a talk to your team over half-time. I'm sure they can play better than this!' This was one of those times when one would be happy for the ground to open under one's feet! When I was duly appointed head of house in my last year my earlier bitterness faded.

The strain of growing fast, working as hard as I could, being responsible for certain teams and being made house captain – all against a background of rationing, which had become more stringent after the war – brought me to a point of exhaustion and this triggered two serious bouts of illness. Rugby boots then had nailed studs and as scrum-half I got raked along my legs quite often. The gashes became infected by a streptococcus and simply refused to clear up. As a consequence, in December 1945 I contracted a kidney disease called focal nephritis, probably due to septicaemia from the infection, which was triggering an auto-immune response. Coming back from sitting the Cambridge scholarship exams in January 1946, the tissues of my face, legs and arms swelled up alarmingly. The means of manufacturing penicillin, the first antibiotic, had only recently been found, and though it was used for war casualties, it had not been made generally available. This meant my illness could have had very serious lifelong consequences for my kidneys, even leading to death. Fortunately, our competent general practitioner sent me to the Glaxo company laboratories, where tests showed my kidneys were not seriously damaged. I was lucky that there were no long-term ill effects.

I was accepted by Cambridge, but the senior tutor of St John's, 'Bonzo' Howland, told me I should wait a year. It later transpired that Dr Howland, the St John's College admissions tutor, had been the Cambridge team's shot-putter and was currently also senior treasurer of the Cambridge University Athletic Club. Not surprisingly, he suffered opprobrium when it was discovered that it was he who had diverted me to Oxford, to become a thorn in the flesh of Cambridge athletics for some years. It was an exultant feeling to receive a handwritten acceptance letter in early 1946 from the Rector of Exeter College, Oxford. He wrote, 'We are pleased to tell you that you have been given a place at the college to read medicine and shall welcome you in October 1946.' That was a turning point. As I sat at home I had the vision of the freedom Oxford would grant me, of social, sporting and academic opportunities. Though then only sixteen, I felt ready.

Chapter 4

Oxford

Arriving in Oxford in early October 1946, I found the Exeter College lodge was crowded with undergraduates looking at the noticeboards and chatting in groups. The noise echoed out into the quad, broadcasting, for all the affected nonchalance, the anticipation of a great adventure. The head porter asked me my name and then looked down a list and said, 'Mr Bannister, sir. You have the room on the top floor of staircase 11, it's just around the corner.' The head porter is essential to the functioning of any college. He was wise, canny and intelligent. Very little happened within the college walls that escaped his eye. It was his role to advise tactfully whenever he felt that an undergraduate's behaviour went a little too far, helping him to avoid dire punishment.

I had a large sitting room with a small bedroom adjoining it. There I met my scout, or shared servant, Dennis. I had no understanding of the relationship between a student and the scout. Certainly no one had ever called me 'sir' before. My first purchase was a white tie and a gown needed for the matriculation ceremony the next day. Clothes rationing and food rationing were still in existence in 1946 – the latter even more severe than it had been during the war because some of our food was redirected to Holland and Greece, where the population was starving. Ration books were collected by the kitchen staff, who doled out the sparse dollops of sugar, butter and marmalade on named saucers, and each morning we walked into the hall for breakfast, precariously balancing all of this on a plate. At dinner, the rector and fellows all looked very grand at high table and the rector spoke the Latin grace before and after dinner.

In no time I was bursting with plans. I went straight down to the athletics track at Iffley Road, wanting to get started straight away, but no one seemed to be in charge. Back in the college lodge I found on the notice board the announcement about the university athletic club, subscription of £1, which I sent off. On returning from the Iffley Road track, I found a tall, athletic-looking student and asked him, 'Are you thinking of training for any sport?' He said he wanted to be an oarsman but I persuaded him to come with me for a run round the college's own athletic ground on the far side of the Isis. After we had circled the field a few times, the Exeter groundsman came up to us.

'Excuse me,' he said. 'I suppose you're freshmen, can I help you?'

I said, 'Thank you, my friend wants to be an oarsman and I want to be a runner.'

'Perhaps I can help you because I remember the great Jack Lovelock.'

In my innocence I asked him, 'Who was Jack Lovelock?'

He replied, 'He was the greatest miler Oxford has ever seen. He was at Exeter College and won the Berlin 1500m Olympic gold medal.' He went on, 'If I may say so, your friend here who wants to take up rowing has a good running style but,' looking at me, 'if I may say so, sir, you don't have the neat style that Lovelock had and perhaps running may not be not your best sport.'

I felt I had heard enough from him and my new-found friend and I ran back to the college.

On my second visit to Iffley Road, I was introduced to a gruff figure wearing a bowler hat and an overcoat: Bert Thomas, the middle-distance coach for Oxford. I was told he had been coach to the great Jack Lovelock and had travelled with him to his races in America. Rather peremptorily, he asked me to run a lap. I asked him at what speed and he replied, 'That doesn't matter, just run a lap.' Naturally, I ran it as fast as I could and went up to him afterwards, breathless, asking him what my time was, to which he replied, 'I'm the coach, you're the runner,' and snapped his stopwatch closed and put it on its chain back in his pocket. Our relationship held no promise.

The secretary of the Oxford University Athletic Club, Russell Grice, was much kinder and more helpful. I duly came second in the freshman's mile race in November 1946, with the very modest time of 4 minutes 52 seconds, but I was on my way. The secretary of the Achilles Club, an Oxford long jumper at the Berlin Olympics, commented then, 'If you stop bouncing like a kangaroo, you could knock off 20 seconds.' That term I also ran some cross-country races. On one training run I found the pace so fast that I turned to the runner next to me and asked, 'Do they always run as fast as this?' He said, 'They do... But we could walk for a bit if you like.' This we did. It was the start of a lifelong friendship with ex-serviceman Charles Wenden, who, though he never spoke of it, had won the Military Cross in the Ardennes battle during the war and was history scholar at Wadham College. Our friendship was so close that it was with his family that I found a haven for lunch on the day of the four-minute mile. It is he in the photo of the four-minute mile who is crouched, covering his face with his hands, unable to lift his eyes to see whether or not I had made it.

Though racing and training became quite important from then on, there were lulls when I did not compete much. I never wanted training to take up too much time – not more than a forty-minute session of vigorous running four times each week.

In the meantime, I was delighted to be at this cheerful college on the Turl, right in the heart of Oxford. At Exeter there were two other medical students in my year and about 180 undergraduates altogether. Most were ex-servicemen. It was absurd that some who may have risen to become active brigadiers during the war should have to submit to ludicrous rules of being back in college by ten o'clock. Men who'd driven tanks still weren't allowed to have a car within two miles of Carfax, the centre of Oxford. They tolerated those of us straight from school with cheerful generosity. The college had various clubs including the athletics club, which I discovered was the first athletics club in the world. I organised a centenary sports in 1948, including events from the calendar of 1848.

Work and social life were very happily intertwined and the only athletics I did was some cross-country matches at weekends. Combining work and sport was a constant struggle but well worth it. I would not have been able, aged nineteen, to captain the Oxford–Cambridge team to the American universities had I not been able to juggle the order of the exams expected of me.

One of the most colourful – literally – members of the team was a Fijian 6 ft 5 in. high jumper called Ratu Tumurali Mara. When jocularly asked his nationality, he replied, 'Scottish – by absorption. You see, my great-great-grandfather ate the Scottish missionary.'

But the hub of life at the centre of Exeter College life was the junior common room (JCR). Students constantly floated through these crowded rooms, opening from the main quadrangle, to jostle, argue and laugh. They celebrated when they passed an exam and commiserated with those who had failed. Students *were* the college and they loved that untidy pair of rooms with their damaged chairs and sofas with torn leather upholstery, which the college seemed reluctant to repair as they would soon return to their battered state.

The rooms were always littered with partially destroyed newspapers and journals. High emotion was always aroused by the contents of certain newspapers, resulting in the suggestion that the JCR should terminate its subscription. At every JCR meeting, the offending papers changed, but this was an excuse for a debate on politics. Yet no one, whether from right or left, would countenance ending the subscription to the Communist *Daily Worker*.

There was a large leather-bound 'Suggestion Book', where members made all kinds of requests and comments, from the serious to the absurd. The right-hand page was left for the president of the JCR to comment. He rarely felt it necessary to add anything other than 'noted'. However, I remember one contribution, several pages long, by Correlli Barnett. This earned a gentle reproach, 'May I suggest you save your literary gems for your tutor and not take up valuable space in the Suggestion Book.' Correlli Barnett later wrote one of the first critical historical books about First World War generals and became a fellow of Churchill College at Cambridge.

Unlike the younger students among us, whose attitudes to the university and the college spanned varying levels of respect, the ex-servicemen had little time for some of the petty rules governing college affairs. Some engaged in foolhardy if not dangerous ventures. One known prankster, a former army man, noticed a steamroller parked, still hissing away, down the Abingdon Road one evening. He had the bright idea of driving it into town to form a sort of traffic blockade. He returned at 2 a.m. the next night with a bag of coal and fuelled up the furnace. He managed to drive it all the way into the centre of town without detection and abandoned it, causing a block all the way along the High Street. He then climbed back into the college, went to bed and was never caught.

Our supposed habitual rivals were Jesus College, across the Turl. An exuberant Exeter student once stole the portrait of their founder from their dining hall by entering the back door with a coal lorry. After much speculation as to the culprit, he then returned it surreptitiously when the police got involved. There were always scuffles with Jesus College on Guy Fawkes Night. But after a while students from both Exeter and Jesus drifted down to the Broad to watch the more serious battles between 'Bloody' Balliol and Trinity, who decried Balliol's academic success and policy of accepting foreign students. The worst offenders, if caught, were, in Oxford vernacular, 'progged' by 'bulldogs', and faced fines from the proctors, the university's guardians of order.

Food, or the lack of it, played a large part in those early post-war years but I am sure the college did its best. We enjoyed the dinners before a blazing log fire and the tradition of 'sconcing' was alive and well. This consists of punishment for offences such as spilling the salt, mentioning the same girl's name more than once, or referring to your work. The offender was forced to sink a yard of ale without removing the tankard from his lips. If he failed he had to buy beer for the whole table.

Women could be invited into our rooms only during the afternoons. Crumpets would be toasted in front of the gas fire, which would only function if the meter was filled with shillings. Tea parties were rounded off with a Findlater's Dry Fly sherry. Lunch for me was often at the state-funded 'British Restaurants', communal kitchens established during the war by the Ministry of Food. There was one such restaurant opposite Somerville and close to the medical school. The main course of the meal cost a shilling and consisted largely of Spam, potatoes and cabbage. It was cheap and filling and was a great boon in those bleak years. If a girl invited you to one of the women's colleges' end-of-term dances, it was the custom to take her out to dinner. The Eastgate Hotel was regarded as sufficiently respectable, dinner costing around fifteen shillings for two.

Students revelled in passing on stories of the fellows' eccentricities. One absurd story was about the Master of another college and his dog. It passed into college and university lore. A head of house was in the habit of taking his dog to the Phoenix cinema, where he solemnly bought a ticket for the dog. He placed the dog on a cushion he had brought with him and together they watched the film. As he left the cinema one day, he met a fellow of the college, who remarked jocularly, 'Did the dog enjoy the film?' The dog's owner replied, 'Yes, but not as much as the book.'

One of the most well-respected Exeter College fellows was Nevill Coghill, who was famous in the wider world outside the university. One of Oxford's legendary post-war figures in the world of the arts, he inspired generations of students to become actors, producers and writers. Born a baronet's son in an Irish castle, he revived world interest in medieval poetry, especially Chaucer's *Canterbury Tales*.

Coghill even produced a musical version of the *Tales*. Prior to its production no one dreamt it could be a financial success and none of London's established producers would back it. So

Coghill's friends put in what small sums of money they could afford, usually less than £100, to get it started. It had, however, just the right mixture of colour and vulgarity to become an instant success and it ran for five years at the London Phoenix Theatre, then toured the world for years and made the 'angels' who backed the show thousands of pounds. Only Lord David Cecil, Kenneth Clark and Isaiah Berlin were equally well known among the post-war fellows.

The senior college fellow, Dacre Balsdon, was a classicist who wore a loud brownish-orange tweed suit and whose pompous accent boomed across the quad. He was also a repository of college traditions. He had his favourites among the undergraduates and held breakfast parties, trying to revive some traditions of civilised pre-war college entertaining. At times he rather aped the eccentric warden of Wadham, Maurice Bowra, the subject of many a tale. One example was when he claimed to get his exercise by climbing the 'hill' to the Bodleian Library, which was all of fifty yards away, and which a fellow proved was precisely two inches higher than Wadham. Another story was told of a student he interviewed for admission. At that time, some Latin, as an O level or equivalent, was a compulsory requirement for admission to Oxford. In 1946, a candidate who had been in the army, said to Bowra, 'I'm afraid I never studied any Latin.' Bowra replied, 'That's alright, "war" equals Latin.'

On one occasion I banded together with some Exeter friends, had some cards printed and gave a drinks party in the fellows' garden. As a small college, we all got to know each other well, giving us a chance to learn from each other beyond our respective academic subjects. It helped that with clothes rationing we all dressed very much the same, usually in tweed jackets and grey flannels or corduroys, minimising any feeling of social divisions.

Many stuck to college activities but a few became orators in the Union or were prominent in the dramatic society (OUDS) and *The Isis*, the undergraduate magazine. But none of my contemporaries at Exeter set out to shock like Kenneth Tynan at Magdalen, who spent his time as an undergraduate strutting round Oxford in a purple suit, aping Oscar Wilde. He went on to be London's most acerbic theatre critic.

I can imagine that Alan Bennett, a student at Exeter College in 1959, drew on his experience of Exeter for one of his wickedly funny sketches, performed in his *Beyond the Fringe* revue, in which he imitated a priest giving a sermon. After droning on, he ends with phrases like 'Understanding faith is rather like eating from a tin of sardines – however hard you try, there is always a little bit left in the bottom of the tin. But it's that little bit that is the message to us all, that is always somewhere deeper than you are looking.'

There was no medical fellow at Exeter, so I was 'farmed out' to a biochemist, Dennis Parsons, a fellow at Merton, for whom I wrote weekly essays. I was enjoying Oxford; after the full day of lectures and dissections, I was going to meetings of clubs at night, and in my first term I was on a cross-country team, training and travelling away at weekends for matches.

My life at Oxford changed substantially in March 1947. The winter of 1946–7 had been the coldest for a generation and all the snow and ice had prevented proper trials. Having been seen enthusiastically shovelling snow from the Iffley Road track earlier in the term, I was selected almost *faute de mieux* as the third string for Oxford in the mile against Cambridge, which took place on 22 March 1947 – the day before my eighteenth birthday – at White City Stadium. This is my description written at the time:

When the gun fired, the Cambridge runners shot into the lead so, as ordered, I stayed back at a respectful distance and remained there until the middle of the back straight after the bell, marking the start of the last lap. I suppose I was as tired as everyone else, but suddenly I felt a crazy desire to overtake the whole field. I raced through into the lead. A feeling of great excitement swept over me. I forgot my tiredness. I had suddenly tapped that hidden source of energy I always suspected I possessed. I won by twenty yards in a time of 4 minutes 30.8 seconds.

I had rediscovered my gift for running and now enjoyed the new status of being a full Blue. That evening I met Harold Abrahams, the 100m champion from the Paris Olympics of 1924 – and now made famous by his portrayal in *Chariots of Fire*. I also met, at last, the great Jack Lovelock, who had also studied medicine at Exeter College and St Mary's Medical School in London. The next day the national press reported that my surprise victory showed great promise.

Oxford had a good record of creating middle-distance runners and athletes who managed to reach the Olympics and also to lead full academic and social lives. It was my fervent hope that achieving the same balance was to be the theme of my own life. It was helped by the fact that, to the irritation of the press, I competed relatively rarely in athletic events and chose not to enter many national or international competitions. I took this as the prerogative of being amateur, but it did not make me popular with the press.

Our first ever visit abroad was billed as a 'goodwill tour' to German universities in the summer of 1947. The wreckage wrought by Allied bombers was so much worse even than that of

London and Bath that we were stunned. Going round Germany only two years after the country's defeat demanded sensitivity and compassion. Unforgettable was a one-legged German high jumper. The German distance runners dropped out of the race after a mile or so and would lie on the grass in distress. We suspected they were making a political point about the inadequacy of their rations. On our return from this tour we all felt shaken. To win my races against men who had faced several years of war and starvation did not bring me any satisfaction.

Athletics created a whole new range of surprising opportunities, including new friendships, travelling abroad and trying my hand at journalism. At that time, British citizens were not allowed to spend more than £25 of their own money each per year outside the country, owing to the balance of payments crisis. Sport provided an easy travel opportunity. My closest athletic friends at that time included Norris and Ross McWhirter, Christopher Chataway and Christopher Brasher.

In 1947 I started to become involved in Oxford sporting administration. I became secretary and a few months later I was elected president of the university athletic club. In my first, initially faltering, speech as president I proposed a scheme to replace the hopelessly uneven third-of-a-mile-long university track at Iffley Road with a new quarter-mile track meeting international standards. To add to the odd length of the track, there was also a large elm tree at the far end whose roots were entangled with the cinders. Visiting runners, unaware of this hazard, had been known to trip and fall. Many professed sorrow to see the three-lap track disappear, but the proposal was accepted.

My secretary Derek Steel and I then set about finding a contractor. In retrospect, we probably should have gone to the university surveyor. But that would have meant delaying the whole scheme while detailed plans were drawn up and formally put out to tender and would risk getting stuck in university committees. I already knew only too well that Oxford's committees ground through agendas at a lethargic pace.

Derek and I had to get on with it quickly and so we decided to manage the project ourselves. We went through the Yellow Pages and phoned several contractors. We then went to see three contractors to make sure they had the necessary earth-shifting machinery. It seems odd now that two undergraduates were given free rein to negotiate this £50,000 contract. We had a time deadline that the work must be done within the next long vacation, before the start of the next soccer season, because the university's soccer pitch was in the centre of the old track. This was the year that a team of Oxford and Cambridge soccer Blues formed the Pegasus Club and won the FA Amateur Cup in front of some 100,000 spectators at Wembley. Unwisely, we accepted the lowest tender. The turf was stripped off the whole pitch, rolled up and put on one side and they brought in the bulldozers.

Then disaster struck. After three months the contractor, not a big enough firm, went bankrupt. The turf dried up and died. We were then forced to get other firms to tender quickly. Tommy Thompson, chemistry tutor at St John's and senior treasurer of soccer, was understandably furious with us and with me in particular. He had to hire Oxford City Football Club's pitch for university matches, including Pegasus matches, for the whole of the next season.

In the end it was completed three months late. In December, the Pegasus Club used the new pitch for the first time. As a club, they remained a force in national amateur soccer for several years.

In 1947, my administrative skills as secretary of the Oxford second team were put to the test at an away match. We had taken a bus to Cambridge and after the match, which, incidentally, we won, each member of our team was entertained at dinner by their opposite number. I asked them to be back at the bus by 9.30 p.m. at the latest. I had underestimated the warmth of the hospitality at Cambridge and they arrived back at the bus in dribs and drabs. They were 'tiddly' if not drunk, but as the body is only able to absorb alcohol at a fixed rate, someone who has consumed a lot of alcohol will actually get progressively more drunk after they've stopped drinking.

Waiting for the last remnants of the team, we sang a few lusty songs to discourage anyone from leaving the bus. Then, one of the party suggested taking a few street signs back to Oxford as souvenirs. I was quite unable to control them. They managed to take signs from the streets nearby, but then got more ambitious and started pulling at a Belisha beacon. When the police arrived, following a tip-off by some passer-by, we were saved by the senior treasurer of the Cambridge Athletic Club, none other than the Dr 'Bonzo' Howland who had offered me a deferred place at Cambridge. We managed to get everyone back into the bus and the senior treasurer gave all of our names to the police, kindly accepting personal responsibility for any damage. Somewhat deflated, we made our way back to Oxford and, thanks to Dr Howland, no more was heard of it.

❧

1948 was the height of post-war austerity in Britain. Food rationing was even worse than during the war. Winston Churchill, when an ordinary citizen's rations for the week were laid out in front of him, is said to have mistaken them as the rations for a single day. Our national debt was almost four times as large as it is today, largely because we were forced to pay America for all the war supplies received before she entered the war. As Wellington said, 'Nothing except a battle lost can be half so melancholy as a battle won.'

I was a typical student and, like so many other students, yearned for foreign travel as a right – a rite of passage. My plans for the long vacation in 1948 were quite complicated and, after the London Olympics, I cleared several weeks from any competitive athletics in order to travel to Switzerland. To get across France I would have to hitch-hike. Today it is considered very dangerous, but in 1948 it was the student's only way to travel. Resourceful, if naive, I wondered whether I could earn some money to pay for the holiday by writing a light-hearted beginner's guide to hitch-hiking.

I could already see a slim volume taking shape, *Hitch-hiking: The Science and Art*, as I stood by the road outside Calais. Having crossed the Channel, Dover to Calais, by ferry, I stood with my arm extended, beckoning towards every vehicle with my thumb, the universal hitch-hiking signal. But for an hour cars and lorries sped past me, totally ignoring my increasingly frantic efforts to persuade them to stop. The idea of writing a book faded, but I came up with a list of simple rules to follow.

Rule One: Take any lift in the general direction of travel. All offers should be accepted. A short hop is better than a night sleeping by the roadside. As darkness threatened, I now realised I'd be very lucky to get to Paris that evening and I didn't fancy sleeping in a haystack. Then, suddenly, my luck changed. An ancient Bedford 3-ton truck drew up with 'George Boussonier of Paris' written on the front. A man with a flamboyant moustache and a blue workman's cap stuck his head out and, sucking a tobacco-stained pipe, asked, 'Where are you going?' in English.

I thought it odd he spoke English but doubtless in time all would be revealed, and I replied, 'Paris, please.'

'Hop in,' the driver said, and I was on my way.

Rule Two: Don't ever be the first to start the conversation. Wait for the first question. The driver is the boss. If he's in the mood to talk he'll start in his own good time. And if he isn't, you will just have to suffer in silence.

'Where are you from?' he asked eventually.

I said, 'I'm a student from Oxford.'

The lorry driver paused to consider this.

After about five minutes' silence, perhaps because his curiosity got the better of him, he said, 'I guess you're surprised my English is so good.'

'Actually, I was, especially since I saw the French name on the front of your lorry.'

He said, 'You know, you're damned lucky I picked you up. Most of my friends hate the English. They still think you let us down at Dunkirk and when Winston Churchill blew our navy fleet to bits at Oran. But I don't share that view.' He spoke quickly, as if anxious to impress me with his Anglophile credentials. He clearly wanted my respect, though it was obviously unnecessary as circumstances dictated that for the present I was totally dependent on him.

I told him I was a medical student, but interested in politics. Clearly there was no point in talking about medicine, so I went on, 'We've had some strikes by our Labour parties in Britain, not by the Communist Party. In Britain, Communism isn't a threat at all.'

Rule Three: In hitch-hiking, a bond of commitment starts with the driver making his own choice to stop and he is then the boss in the partnership. It is he who decides how far he wants to take any revelation of his own private life. He said, 'In France, we love our politics. We think, eat and sleep politics. We love arguing. I was a Gaullist during the war and hated those vile Vichy collaborators. My wife is half-English, so we speak English at home.'

'I think we understand that you were powerless during the German occupation,' I answered.

Rule Four: Don't interrupt your driver. Often he needs no priming to talk, so just let it flow. Hitch-hiking can give a window to other worlds you may never experience again. Savour it.

Soon I felt he was beginning to take a liking to me. Then there was an ominous slowing of the lorry and the engine lost power for a few seconds. It picked up briefly, but seconds later it faltered again and then stopped. Georges, the driver, just managed to pull in to the verge.

Rule Five, perhaps the most important rule of all: Breakdowns may be bad luck, perhaps even the driver's own fault, but it doesn't mean you should, or can, quit. Only rats leave sinking ships. George took a bag of tools from behind his seat, climbed down and opened the bonnet and plunged around in the dark. He said, 'If you want to make yourself useful, take this torch and shine it down where I'm working.'

Then, perhaps feeling guilty about the breakdown or grateful for my help, he said, 'If you've nowhere to sleep tonight we can give you a folding bed. And if you want a lift south tomorrow I've got a friend, François, who's going to Lyon in the morning and I could take you round to him.'

Rule Six: The offer of a bed and a lift the next day must be accepted. To reject it would imply a lack of trust and you could give unpardonable offence.

The engine mended, at any rate for the time being, we were now on the outskirts of Paris. Georges at last stopped the lorry outside a three-room bungalow with a garage. He put up a truckle bed for me at the back of the kitchen and told me before bidding me goodnight that he had phoned his friend, who would be happy to drive me to Lyon in the morning.

Rule Seven: A hitch-hiker is not without honour except in his own country. Abroad, he is welcomed as the only traveller who gives his company instead of his money. In return he may receive insights that can change his ideas, if not his life.

It took me a week to hitch-hike across France to Switzerland. What exhilaration to see those mountains for the first time – I could not have imagined then that I would make a dangerous climb with Brasher seven years later. I had saved enough money to return home by train. It was fun to see my first article published in a magazine, now defunct, called *Travel*, as a mild reward.

At the start of Michelmas term in 1948, I asked the captain of the cross-country team if he needed me for the race against Cambridge in December. His reply was, 'Oh no, we've got a terrific team and won't need you.' Then, a week before the race, the captain came back to me rather sheepishly and said, 'I wonder if you'd mind running next week? Cambridge have discovered a fellow called Chris Brasher, he was the best distance runner at Rugby. He's really very good.' So I said, 'Yes, I'll do my best, but I haven't been training because you said you wouldn't need me.'

The Oxford–Cambridge match is over seven and a half miles on Wimbledon Common. At one point the runners splash through a stream and then across a ploughed field so that the mud sticks to their running shoes and legs, making each step unbearably heavy. Then, as if to add insult to injury, there is a half-mile hill we called the 'Toast Rack'. This was by far the most strenuous part of the race. Riling an opponent can often play a part in long-distance running. The most famous instance was in the 1952 Olympic matathon. Zátopek was running at the shoulder of Jim Peters, the British champion, and at ten miles Zátopek turned to Peters and said, 'Excuse me, Mr Peters, but I have not run a marathon before. Surely we should be running much faster than this?' He then put on a brief burst of speed that took him ten yards ahead, before slowing down again. Jim Peters was psychologically defeated. In my 1948 race, Brasher was leading from me by a few yards. I came up to Brasher's shoulder halfway up the Toast Rack and said cheerfully, 'This hill doesn't seem as steep this year.' I then, despite feeling extremely tired, accelerated away from him for fifty yards. I was able to hold this lead and won the race in a record time. After this race Chris and I began a lifelong friendship. He was best man at my wedding.

My third year became unbelievably busy, crowded with becoming president of Vincent's Club, an elite Oxford sporting club said to open many doors in the future for its members in the wider world. You have to be elected and the tie is recognised in far-flung places by fellow members, with pleasant links immediately forged. In 2013, we celebrated its 150th anniversary.

In 1949 I was proposed for the presidency of the junior common room (JCR) at Exeter College. The election itself was usually a noisy, rather drunken affair. The previous president was a tall, imposing ex-service figure and his natural authority kept the meeting under some semblance of control, though seeming to allow everyone to let off steam. He had become a much respected member of the college during his presidency, being less conservative than he looked, and he ended up as a comprehensive school headmaster. The election meeting was, as usual, accompanied by leg pulling, hilarity and occasional goading of any reluctant candidate for office.

It fell to me as president to organise the summer ball. At that time, thirty years before women were admitted to men's colleges, only one in eight undergraduates was a woman. On the night of the ball, many girls came from London, but the Oxford girls from the university and some nurses and physiotherapists of course came too. Wine, women and song was the order of the night.

We decided that the ball should have an Elizabethan theme, as befitted a new Elizabethan age when Princess Elizabeth II would soon become Queen. As guests arrived at the lodge they were greeted by a student dressed as Sir Walter Raleigh who waved his cloak as if to protect the ladies' dainty shoes from the ground underfoot. As couples entered the front quadrangle they saw four coal braziers aflame, fixed at the corners of the lawn. After dinner there was a fireworks display.

A transforming experience for me was going to America for the first time in the summer of 1949, as captain of a joint Oxford–Cambridge team visiting Yale, Harvard, Cornell and Princeton. The first shock was the country's affluence. We were given lavish meals, in stark contrast to the position in England, still under general rationing. At first we were in danger of eating our way to defeat! The scale of the universities' training facilities, stadiums and coaching support were unlike anything at home. We arrived at Princeton at the time of the commencement ceremonies, in which each year of Princeton students came back to celebrate the year they joined the university. They wore silly hats and marched behind vans and at the end of the celebration were expected to write out big cheques to Princeton. There is a story of an alumnus who got so fed up with appeals from the university that he asked his secretary to ring the university's office to say he'd died. Months later, he was furious that his tickets for the Yale–Princeton football game had not arrived.

After that I was dazzled by the Americans' informality, enthusiasm, good humour and openness to new ideas. These traits seemed to promote rather than impede success in academia and the burgeoning economy. At first it was quite disarming, coming from England's more formal and hierarchical culture.

For some foreign tours in 1950, when no professional sports journalist could be flown out specially, I was commissioned by *The Times* of London to report on the races, including my own. This required anonymity, as all *Times* correspondents laboured under at the time, so the editor used the byline 'Special Athletics Correspondent'. It was my first chance to be a journalist, though under the strictly enforced rules for amateurism then prevailing, I could not be paid for it.

On this tour I got gastroenteritis in Greece and then faced a race in the Soldiers Stadium in Belgrade in front of about 70,000 spectators. I had beaten their best miler, Otenhajmer, in the British Games mile at Whitsun earlier in the same year. Of course he beat me, but I had the satisfaction of writing a report of the race in *The Times*, in which I wrote, 'Bannister, who was far from his best…'

On one occasion, Chris Chataway and I accepted an invitation to go to Morocco in the middle of the winter, where we could expect the twin bonus of warm sunshine and a lack of serious competition. One morning we drove out to a beautiful Mediterranean beach, donned swimming trunks and waded into the sea. Foolishly, and without thinking, I swam out some distance and then felt myself being swept by a strong tide away from Chris, who had not ventured as far. With all my might I struggled to swim across the tide and it was ten minutes, by which time I was nearly completely exhausted, before I found that I was closing the distance and eventually I managed to reach him. It was one of the four occasions I recall feeling I might lose my life, the others being when climbing or sailing, not counting the risks of bombing in either Bath or London.

Under the usual schedule for medical undergraduates, I would have taken my physiology exams in the summer of 1949, but I received a dispensation to delay them for a year so that I could leave in May for the American tour. In the meantime I had polished off in advance my pathology, pharmacology and bacteriology exams in March 1949.

In October 1949, the new school of Philosophy, Psychology and Physiology (PPP) was started. At the time, I was fascinated in the physiology of the brain and I moved to this new school. But then I found that it had an emphasis on behaviourism. The faculty wanted to get away from psychiatry or the psychology which had been introduced by Freud and instead analysed behaviourist aspects of brain function. Most of the other students on the course had been reading Politics, Philosophy and Economics (PPE) or Ancient Philosophy. The head of the new school was a classicist and of course the ancient philosophers had many ideas about how the mind works, but without knowledge of – or deep interest in – anatomy or physiology as they had to rely on logic. The course was not as I had envisaged it and so, after a term, I switched back to straight physiology. I had good reasons to come back into the mainstream of physiology, and in the end was convinced it was the right path for me to follow.

Oxford at the time had one of the strongest departments of

neurophysiology in the country. Sir Charles Sherrington had only relatively recently retired from Oxford. Over the course of thirty years, through experiments with animals, he worked out the basis of the control of movement by reflexes in the spinal cord. Then he discovered at what level in the brain the upper control of the reflexes exists. This was research of the highest standard, for which he was awarded a Nobel Prize. His was the kind of approach we were taught and it heightened my interest in the brain and neurophysiology. On account of this interest, in my fourth year I went for tutorials to David Whitteridge, another prominent neurophysiologist. His research interests were also in control of the heart and circulation.

After living in college for three years, I went to a room at Vincent's Club. But being there distracted me from my work, so I moved to a room in Charles Wenden's house in Bradmore Road in north Oxford. Here, without immediate diversions and no longer administering any sports, I could devote myself to work, taking my delayed physiology finals in June 1950. This was the same house in which I had lunch and waited all afternoon before the four-minute mile, staring gloomily out of the window and hoping for an improvement in the weather.

I spent another year at Oxford after taking my degree, as a Harmsworth Senior Scholar at Merton. These scholarships, with senior common room dining rights, were awarded to a few graduates who were conducting research and hoping for an academic career at Oxford. My research was in human respiratory physiology, specifically on the problem of breathing control in exercise. The choice of this topic might suggest a connection with my athletic career, but in fact my interest was purely academic and had no particular benefit to me as an athlete. Indeed, I spent hours each day sampling gases and was then unwittingly exposed to high levels of mercury vapour, which could well have been harmful to my lungs and general health. From time to time, I glanced at my gums in the mirror to see whether there was a blue line, which is one indication of mercury poisoning.

I chose this problem because it also had a neurological dimension: the brain's control of breathing, that is, how the rate and depth of breathing naturally adjust to the needs of the exercising muscles. The link is mainly the increase in the carbon dioxide concentration in the blood, resulting from breakdown of glycogen in the muscles. If not enough oxygen can be provided from the lungs and blood, lactate accumulates, altering the acidity of the blood circulating through chemoreceptors in the brainstem and increasing the rate of breathing still further. There is also an increase in nerve impulses to the brain from sensory receptors in the muscles, tendons and joints. In extreme exercise there was a possible third element that was then in dispute. Could the demands for oxygen in the muscles become so acute that blood could not be fully oxygenated by one passage through the lungs so that the partial pressure of oxygen in the arterial blood would actually fall? Or did the mechanism for transporting oxygen to the muscles remain adequate even in extreme exercise? At that stage it was not yet possible or safe to sample arterial blood directly from a subject as he exercised and so, in an attempt to answer this question indirectly, I arranged for the subjects to breathe levels of oxygen higher than the 20 per cent in ordinary air: 33 per cent, 66 per cent and 100 per cent. If the transport mechanism were efficient enough, increasing the oxygen content would not increase how long the subjects could run until reaching exhaustion. In fact, up to 66 per cent oxygen allowed them to run for about twice as long before exhaustion, seeming to indicate that oxygen supply did fail in extreme exercise. One subject on 66 per cent quit due to boredom and another because he 'had a train to catch'. The failure of 100 per cent oxygen to be better than 66 per cent oxygen was puzzling, but we attributed this to an irritant effect of pure oxygen on the lung passages. This research formed the basis of my thesis for the MSc degree. My supervisor was Dr Dan Cunningham. Much later, Professors McDonald and Wade at Birmingham later proved that arterial blood oxygen was lowered in hard exercise by catheterising an artery at the elbow.

One of the most frequent questions I am asked is 'What are the limits of speed for a runner over different distances?' What makes one runner a winner and the other a loser?

Sprinting is simpler than middle-distance running. It depends on the wasteful, but massive, phosphocreatine release in fast-twitch muscle fibres. The principle, unchanged since 1920, when Professor A. V. Hill of University College London proved the point, is that there was an 'oxygen debt' incurred and then 'paid off' after the exercise, as lactate is converted to carbon dioxide and water. In racing over 400m, 25 per cent of the energy is provided by aerobic means and slow-twitch fibres start to be recruited. As the distance increases, the proportion provided by anaerobic sources of energy falls to 50/50 in the mile, and only to 1 per cent aerobic in the marathon.

So, in summary, there are two limiting factors in running: the first is an intrinsic muscle power release factor. The second is a mental factor. I have said the winner is the runner who can take out more than he has; he may 'faint' or collapse at the end of the race. He may collapse briefly after driving himself harder, but it does not matter. There are many runners with a high aerobic capacity who break world records but are beaten at the finish because they cannot drive their body as hard as their rivals. What determines this mental phenomenon? A French journalist once asked my wife, ''ow did 'e know 'e would not die?'

Though I spent nearly two years doing research into the control of breathing in exercise at Oxford, the conclusion I reached was: the human body is millennia ahead of the physiologist. My studies were more concerned with the fundamental control of breathing and whether lowered arterial oxygen occurred as a limiting factor in the final stages of all exhaustion, rather than whether a particular athlete had a physiological advantage. A leading physiologist of exercise, Professor Tim Noakes of South Africa, made an intensive study of my papers, published in the *Journal of Physiology* in 1954. When he asked me what the limiting factor in human exhaustion was, I said, 'Of course, it is the brain, which determines how hard the exercise systems can be pushed.' He concurred.

By the summer of 1951, when I left for London, I had been at Oxford for almost five years. My choice of medicine as a career had been confirmed; I had started along the path to publishing research, and had already discovered a strong interest in the brain and neurophysiology. It had also taught me that I was unsuited to laboratory research into physiology and so was looking forward to starting clinical work in London. I had also been able to reach an Olympic standard without sacrificing several other dimensions of university life, foremost among which had been administering the athletics clubs and seeing to the building of the new Iffley Road track.

For the opportunities Oxford opened to me, I felt grateful.

My parents took great pleasure in visiting me at Oxford and my sister at Reading University and seeing that it would serve us in good stead for the future. I still recall the sense of fulfilment my father quietly showed on one occasion when he was working near Oxford and I could invite him to have lunch with me at Vincent's Club, and we sat together chatting, surrounded by the members.

Chapter 5

Early Experiences in
International Athletics

In the summer of 1945, aged fifteen, I saw my first international athletics race when I was taken by my father to the White City Stadium. I had never been to any big sporting occasion before, not even a football match. There was tremendous excitement about this meeting because after six years of war every sports enthusiast wanted to turn with relief back to watching sport again. Perhaps my father, who had won the mile in his own school sports in 1910, wanted me to have the chance he missed to become a runner. But being a wise parent he never, as far as I can recall, voiced any expectations or hopes for me at this early stage, although I had already won several school races.

We arrived at the White City Underground station in good time, but as we walked into the road leading to the stadium we found it was already packed with a milling crowd, the largest I had ever seen. It seemed that the stadium was full and a barrier had been put up across the entrance. We were facing the disappointment of a long journey back to Harrow when the barrier broke, and I soon found the crowd behind was pushing us inside the ground, happy to stand for four hours. We were rewarded by seeing the race that fired my ambition.

In the field for the mile race was a spare, small, black-vested British athlete, Sydney Wooderson, our best-ever miler. He missed the Berlin 1936 Olympics because of a sprained ankle but broke the mile world record in 1937 with a 4.64-minute time and in 1938 set up a new world half-mile record of 1 minute 49 seconds. However, he was cheated of his expected Olympic success when the Games scheduled for 1940 in Tokyo were cancelled at the onset of war. Wooderson had disappeared somewhere into the British Army, where he had become a lance corporal, and now here he was in his first post-war race, though no one knew whether he had been able to continue his training.

He faced another former world-record holder in the mile, the Swede Arne Andersson. The Swedes were neutral during the war and so they were able to run repeatedly against each other and lower the world record several times. One of Arne Andersson's rivals, and often a 'hare' (or pacemaker) in record attempts, was Gunder Hägg. In 1942 he broke ten world records in eighty-two days, starting with Wooderson's mile record. Often, he had a sustained final sprint of some 300 yards which Arne Andersson could rarely match. His 1945 world record of 4 minutes 1.3 seconds meant he had only been about ten yards short of the tape when the clock passed 4:00.0.

The Swedes had adopted a new training method learnt from Woldemar Gerschler, the pre-war German coach of an earlier world half-mile record holder, Rudolf Harbig. They modified his method slightly, by continuously varying the speed of running, between sprinting and jogging, over soft grass in the country-side. They called this *fartlek* or speed play. It seemed to increase both speed and endurance and avoided pain in the legs which occurred if runners spent too much time on roads or cinder tracks. I later adapted this form of training for myself.

In the race at the White City Stadium, Arne Andersson and Sydney Wooderson broke away from the rest of the field on the last lap and it looked for a few strides as though Wooderson, some six inches shorter than the graceful lanky Swede, might daringly beat him. The stadium was filled with a roar such as I had never heard before. But it was not to be. Andersson caught Wooderson and won in 4 minutes 8.8 seconds. The drama of this confrontation crystallised my sporting ambitions. I resolved then to become a miler.

The first Olympic Games in which I could have competed were held in London in 1948. I was nominated as an 'Olympic possible', but forgoing the extra food ration available to 'possibles', I withdrew myself from consideration on the grounds of my age. At eighteen, I held the notion then traditional in Oxford athletics that over-competition too young could produce 'staleness'. I decided that I could not win a medal in London as my times were then equivalent to a 4-minute 10-second mile, whereas I expected the winner of the final to run the equivalent of a 4-minute 6-second mile. This was indeed how it turned out in the end.

I was then offered the post of unpaid assistant to the British Olympic Association. I readily accepted, hoping to gain some experience of the Olympic organisation.

One dramatic moment stands out. On 29 July 1948, the day of the opening ceremony, the commandant and I were about to drive over to the stadium. We had been told that a car carrying the flags of all the nations was to drive along the line of assembled teams just before they marched into the stadium. In this way there would be no danger of any team forgetting its flag. As we were leaving Uxbridge, my eyes caught sight of an old Union

Jack which our commandant had used for minor flag-raising ceremonies with British teams in the past. We kept it rolled up in a corner of the office. I suggested we should take it with us, 'just in case'.

On arrival at Wembley we saw the car park was crowded and we left it to the driver to find a place. The commandant and I made our way to the British team. The flags for the parade had just been handed out, and horror! – there was no flag for the British team. A mistake had been made. In another twenty minutes the British team, parading last as host nation, would enter the stadium. The whole ceremony culminated in placing the flags of the various countries in a semi-circle round an athlete who would take the Olympic oath on behalf of all competitors.

The commandant ordered me to find the flag we had brought from Uxbridge. He gave me a jeep and a British Army sergeant. Together we tore off towards the car park. We drove furiously through the crowds which still packed the approaches to the stadium. I kept my hand on the hooter so that it sounded continuously. We reached the car park. There were thousands of cars and to find ours in time seemed an impossibility.

Everyone stared as we rushed like madmen up and down the lines of cars. It took us ten minutes to find our own. It was locked, so I smashed a window with a stone while the sergeant restrained a policeman who wanted to arrest me.

Seizing the flag, I rushed back to the jeep and we set off for the stadium. But the entrances were blocked by last-minute arrivals and the jeep was soon hemmed in on all sides. Hooting was useless. Time was perilously short, and I could see the British team having to parade without a flag. I jumped out of the jeep. Using the flag as a battering ram, with brass spike foremost, I charged through the crowd and reached the British team just before they marched into the stadium. The official film shows the British team with a smaller flag than all the others.

In 1948, facilities were simple and conditions spartan. The teams and the administrators lived in RAF huts in Uxbridge. Teams from the defeated enemy countries, Germany, Italy and Japan, were excluded. Russia was ill-prepared to compete after its war efforts and the loss of more than twenty million people and so stayed away. This decision was compounded by the international quarrel over Stalin's move to blockade the Allied-controlled quarter of Berlin. This was successfully countered by the Berlin Airlift, which saw Allied planes dropping food and supplies into the city until May 1949.

The stars who made their names in 1948 included the greatest ever Czech runner, Emil Zátopek, and the Jamaican Arthur Wint, the 400m winner, and the brilliant Jamaican 4 x 400m relay team. The Belgian Gaston Reiff just beat Zátopek in the 5,000m. Inexplicably, Zátopek allowed Reiff to get forty yards ahead at the bell but then caught up all but one metre in a desperate 62-second last-lap sprint. Women were also prominent, especially Fanny Blankers-Koen, the Dutch mother of two, who won three gold medals. This performance was even more astonishing in light of the fact that the Dutch population had been subjected to some of the worst starvation in Europe during and just after the war. The Australian sprinter Shirley Strickland won two gold medals at the 100m and 200m. The London Games were an undoubted success, despite the modest organisation, partly because the number of athletes and accompanying journalists was kept within manageable limits. The entire cost of the Games was £780,000, as opposed to the £10 billion for London 2012. The White City Games actually turned a profit of £20,000!

In 1937, Ludwig Guttmann, a German Jewish Professor of

Neurology at Breslau, fled Germany and came to Oxford. Like a number of German doctors and academics, he was generously treated by the university and he was given a post at the Radcliffe Infirmary. He was lodged by Lord David Cecil in the Master's lodgings at Balliol for two weeks, given £2,000 and then found a house in north Oxford. There was no doubt about his competence as a neurologist. In German hospitals, 'Herr Professor' was a title held for life and he was powerful in promoting his juniors. In Oxford, Guttmann was found to be prickly.

Dr Ritchie Russell, the senior neurologist in Oxford, besides his work at the Radcliffe Infirmary was in charge of the Armed Services Head Injuries Unit built during the war in huts at Headington, on the edge of Oxford. Brain injury casualties were flown back from every sector of the war, assessed there and, if necessary, operated on by Oxford's neurosurgeons, under Sir Hugh Cairns. Ritchie Russell had an increasingly serious problem. His beds were becoming 'blocked' by paralysed chronic spinal injury patients.

This type of injury in peacetime was an uncommon consequence of riding and motorcycle accidents but now the war brought patients flooding back to Headington from all war zones. Their prognosis was bad and many died within months of injury, from infected bedsores, pneumonia or bladder infections.

One morning a 'eureka' moment came to Ritchie Russell. In an instant, he realised that Dr Guttmann could solve the paraplegia problem. The solution lay in appointing Dr Guttmann to Stoke Mandeville, a small district hospital outside Oxford, but part of the Oxford regional health service.

A totally new national spinal injury unit was created at Stoke Mandeville. Guttmann became the sole director, with wide powers. Ritchie Russell made the case to government for funding, which was unanswerable. It fulfilled a national need. These paraplegics were holding up vital treatment for other needy patients, so money had to be found for the new buildings Guttmann required.

The government accepted the argument of 'national need', but little did they know what they had let themselves in for. Guttmann almost parked himself on the doorstep of the headquarters of the National Health Service at the Elephant and Castle in London until he got what he needed. He was, as someone said, more dangerous than a Rommel Tiger tank parked on their lawn and nearly always got his way. Apart from new buildings, new equipment had to be specially designed. Better mechanical respirators were needed than the 'iron lungs' then used for patients whose breathing was weak because the upper spinal cord controlling breathing was damaged. He had new designs for steel beds that could be rotated through 180 degrees to nurse patients with bedsores on either side or on their faces. Guttmann told the nurses, 'You can put anything you like on a bedsore, except the patient.'

Ludwig Guttmann was a rigid disciplinarian with whom it was sometimes not easy for other doctors to work, but his patients were devoted to him, nicknaming him 'Poppa'. He allowed no authority to stand in his way as he strove to obtain the best equipment for his patients.

Everyone realised that Guttmann was quite brilliant in his new role. Within a year he devised entirely new treatments for paraplegics that revolutionised world medical practice for treating spinal injuries. Patients who would almost certainly have died in three months now left hospital in six months in a wheelchair, filled with hopes for a new life, reprieved from the likely sentence of early death.

The changed atmosphere was catching and the ripple effect gave courage and hope to all those soldiers wounded in our recent wars, let alone the civilian victims of a car crash or any untoward accident.

Guttmann became more famous as his power and success grew. In time he collected a coterie of loyal disciples, some also German refugee doctors who respected him and acquiesced to his manner and style.

When I was a medical student in Oxford in 1947, Dr Guttmann invited me to Stoke Mandeville. He wanted me to see the way he was using sport to help bring hope to his paraplegic patients. He told me that one day he saw one patient throwing a ball to a patient on the other side of the ward who caught it neatly. He also told me that he found some patients had invented a form of hockey, using walking sticks and hitting a puck around the asphalt car park while seated in their wheelchairs. These simple incidents made him realise that the skills of the arms were usually normal and could be used to play various kinds of adapted sports, including archery and pistol shooting, just as well as able-bodied athletes. Furthermore, most of the early patients had war injuries and so were young, well-motivated and willing to take risks.

On that first visit in 1947, I saw wheelchair netball was difficult in the heavy wooden wheelchairs that were the standard issue for paraplegic patients. In 1948, Dr Guttmann held his first Paralympic Games at Stoke Mandeville and by then he had persuaded the Ministry of Health to provide them with metal chairs which were much more manoeuvrable and enabled the British wheelchair volleyball players to take on the American teams with their state-of-the-art chairs on equal terms. The whole emphasis then became a realisation of what the disabled can do despite their disability, rather than what they are unable to do by virtue of their disability.

There was widespread national and international publicity for Guttmann's ideas. They were widely applauded and enthusiastically supported. In time, the theme of 'sport for the disabled' swept through more and more sports: swimming, horse riding, sailing and skiing – there seemed almost no limit to what paraplegics could do, with proper modification of the events. And it was spreading to other countries too, just as Guttmann's pioneer methods of treatment had done.

The sea change in attitude to the disabled reached its zenith at the 2012 London Paralympics. Every heart was stirred by the obvious joy of so many Paralympic competitors. The Paralympics had all the ingredients of sport, but of a different kind. For the first time, a whole generation was exposed to the thrill of watching a new sport. Just as Baron de Coubertin is rightly called the founder of the modern Olympic Games, Dr Guttmann is the founder of the Paralympic Games.

Chapter 6

International Running Career:
Oxford to Helsinki

Just like any explanation of the things we enjoy – like the description of a rose to someone who has never seen one – attempts at analysis of the joy of running are never adequate.

The scientist may try an objective approach. The sense of exercise is an extra sense or perhaps a subtle combination of the others. It is one which most of us ignore. Small electrical impulses, so the scientist tells us, pass from our contracting muscles and our moving joints to our brain. The electrical rhythm produced in the brain is a source of pleasure. Like that caused by music, it has some interplay with the rhythms inherent in our nervous systems. But no explanation is satisfying that does not take account of feelings of liberation.

The satisfaction we derive from different games is complex. We enjoy struggling to get the best out of ourselves, whether we play games of skill requiring quickness of eye and deftness of touch, or games of effort and endurance like athletics, cycling and rowing. It is not just the desire to succeed: there is also the desire to find in sport a companionship with kindred people. I have found all these.

Paradoxically, the sportsman enjoys his sport even if he has absolutely no prospect of becoming a champion. In athletics there are many events – running, jumping and throwing – which call for different physiques, the long and thin, the broad and strong. Industry and perseverance, without any great natural aptitude, bring greater success in athletics than is possible in ball games.

For nearly ten years I ran about twenty-five miles a week. The more I ran, the longer my list of reasons for running grew. Running through mud and rain is never boring. I found in running – win or lose – a deep satisfaction that I could not express in any other way. In 1948 it was difficult to find 100 runners to take part in the annual national marathon from Windsor Castle to the White City Stadium. Today, every weekend around the country there are 10km races, half-marathons and marathons. This is historically one of the most extraordinary changes in human behaviour, which started originally with James Fixx in America, a *Time* magazine editor who wrote an inspiring book simply called *The Complete Book of Running* in 1977. There are now over a million recreational runners in the UK, and ten million in the USA, often racing for their favourite charity, for whom similar feelings about running also apply. However strenuous our work, sport brings more pleasure. It brings a freedom and challenge which cannot be found elsewhere.

Was it a remnant of this primitive feeling that spurred me on, when I put on shoes with nearly half-inch steel spikes, and ran round a cinder track, only to come back to the starting point? What is it like to have the excitement of competitive struggle grafted onto the natural freedom found in movement? To champion the cause of club or country and to have their honour, as well as your own, at stake? What difference does it make when the sound of breakers on the shore is replaced by the roar of a crowd of 50,000 spectators in a stadium, crying out for more and more effort and identifying themselves with their country's success or failure? What does it mean to wait weeks or months for a race which only lasts for a few minutes, or for a sprinter to travel thousands of miles for the few seconds of supreme exertion before reaching the finishing line?

It becomes more difficult to experience again the earlier pleasure in running when facing the complex challenges of organised championship racing. With your mind on race tactics, on the line you will take on each corner, and with the opponents breathing down your neck, part of the primitive sense of freedom is inevitably lost.

If I had been asked before my retirement from athletics what running meant to me, I should have replied, 'I don't know.' Life must be lived forwards even if sometimes it only makes sense as we look back. Before my retirement, it would have been impossible for me to attempt to write about running, but now I can see a pattern of striving – of success and failure – which has grown clearer. Though I only have experience of my own running, this story, I feel, applies to athletics in general, to other sports and I hope even beyond. I write mainly as though running were all-important. It is difficult to describe how moments when running seemed insignificant alternate with moments when it threatened to engulf me. Of course, this applies to competitive running. When my racing career was over, my love of 'fun' running as a recreation never left me.

My early training at Oxford was very light and, in retrospect, ridiculously inadequate. My first system of training was taken from a small paperback pamphlet written by Sydney Wooderson in the 1940s and priced at 'two and sixpence'. I thought it more reasonable to listen to the 'greats' of the sport than to the theories of coaches of whom I'd never heard. I trained four days a week, running mainly on grass, continuously varying the speed and length of sprints. Once a week I trained on a track, alternating slower runs of 1¼ miles on the track with faster runs of ½–¾ mile. Every fortnight I would have a fast time trial of ¾-mile, from which I could predict the likely speed for the next race.

This schedule had several disadvantages. It kept me in steady condition, but did not strengthen me. Provided I did not race too often I was able to run races near my best times, but without showing any definite improvement. I clearly ran largely on nervous energy summoned up for the occasion and, as a result, I needed time afterwards to recover. The night after my races I was often too tired physically and too excited mentally to sleep. If I did not take enough salt to make up for what I had lost through excessive sweating, the muscles of my legs would ache and I would be racked with cramps.

It was in early 1950 that the AAA coach Jim Alford, who had been a 4-minute 15-second miler himself, lent me an account of the training methods of Gunder Hägg, the Swedish world-record holder for the mile. Hägg used the *fartlek* ('speed play') method, running almost entirely on grass. He alternated gentle running with fast running over distances from 100 yards to a mile. The aim was to give both speed and stamina to the athlete, imitating the games which children play in the playground involving short bursts of running until breathless, followed by a pause for recovery. The success of the method depends on pushing yourself as hard as you can during the bursts, running to exhaustion before allowing partial recovery, but not finishing so exhausted that you have no wish to train the following day. I was glad to have my own training pattern confirmed and this principle formed the basis of all my subsequent training. It was so simple, but also proved to be highly effective.

In the AAA championships on 15 July 1950, I ran a half-mile against the great Arthur Wint, the Olympic 400m champion from Jamaica. It was like leaning out from our respective events below and above this distance, he from the 400m and me from the mile, to shake hands with each other. We were good friends but this was the only occasion when I was able to make any challenge.

I had a strange feeling when running behind him. He was six feet four inches, with legs long in proportion even for this height. His length of stride was so great that it interfered with the natural rhythm of my own running. Arthur Wint had been a Spitfire pilot during the war, though folding himself into the cockpit must have been difficult. He was the only runner I had met who could influence my length of stride. At the time we raced each other he was a medical student. As a runner he dominated me so much that I almost wished I could fit in two strides to his one. I had to keep at a respectful distance to avoid getting spiked – it was like running against a giant.

He was one of the greatest natural athletes I have seen, with a broad chest and an easy, graceful stride. His stature and physique can be compared with that of Usain Bolt. His charm endeared him to fellow athletes and spectators alike. I am told that when I or any other English half-milers were running behind him we looked like little boys chasing our big uncle. Despite his usual ease of movement, on occasions he looked ungainly when he ran, like a big man attempting to run more slowly than he should. He relied mainly on his natural ability, not training anything like as much as other half-milers of the time.

The outcome of our championship half-mile was that he beat me with ease in 1 minute 51.6 seconds, though I ran my fastest time to date of 1 minute 52.1 seconds. I put in a good burst over the last 250 yards but it was insufficient to catch him.

My first taste of full international competition came in the final of the European Games 800m in Brussels on 26 August 1950. I was ill-prepared for such an important race. John Parlett, who ran a 1-minute 50.9-second 800m in the Olympic semi-final at Wembley in 1948, was the other British representative. Our opponents included Audun Boysen, a Norwegian who had startled the world some weeks before with a 1-minute 48.7-second 800m. There were also Marcel Hansenne of France, who took third place in the Olympic 800m final of 1948 Wembley, and Josy Barthel of Luxembourg.

This was my first experience of an international 'scrambling' race, by which I mean a crowded field with runners jostling for position, with the risk of falling or being 'spiked'. Boysen rushed into the lead with a suicidal first lap of 50.9 seconds. I lay fourth in 53.8 seconds. The extent of the jostling took me by surprise and I found myself in the middle of the runners, with elbows pushing me on all sides. After moving up on the back straight I held the lead round the last bend and into the finishing straight. Then Parlett came alongside and edged past me as if blown along by a private gust of wind. Thirty yards from the tape I had no strength left. Somehow I staggered on, taking an overdraft from some hidden source. Just as I tottered over the line Marcel Hansenne came up on the outside. Parlett had won by inches in 1 minute 50.5 seconds and I was declared second. There was an appeal. The jury met, the photo finish was examined and Hansenne was given the second place, with the same time for all three of us of 1 minute 50.7 seconds.

After this I decided that it was not tactical sense I lacked but strength to sustain my finishing speed without fading. I had survived the elbow battle and had reached a winning position. The situation in each race is different and it is a question of thinking quickly. I doubt if this ability is improved much by practice. I simply lacked the strength to make use of a good position. This strength could only come from harder training. After this meeting I became far more aware of the strain of international competition and the far greater intensity of nervousness it produced beforehand, relative to university matches.

Over the course of two months in summer 1950 I was beaten in five major races. Whereas in previous years winning was my stimulus, now I was becoming accustomed to defeat, to the point of being casual about it. I was frustrated by the racing schedule, which had dragged me across six European countries in that period. This was a turning point that could have seen my career as a runner coming to a premature finish. Luckily, my enjoyment of the sensation of running, the elation when I did win and the prospect of the Olympics in Helsinki in two years' time, taken together, were enough to carry me forward. I worked out a plan which would, I hoped, bring me to a peak for the great Olympic race in 1952. Having stepped up my training programme, the first phase of this would involve running in as many first-class meetings as possible during the 1951 season. I intended also to travel widely so that I could get used to changes of food and climate. I hoped to meet most of the opponents I was likely to race against in Helsinki. This would help me to find out their individual strengths and weaknesses. After a year of this, culminating in the AAA mile at White City in July 1951, my Olympic preparation would begin in earnest. This second phase would see me remain in England and rely on training rather than racing. I hoped this would give me strength without draining my nervous energy. It was a lack of strength that I had struggled with during my first year of international racing.

At Christmas 1950 I travelled out to the Centennial Games in New Zealand with Arthur Wint and Emmanuel McDonald Bailey, taking on the extra duties of team manager. McDonald Bailey came from Trinidad and, with Wint, dominated Commonwealth sprinting and shorter middle-distance running between 1946 and 1952. McDonald Bailey had perhaps the most consistently successful record of any sprinter of that era and his career was crowned by his world-record run of 10.2 seconds for the 100m at Belgrade in 1951. They were both considerably older than me and much more experienced athletes.

The 36-hour flight to New Zealand by slow propeller aircraft provided much greater interest than my only other major tour, to America in 1949 with the Oxford and Cambridge University team. We flew over the snow-capped Alps and circled Vesuvius on our way to Egypt. We saw the pyramids in the twilight and the sun-baked city of Cairo looking fresh in the early morning air.

We stayed one night in Singapore. Cars were upturned in the street – the result of riots. The sights and sounds of an Eastern city, the crowded streets and hubbub, were too much to absorb on such a short visit. We spent the next night in the tropical humidity of northern Australia at Darwin, in huts built on piles to guard against the ravages of the white ant. Three days of continuous flying coupled with sightseeing when we should have been sleeping had brought us to a stupor of fatigue. Sydney Harbour Bridge, ranked as one of the wonders of the modern world, raised barely a murmur of excitement in us. We spent an hour or so watching the Ashes Test match in Sydney in a boisterous atmosphere that contrasted with the silent, stolid respectability of Lord's. Our curiosity was temporarily sated and we were impatient to complete the last stage of our journey to New Zealand. It was midsummer in New Zealand and soon we were eating our Christmas dinner and sunning ourselves by the stream that lazed through the grounds of the school in Christchurch where we were staying.

The Games were founded to celebrate the 1851 settlement in Christchurch, South Island, by an Anglican group from Canterbury, England. Aiming to escape the industrial revolution, they brought with them what they felt was a perfect cross-section of English rural society. Ironically, the country was consumed by a labour strike at the time of our visit.

I won my race from a field which included Willy Slijkhuis from Holland, the European 1,500m champion. We ran on a grass track and my time of 4 minutes 9.9 seconds was my fastest so far. When I chatted following the race with Don MacMillan, the Australian miler who came second, he commented to me, 'I've noticed, Roger, you only become really friendly with your opponents after you've beaten them!' This was true. I naturally eyed my rivals suspiciously, wanting to win after travelling 11,000 miles to a race against them lasting some four brief minutes.

In the anticlimax after this effort I was beaten the following day in a half-mile race. This defeat received almost as much attention as my victory in the mile. At the time I thought I felt relatively impervious to unfavourable press comment, which takes no account of individual temperament or the athlete's own planning. I preferred to reserve myself for the important races.

From each race there were lessons to be learnt. Often it was from mistakes that I discovered my instinctive reactions to many of the situations I was likely to meet in future big races. It was my aim to make these reactions to many of the tactical problems so automatic that I might experience again in races the same spontaneity that I had as a boy running wildly along the shore.

I settled eventually on my own 'interval' method of training, which meant running five to ten miles per session five times each week. The first phase of my preparation had been a success. I had learnt how to enjoy the travel aspect of international touring and had come across many of the competitors I was likely to face in Helsinki. I had also improved my speed, and the changes to my training left me feeling fitter and stronger.

These improvements brought with them an unexpected urge for the competitive races I had been trying to avoid earlier. This revealed a pent-up, aggressive energy that I had not been aware of before. As a result I accepted an invitation to run in the Benjamin Franklin mile at the Penn Relays, one of America's biggest track meets.

Two weeks before leaving England, on Tuesday 18 April 1951, I ran a ¾-mile trial at Motspur Park in 2 minutes 56.8 seconds. Andersson's world record stood at 2 minutes 56.6 seconds, so I was getting close. My time was nearly 3 seconds less than Wooderson's British record of 2 minutes 59.6 seconds, made in 1939. It was a very quiet affair, an evening meeting between my friend Chris C's club (Walton) and Imperial College. I had always found it easier not having to lead from the front and this was the first of many occasions when Chris C helped me with the pacing.

I felt that I had reached world class at last. After this run, *News of the World* journalist Joe Binks wrote that the four-minute mile could no longer be regarded as a joke, but I knew that in fact it was still a very long way off. Nor was I even prepared to think about it until the great hurdle of the Olympic Games was passed.

I underestimated the press interest in my visit to America

and I arrived alone. The general press reaction was summed up the following day by one reporter who wrote, 'No manager, no trainer, no masseur, no friends! He's nuts or he's good!'

My main rivals in the race would be Fred Wilt and Don Gehrmann, both of whom had run faster miles than me. Before a big race a minor incident is apt to seem like a grave threat. I was training with some sprinters on the Wednesday before the Saturday of the race. I seldom sprint in normal training, but on this occasion I was eager not to appear too slow. The unusual speed training left me very stiff. I spent the next two days having alternate hot and cold baths, but the stiffness remained. However, when the day of the race finally came, this trivial upset was forgotten in the excitement.

Held on Saturday 28 April 1951, the race was the successor to 'Miles of the Century' in the 1930s at this same Penn Relays event in Philadelphia. There was a crowd of 40,000, very large for an American track meet. Track and field athletics were not as popular with spectators in America as in England at the time, but advanced press coverage of my event must have had some effect. Just before the race I talked with forced confidence to Wilt and Gehrmann. To me, neither looked particularly happy and this gave me hope.

For the first two laps I ran mechanically, feeling too uncertain to want to set the pace, and I hesitated until the middle of the third lap, when we began slowing down. I was concerned that soon Wilt and Gehrmann would pass me, so I moved quickly into the lead before the bell. As I accelerated, I felt something of that experience of running in childhood, with the surge of adrenalin added. I was liberated from a world of stopwatches. I was transformed by the pure joy of making a physical effort for which my body was well prepared. The last lap of 56.7 seconds was the fastest last-lap time to date in a mile race of this calibre and I won in a new record time for this event, of 4 minutes 8.3 seconds. This brought me to twentieth in the all-time list of the world's fastest miles.

Some of the American sports reporters complained that I made a mockery of the race by exploding in this unseemly fashion in the last lap, leaving Wilt and Gehrmann twenty yards behind. One said, 'Just keep Bannister in England, that's all. That guy's murder over here.' But most of them, with great respect for England's middle-distance running, as typified by Wooderson and Lovelock, regarded my race as a victory in 'the classic English manner'.

In England, Harold Abrahams wrote in the *Sunday Times*:

> What Bannister needs now is confidence in his own ability. Modesty – a characteristic of Wooderson – in Bannister amounts to an almost complete reluctance to acknowledge his greatness. He has the brains to plan and dominate the Olympic final as Lovelock did in 1936. To beat the world – and I believe he can – he must cultivate a purposeful aggression.

Having respect for Harold Abrahams's judgement, I hoped that I was beginning to show more of the necessary aggression.

On 5 July, only a week before the AAA Championships, I flew to Finland; the opportunity of running on the new Olympic track at Helsinki was too good to miss. I wanted to be prepared for all eventualities. Before the race, Paavo Nurmi, the world's greatest distance runner in his time and still very well preserved, took away my split running shoes and arranged to have them stitched. It was a rain-soaked track and my time was 3 minutes 52.4 seconds for 1,500m, equivalent to 4 minutes 10 seconds for a mile.

Next came the big test of 1951, the British AAA Championships. My American race had given me a reputation abroad, but an uneasy doubting of my ability lurked in the minds of many at home because I had not yet raced against my toughest British rivals. There were six British runners who had beaten 4 minutes 15 seconds in 1951. Bill Nankeville, for whom I had great respect, had already won the British Mile Championship in the three preceding years. When we were together in Oslo he had told me that he was in good form and ready for anything. John Parlett, European 800m champion, had also turned to miling. He had beaten Chataway in Oxford in a 4-minute 12-second mile and had recently run a 4-minute 9.2-second mile in Paris to beat Patrick El Mabrouk, the French-Moroccan runner. I was called 'the champion without a title', because I had still not won the British Mile Championship, which had become one of the toughest of national titles. Yet because of my racing abroad I had more prestige as a runner and stood to lose more than the other competitors if I did not win. I was worried, lest I had done too much racing and travelling.

During the season I had competed in nine major races and travelled thousands of miles. In my mind, the AAA Mile became a test race for the Olympic final. If I lost this race I should not feel hopeful about the Olympic final a year later. This was to be my last serious race before the Helsinki Games. If I won, I decided I would temporarily stop racing in order to carry out my winter Olympic training programme.

I felt more alone on the starting line at White City than I had when away in America. At first there was a great deal of timidity in front and pushing from behind. Then Alan Parker of England took the lead. As he did not have a fast finish over this distance, his only hope was to speed up the pace from the start.

Just after the bell there was a moment of pleasure, because I now had a sense of command. Parker was still leading and I could distinctly feel Parlett hesitating at my shoulder. For a moment I was wedged between them and nearly boxed in. I took the lead decisively, slipping between them and brushing their shoulders as I did so. This was the correct moment to seize the initiative. I had to make the first move, but keep enough strength to resist the late challenge I expected from Parlett, I rested for a moment round the next-to-last bend, knowing that I could not sustain my sprint for the full 440 yards. Just before the back straight I had enough reserves left for a weaker burst, which I maintained to the finish. I had never been so exhausted before in a mile race as I was when I crossed the line. The time was 4 minutes 7.8 seconds, my fastest and a best championship performance, but my last lap of 59.1 seconds was slow for me and lacked fire. I was racing to the limit of my strength and my main feeling was relief that I had won.

The 1951 season was my best yet and after eight successful mile and 1,500m races I decided I had raced enough. But each season now, even during successful periods, sooner or later the moment came when I almost hated athletics because of the publicity attached to my track appearances. It left me no freedom to run as I pleased. So in August 1951 I lost myself in Scotland for two weeks, walking, climbing and sometimes sleeping in the open.

One day I had been swimming in the sea and to warm myself I started running. Soon I was running across the moor to a distant part of the coast of Kintyre. It was near evening and fiery clouds were chasing over to Arran. It began to rain and the sun shining brightly behind me cast a rainbow ahead. It gave me the feeling that I was cradled in the rainbow arc as I ran. I was running back to all the primitive sense of contact with nature that my season had destroyed. At the coast the rainbow was lost in the particles of spray, beaten up by the breakers as they crashed against the granite rocks. I grew calmer as I sat watching pebbles rolling to and fro where the fury had gone from the waves and I turned back.

❧

In the autumn I began my clinical training at St Mary's. I moved into a room in Earls Court, in the basement of a friend's flat. I ate mostly home-cooked stews in the evenings and at weekends I went back to my parents' home in Harrow. The move could have proved disruptive to my training, but in fact the change of situation refreshed me. St Mary's also provided me with a wide range of social distractions, from cross-country running to an unlikely appearance onstage as Lord Darlington in *Lady Windermere's Fan*. These provided a counterbalance to the daily athletic training.

In the winter of 1951–52 I started on the second phase of my Olympic preparation, having completed my travel programme. Because of the nervous strain I suffered during races, I believed that excessive competition was essentially harmful to someone of my temperament. So I did not run in any cross-country races during the winter. I decided not to start running on the track until February and did most of my training in Harrow round the grass cricket field of Harrow School. I was technically trespassing, but no one stopped me, and after the four-minute mile, the headmaster of Harrow wrote to give me permission!

This cricket field was nearly a mile round, enlivened by its slope and by the variety of elms and poplars that surrounded it. I did not have time to train until evening, when it was dark. Often I was tired from standing in hospital wards, operating theatres or tube trains. It needed an enormous effort to make myself change into my running kit, but once I had taken the plunge the run always refreshed me. I never ran for longer than half an hour and never timed myself with a stopwatch.

At Christmas the American rankings for the Olympics appeared in the press – I was given fourth place. Willy Slijkhuis of Holland, the reigning European champion, whom I had beaten in New Zealand, was selected as the winner, Landqvist of Sweden as second, with the equivalent of a 4-minute 3-second mile to his credit, and Otenhajmer of Yugoslavia, who had beaten me in Belgrade, in third.

One afternoon I spent watching Oxford's victory over Cambridge in the Boat Race. I felt frustrated that I had not been able to take part in their inspiring struggle. I remembered from my schooldays the intense pleasure of utter exhaustion from rowing in time with the rest of the crew. I went out running as soon as I reached home. The snow was falling and already lay about four inches deep. No one had crossed it and every step I took left its impression behind. I ran and ran until I was exhausted.

In the spring of 1952 the furore over my training methods was let loose again and continued through into the summer. One writer said, 'Bannister needs serious tests' and another, 'Is it fair to take Bannister's record as good enough?' Some light relief was provided by a third writer, who, under the headline 'Bannister won't turn a hair', reported that I was likely to be paced by an electric hare at the White City (which was used for greyhound racing) as part of my training for the Olympic Games! An appearance of truth was given to this rumour by a photograph, obviously faked, showing me panting behind just such an electric hare.

I was building myself up for one supreme explosive effort on 26 July 1952 in the Olympic final at Helsinki. I had intended that the AAA Championships of 1951 should be my last fiercely competitive mile until Helsinki. I decided that I would not defend my AAA Mile title in the summer of 1952, but would run in the half-mile instead. This would take away none of my freshness or strength and would give me sharper tactical experience. There was much surprised comment, but I did not allow it to disturb me.

I did not expect people to understand my scheme of training. I only hoped that they would be patient with me and trust that I was doing my best to prepare for the Olympic race. But everyone seemed to know better than me how I should train. There was no coach or adviser and hence no alibi for me if things went wrong. I had to carry the full weight of decisions myself. I now regretted that by running so fast the previous year I had added fuel to the fire. Everyone wants to give good advice to a favourite and, if there is a mishap, they enjoy the sense that it arose as a result of his not following that advice. I myself knew I must store enough nervous energy to take the lead at the right moment. I could not afford to squander preciously hoarded nervous and physical reserves beforehand in unnecessary gladiatorial combats. An Olympic victory is an honour that may come only once to an athlete. For me, to achieve it, I had to have an absolutely single aim.

I was also accused of harming my chances by avoiding my most serious rivals. My answer to this would have been that because of my way of training for and running a race, the nervous strain of the AAA Mile final would prejudice my performance in the Olympic Games. I did not want to throw away an Olympic title for a lesser crown! I respected my rivals in this country, but I had beaten them all the previous summer and did not consider them as serious challengers at Helsinki. The Olympic standard was quite different and I saw no useful purpose in exhausting myself needlessly.

So I went on alone, but I knew that in the bitterness and criticism that had been aroused I had exchanged the sympathy of the public for a begrudging permission to go my own way in training. This seemed implicit in the final press plea to 'leave Bannister alone'. Only by success would my lone furrow be justified. Why did my freedom of decision always seem so hard to win? I was now cornered. Victory at Helsinki was the only way out and then I would retire. Perhaps I strove to create this situation, so that in desperation I would be forced to get the last ounce out of myself. It was probable that the 1952 Olympic Games would be my only Olympics. Running was only my secondary interest and I could not afford to spend another four years jeopardising my medical future with this exciting distraction. I was glad in a way that the chance could only come once. Success or failure at one throw, this seemed right.

The Queen and Princess Margaret came to see the AAA Championships on 21 June 1952. Nankeville won the mile race in 4 minutes 9.8 seconds from John Landy of Australia and I won the half-mile in 1 minute 51.5 seconds with Albert Webster second. 'Isn't it more usual for you to run in the mile?' the Queen asked, as she handed me the massive cup. 'Yes,' I replied. 'The race over half a mile today was entered to sharpen my speed for the longer race in the Helsinki Olympics. I am told something similar is done in horse-race training.' She smiled and said, 'Yes, it is.'

My training was going well. Ten days before the Helsinki final I ran my last time trial at Motspur Park. Chataway led for the first lap and a half and I completed the ¾-mile in 2 minutes 52.9 seconds. The time was unbelievable, with each lap faster than the previous one: 58.5, 57.5 and 56.9 seconds. I had never run at such speed before and I rank this as equal to – if not better than – a four-minute mile. I felt so full of the running that I had restrained for so long. Though this trial did not take much out of me, it was nearly four whole seconds better than the unofficial world record of 2 minutes 56.6 seconds, set up by Arne Andersson of Sweden in 1945, and my own English native record of 2 minutes 56.8 seconds, at Motspur Park on 17 April 1951. Athletes all have a 'best' distance, based on their physique and temperament. I knew that my best distance was ¾-mile, but I never imagined I was ready to run as fast as this.

The Olympic 1,500m distance is only 320 yards longer than the ¾-mile. I felt now that in a final race, with a day's rest after the heat, I might even beat the world record. This should be fast enough to win at Helsinki. I said to Norris McWhirter, 'Please don't tell anyone about this. If I win in Helsinki it will be irrelevant. If I lose in Helsinki it will sound like sour grapes. Its purpose was to find out if I was ready for Helsinki. The answer is yes. I'm ready.' It was only valuable as a boost for my own state of mind.

The blow to my Olympic hopes came shortly after my blistering ¾-mile run at Motspur Park. A decision had been made to hold the heats, the semi-finals and the final of the 1,500m on consecutive days. It was impossible for someone training on my schedule to run three good races in such a short space of time and I felt sure that the organisers knew as much. Just when I had become sure that my training methods were correct, this new Olympic programme made a mockery of them. It has never been scheduled like this in any Olympics since.

The atmosphere in Helsinki differed from that at Wembley four years earlier, primarily because of the unease caused by Russia deciding to enter a full team. The Russians were so worried about some political complications at the height of the Cold War that they refused to stay with the other athletes in the camp and instead hired their own hotel between Helsinki and the Russian border. We were told Helsinki was within range of Russian guns in Leningrad. Having their own camp would also make defections impossible.

One evening the British team was invited to have dinner at the Russian base, some twenty miles from Helsinki. We were greeted by interpreters, who guided us into the large technical school in the middle of some pine woods. On the front stood a gigantic portrait of Stalin and 'CCCP' ('USSR') in foot-high letters. Apparently there was supposed to be some sort of ceremony but it never materialised. My interpreter showed me the honours boards above the dining tables, where the names of Soviet medal-winners were embossed in gold, silver or bronze each day. Making conversation, I said that we were yet to win any golds. 'But you are such a small country,' he replied, not very tactfully.

We expected caviar and steaks but instead were served cakes and oranges, along with the traditional Russian spirits. These we forced down while the Russian director delivered a speech, each sentence of which garnered generous applause from his own team. This applause was then mimicked by the British team after each sentence had been translated. I suddenly felt great sympathy for those who have to sit through United Nations summits and other such international proceedings.

The heats for the 1,500m were held on Thursday 24 July. I qualified for the semi-finals comfortably in third position. The effort did not tire me unduly, but I had not slept well the entire week. I was sharing a room with Chris C. Our room became a haven for other athletes seeking light relief from the tension. They would walk in to find us lying on unmade beds, chatting lightly about our chances.

Chris raced against the great Emil Zátopek in the 5,000m final. A brave effort carried him to the front coming down the back straight for the final time, but he had struck too soon. Exhausted, he stumbled and fell on the last corner, gallantly struggling to his feet to finish fifth. It was a warning to me not to make my own overtaking move too early. Zátopek went on to take gold medals in the 5,000m, 10,000m and the marathon.

In my semi-final on Friday, José Barthel romped home in 3 minutes 50.4 seconds. He was looking dangerous, known to belong to the toughest training school, and seemed very fresh afterwards. I finished fifth, breathless and unhappy, but was in the final nonetheless. That night my legs ached and I was unable to sleep. The suspense was agonising as I tried to picture the stadium, filled with 70,000 people, and ran through in my mind the moment in the race when I would have to galvanise my tired limbs for the final effort. Saturday brought the final. I was the only British representative to have made it through.

My opponents included two Germans, Lueg and Lamers; two Americans, McMillen and Druetzler; two Swedes, Aberg and Eriksson; Johansson of Finland; El Mabrouk of France; Boysen of Norway; McMillan of Australia and Barthel of Luxembourg. I felt I hardly had the strength to warm up. In front of the crowds I had pictured the night before, my legs had no spring. The ruthless fighting of the semi-final had exhausted me, as I had expected it would.

With twelve men on the starting line, at the gun there was a crush of elbows as each runner tried to win a favourable position.

I was too tired to get involved and contented myself with taking the inside track at the back. The two Germans exchanged the lead over the first three laps, then at the bell we were five abreast, waiting for someone to attempt to break away. I forced myself to move up onto Lueg's shoulder going into the final bend so that I lay second, perfectly poised for my final effort. But I could not force my legs to move any quicker. I had a sickening feeling of exhaustion and powerlessness. The freedom had gone from my running entirely, and instead of bursting past the field I saw Barthel and McMillen come past me to take gold and silver. I finished fourth behind Lueg, but my immediate feeling was one of relief that the ordeal was over.

As I became more philosophical over the next few days I was able to appreciate what a great race it had been. Eight of us beat the previous Olympic record and Barthel finished in 3 minutes 45.2 seconds. I felt admiration for José as he climbed the Olympic rostrum. He was a worthy victor, tougher as well as faster than the rest of us. I knew his happiness must be almost without limit as he wiped away the tears. He was strong and courageous and fortune had smiled on him. No one could begrudge him his success.

The Olympics over, the newspapers excoriated me. One reporter said he felt British athletics had broken the trade descriptions act by predicting successes that were not delivered. You can imagine how Chris B, Chris C and I felt when we flew back to a hostile press hammering. Not at all the triumph we had all hoped for. The only gold medal in the stadium was won by Colonel Harry Llewellyn and his horse Fox Hunter, in the show jumping. The three of us gritted our teeth, privately pledging that the day would come when 'we'd show 'em'.

Some writers were more considerate and asked how coming

fourth in a race of this kind and breaking the Olympic record could possibly be called failure. Others suggested that my two-year plan had failed because I had put the stopwatch before running in races. After a headline 'No – Roger wasn't nearly tough enough', one writer ended his criticism with, 'I feel like suing British athletes for breach of promise.' A letter appeared in *The Times* of 13 August 1952, replying to criticism that the press were unfair. And so it went on:

> Staff writers were almost unanimous that the 1,500m final showed this athlete's [Bannister's] training methods to be wrong; an error to which many of them had drawn attention earlier in the summer, only to find it condoned by British athletic officials to the point of Bannister's abstention from competitive running over the distance.

To me, any way you looked at it, it was failure when the immediate relief had faded. But what use was there in revealing the speed of my last time trial before the Games? I did not have second sight. How could I have foreseen the arbitrary revision of the programme at the last minute – a change which at one stroke made nonsense of a long year's training schedule? If one fails in the Olympics there is no second chance – the years of waiting would seem an eternity of hopelessness. Any attempt to explain away a disappointment is taken as an even greater admission of failure.

The Helsinki Olympic Games were a turning point in my life, in more ways than one. Until then I had, on the whole, been successful in most of the races that mattered to me. I do not find it easy to be overconfident, but an Olympic victory might easily have made me so. My opponents were stronger, physically and psychologically. I was hardly able to bear the responsibility thrust on my shoulders, the terrible burden of having to win. I had tried to bear it alone by developing an attitude of isolation without any buffers between me and success or failure. I realised how much luck there is in sport. I had taken myself and my one goal too seriously. My gamble on one event had failed – was it still possible for me to justify the faith that others placed in me?

Chapter 7

International Running Career: The Four-Minute Mile

My running career can be neatly divided into two parts: before and after Helsinki. My failure to win the 1,500m gold medal in Helsinki, when I had been the favourite, was a shattering blow. All of my past planning over six years seemed to have been wasted. It was a huge knock to my pride, disappointing to my friends and family and to the Great British public.

Some have said that one element of courage is dignity in the face of adversity, and I now had plenty of practice. It was some time before I could screw up my self-belief, but within a month I had decided to continue racing until 1954, when I would face the Empire Games and the European Games. If I could win these titles, then I would feel that my training ideas had been vindicated. Paying back my supporters may be a cliché but many clichés have a kernel of truth. I knew even then that part of my life would be inextricably entwined with running and would never detach itself from sport, despite the hard years ahead that I knew I would need to devote to my training as a neurologist.

I felt it was necessary to prove that my attitudes towards training had been right and hence restore the faith that had been so shaken by my Olympic defeat. I could accept being beaten in the Olympics – that had happened to many stronger favourites than me. What I objected to was that my defeat was taken by so many as proof that my way of training was wrong.

Whether we as athletes liked it or not, the four-minute mile had become rather like an Everest – a challenge to the human spirit. It was a barrier that seemed to defy all attempts to break it, an irksome reminder that man's striving might be in vain. The Scandinavians, with their almost excessive reverence for the magic of sport, called it the 'Dream Mile'.

An interest in running races, and in particular the mile, dates back to the mid-nineteenth century, when mile races were won in about 4 minutes 20 seconds, and the discussion ranged over whether a mile in under four minutes was possible. There was an achingly slow progress in improvement in the record, until a British runner, W. G. George, set up the new record of 4 minutes 10 seconds in 1885. The next big step forward came during the Second World War, when the three Swedes, Arne Andersson, Gunder Hägg and Lennart Strand, repeatedly raced against each other over the mile, week in, week out. Whichever of the three was least strong would be pacemaker for the others. By 1944 the mile record had been driven down to 4 minutes 1.6 seconds by Andersson, and then 4 minutes 1.4 seconds by Hägg. They were declared professionals and their records remained unbroken for nine long years until 1954. The idea that this sub-four-minute mile was impossible was, in my view, a myth. From my knowledge of physiology it seemed preposterous that there was some kind of portcullis that would clang down at 4 minutes 1.4 seconds. If seconds could be clipped off over the past half-century, why would that stop now?

Of course, one difficulty was slow tracks. It is impossible for today's runners to understand the soggy surface of a wet cinder track in the 1950s when runners can now bounce along on a modern plastic track. Seb Coe, who ran on both surfaces, said, 'It makes up to four seconds' difference over a mile.'

I felt that in my running I was now defending a cause. It was a kind of fusion of the Greek Olympic ideal and of the university attitude that Oxford had taught me. I coupled this with my own love of running as one of the most satisfying forms of physical expression. I believed that many other potential athletes could experience this same satisfaction. If my attitude was right then it should be possible to achieve great success and I wanted to see this happen – both for myself and for my friends.

Throughout the winter of 1952–53 I further stepped up the severity of my training programme by intensifying the interval method of running I have already described; Barthel used the same system. I had great admiration for him because he was not a semi-professional maintained by his country's government. He was a qualified chemist who did his training after his working day was over. He had shown that it was still possible to reach the top and do a normal day's work in addition – but only just.

In December 1952, John Landy of Australia, who had been knocked out in my heat at the Olympic Games, had startled the world by running a mile in 4 minutes 2.1 seconds. I could hardly believe the improvement from the runner I had known at Helsinki. Landy made no secret of the fact that the four-minute mile was his goal.

If I was going to enter the lists to attack the four-minute mile, the problem was to decide how and where the race should be run. There were four essential requirements: a good track, absence of wind, warm weather and even-paced running. Some have imagined that a four-minute mile might result from normal competition. This could only happen if there was an opponent capable of forcing the pace right up to the last fifty yards: This was what Arne Andersson had tried to do in 1945, to run Gunder Hägg off his feet and to tire his finish. Gunder Hägg held out, overtook Andersson and was able to set up his own world record. Only John Landy could offer me a race of this kind. By the time we ran against each other in the Commonwealth Games in Vancouver in 1954, the four-minute mile might already have been accomplished and it would be too late. It is easier to race an opponent than the clock, but there were no close rivals in Britain so I had little choice but to attempt it before John Landy succeeded.

I had decided some years before that the Oxford track that I had helped to build should be the scene of any attempt at the four-minute mile. The Oxford *v.* AAA match provided the first opportunity of the 1953 season when I might, at any rate, expect suitable opposition in the early stages of the race. The biggest gamble was the weather and I was taking a great chance in hoping for a suitable day in April or May.

When I ran at Oxford on 2 May 1953, I aimed first to break Sydney Wooderson's British mile record of 4 minutes 6 seconds, which had stood ever since he set it up in a paced handicap race at Motspur Park on 28 August 1937. R. H. Thomas, a well-known miler of the time, had ten yards' start and paced Wooderson for half a mile. There were other runners with up to 250 yards' start to help him in the later stages. This may seem far removed from the conditions of an ordinary race, but it was the only approach open to him, because there was no runner in Europe at the time who could have extended him.

Chris C was also running for the AAA in the match at Oxford on 2 May 1953 and he agreed to run as hard as he could for the first ¾-mile. It was our first attempt to run four even quarters and our lap times were 61.7, 62.4, 61.1. Then I went into the lead and ran a last lap of 58.4 seconds to give a total time of 4 minutes 3.6 seconds, a new British record. This race made me realise that the four-minute mile was not out of reach. It was only a question of time – but would someone else reach the goal before me?

Speculation about the four-minute mile gradually increased through 1953. Details of our lives were splashed across the newspapers here and in Australia. There was even speculation as to whom we might marry. It increased through the summer of 1953. It embarrassed any girlfriends with whom we had dinner or went out dancing, only to find our photos in gossip columns. It was even suggested in one flight of journalistic fancy that I might be suitable for Princess Margaret! Speculation about John Landy was no less. Years later, his wife Lynne said to Moyra, 'We arranged to meet at a jeweller's to look at engagement rings and planned to arrive at the jeweller's shop separately. I stood in the shop for some minutes before I realised that the figure on a sofa hiding behind a newspaper was in fact John trying to disguise the fact that he was about to buy an engagement ring.'

Every time after this, when I ran on the track, the public and press expected new records. On 6 May there was a 4 x 1,500m relay attack on the world record, made at Leyton by the Achilles Club, represented by David Law, Chris B, Chris C and myself. We failed to beat the world record, but our combined time of 15 minutes 49.6 seconds bettered by 6 seconds the best time ever made by a British four.

The next race, which I won, was an international mile race at White City on 23 May in 4 minutes 9.4 seconds, with a last lap of 56.6 seconds. This result was greeted with the headline 'Bannister held back so it looked a race'.

In a match between Oxford and London University on 30 May, the wind was hopelessly strong. I ran a half-mile instead in 1 minute 51.9 seconds, a ground and meeting record.

A week later I was attempting to increase my speed by quarter-miling at the Middlesex Championships at Edmonton. I covered the first bend at a speed which was exceptional for me. Just as I was overtaking a runner in an outside lane I felt a 'twang' in my left thigh, like something between a violin string snapping and being kicked by a horse, and limped off the track. I had pulled a muscle for the first time in my running career. Until then I had never been able to understand how athletes pulled muscles. Now it was all too clear – my muscles were unaccustomed to sprinting and I was simply running too fast for them. In the next hour the pain grew worse.

To add insult to the injury, on the same day the American runner Wes Santee threw out a new challenge with a mile in 4 minutes 2.4 seconds in America. There were now three of us in the race, with Landy training in Australia, waiting to make fresh attempts at the record when his own summer season came around in November. How soon could I recover and make another attempt?

The pulled muscle was not as serious as I feared. The muscle fibres were probably not torn, but a small blood vessel supplying them might have burst, which would have made the muscle seize up. M. M. Mays, the AAA masseur, skilfully dispersed any adhesions after I had rested the leg for five days.

In the middle of the following week, after nothing but slow running since the injury, I felt able to run at the speed of a four-minute mile without aggravating the injury. Norris McWhirter persuaded me that I ought to run a paced time trial. To avoid press excitement in case my pulled muscle did not hold out, the event was quietly included as a special invitation race in the

Surrey Schools' athletic meeting at Motspur Park on the follow-ing Saturday, the 27th. I had no idea what would happen, or whether I could last out the distance. I only knew that the same afternoon five hours later, Wes Santee was to run in Dayton, Ohio, and was confidently predicting a four-minute mile.

I was uncertain how I was to be paced, but Don MacMillan, the Australian Olympic runner whom I had first met in New Zealand in 1950, led for two and a half laps. Then Chris B, who had run the first two laps at snail's pace, loomed on the horizon in front of me, a lap in arrears. He proceeded to encourage me by shouting backwards over his shoulder, just preventing himself from being lapped.

Of course, it could hardly be called a race. It was a mistake. I accept full responsibility for running in it though I did not organise the details. My lap times were 59.6, 60.1, 62.1 and 60.2 seconds, making a total time of 4 minutes 2 seconds. This was the third fastest mile of all time, beaten only by Hägg and Andersson eight years before. My feeling as I look back is one of great relief that I did not run a four-minute mile under such artificial circumstances.

Immediately after the run Chris B and I drove off to north Wales. That night we were sleeping in a hayloft under a skylight, looking at the stars and anticipating a day of climbing, blissfully unaware of the drama which was unfolding in London with the rumpus the secret attempt had caused on Fleet Street.

On 12 July, the British Amateur Athletic Board ratified my 4-minute 3.6-second mile run at Oxford on 2 May as a British all-comers and British national record. On my 4-minute 2-second mile run at Motspur Park on 27 June the Board issued a state-ment to the effect that the time could not be recognised, as they did not see the attempt as a bona fide race.

The news of the rejection of my 4-minute 2-second mile for record purposes brought journalists flocking to the family doorstep. 'What are your views about it?' they asked, feeling they were on the brink of a sensation. 'Surely you must have some views on it? Will you appeal? Only say yes or no!' 'No comment,' I repeated. To say more was dangerous. Anything I said could be twisted. 'Bannister will not appeal' is as good a headline as 'Bannister will appeal' when a story is hot. If I were once tempted into the slightest utterance, further amplification would be called for and I should find myself in deeper and deeper waters. I stuck to 'no comment' instead and evaded all further questions. My own feelings were that I accepted the decision without question. I had doubted that the record would be ratified. As it happened, there was really nothing important at stake. If the time had been under four minutes, the fat would really have been in the fire.

This was my last deliberate attempt of the season. On the same day, Santee, under the full glare of publicity, made another attempt to run the four-minute mile and took 4 minutes 7.6 seconds. I could only hope that he would not forestall me before the end of his longer American season.

For the rest of the season I put all ideas of records out of my mind. On 11 July I won the AAA Mile championship in 4 minutes 5.2 seconds, the fastest time for the meeting. After this I was too busy studying to be able to do any serious training, though on 1 August I ran a 4-minute 7.6-second mile in a successful 4 x 1-mile relay attempt on the world record. Chataway, Nankeville, Seaman and I ran a combined time of 16 minutes 41 seconds. It was good enough to beat the previous world record of 16 minutes 48.8 seconds, set up by a Swedish team on 5 August 1949. It was also well within the previous British record of 16 minutes 53.2 seconds, made on 4 August 1952 when I was in a

British Empire team with Landy, Law and Parnell. Two days later, on August bank holiday in 1952, I ran my fastest half-mile, 1 minute 50.7 seconds, against El Mabrouk of France.

Soon it was the end of our season and of the American season too. But in Australia the summer season was just starting and I waited anxiously for news of John Landy, who was just getting into his stride. This was his second season devoted to record-breaking runs and I felt that it was only a question of time before he ran a four-minute mile.

John Landy's training programme was more severe than any other middle-distance runner in the world at that time. It involved weightlifting and running every day, up to a total of 200 miles a week. Percy Cerutty, at one time Landy's coach, has said that Landy has the temperament of a fanatic. He does not consider this a term of disparagement but the highest possible praise accorded to any man. The only other runners he considers to have had this quality are Nurmi and Zátopek. My view is that Cerutty was not entitled to make remarks like this about Landy, even if he was his coach.

In 1953, John Landy had embarked on a course of training that was in the ten-miles-a-session class. He opened the season with a 4-minute 2-second mile on a grass track in December: a great performance, 0.1 of a second faster than his best of the previous year.

But his harder training and selfless physical ferocity brought precious little improvement. Each week I waited for the news of his times. The tension grew and by April 1954 he had won six races, all in times less than 4 minutes 3 seconds, a record achieved by no other athlete in history. Each race, incidentally, was headlined in the British newspapers as 'Landy fails'. After one race in February he lost heart. 'It's a brick wall,' he said. 'I shall not attempt it again.' But he had caught the four-minute

fever and was already planning a summer in Scandinavia, where
the tracks are perfect and the warm climate such that he could
make repeated attempts with all the pace-making he needed.

Landy's personality intrigued me. I was dependent on the
comments of Percy Cerutty, the Australian coach, who said he
had seen in Landy:

> demonstrations of a character capable of the greatest kindness,
> gentleness and thoughtfulness, and on the other side – as there is
> and always must be – a ruthlessness, lack of feeling for others, and
> a ferocity and antagonism, albeit it is mostly vented on himself,
> that makes it possible on occasions for John to rise to sublime
> heights of physical endeavour.

If all this were true, he would indeed be a formidable opponent, provided all went well and we were both selected for the
Empire Games at Vancouver in 1954. A reason for my hesitancy
in putting myself in the hands of a coach was that I had no wish
for anyone to make any such public statements about me. Franz
Stampfl had more discretion and never did this. I could speak
for myself.

Over the autumn of 1953 a great change came over my
running: I no longer trained alone. Every day between noon and
two o'clock I trained on a track in Paddington with a group of
recreational runners and had a quick lunch before returning to
hospital. In order to do so I was often forced to miss a regular
obstetrics lecture at noon. This was the one speciality I was sure
I did not want to pursue. At the back of the lecture theatre was
a comfortably upholstered leather bench, across which students
would habitually recline to escape the lecturer's line of sight,
relaxing sometimes to the extent of sleep. On a wooden panel

above it was carved an ironic quotation from Ralph Waldo Emerson: 'God offers to every mind its choice between truth and repose.' An unintended irony.

We called ourselves the Paddington Lunchtime Club. We came from all parts of London and our common bond was a love of running. I think my willingness to engage in the social side of running was a sign that I had mellowed. I felt extremely happy in the friendships I made there and these training sessions came to mean almost as much to me as had those at the Oxford track.

In my hardest training Chris B was with me and he made the task very much lighter. On Friday evenings, starting in November 1953, he took me along to Chelsea Barracks where his coach, Franz Stampfl, held a training session. At weekends Chris C would join us and in this friendly atmosphere the very severe training we did became really enjoyable. Franz kept us all amused and usually afterwards the four of us went out to the John Lyons Cornerhouse on Sloane Square to eat baked beans on toast, about the best dish available during food rationing.

I realised that the two Chrises were the only pacemakers who could be relied on to help me attack the four-minute mile early in 1954. Between the four of us, with Franz carefully coordinating our trainings, a strategy emerged as to how this ultimate athletic challenge could be overcome. To use a mountaineering analogy, our plan for the record attempt was for Chris B to take Chris C and me to 'base camp' at the half-mile, so that Chris C could then launch me into the attack itself on the last lap. This made both Chris B's pace judgement and Chris C's strength and speed over the ¾-mile equally crucial for success.

In December 1953 we had started a new intensive course of training and ran a series of ten consecutive quarter-miles each week, each in 63 seconds. Through January and February we gradually speeded them up, keeping to an interval of only two minutes between each. By April we could manage them in 61 seconds, but however hard we tried it did not seem possible to reach our target of 60 seconds. We were stuck, or, as Chris B expressed it, 'bogged down'.

The training had ceased to do us any good and we needed a change. Chris B and I drove up to Scotland overnight for a few days climbing with John Mawe, a doctor friend of Chris's. Looking back, it seemed bordering on the lunatic to go climbing with a group of friends to make a break from hard training, chancing exposure to cold weather and dodgy food. The ten-hour drive in John's cramped car, as he himself pointed out, was about as bad an experience as we could put our bodies through so shortly before a big race.

As we turned into the Pass of Glencoe the sun crept above the horizon at dawn. A misty curtain drew back from the mountains and the sun's sleepless eye cast a fresh cold light on the world. The air was calm and fragrant but it would not stay that way. Rain set in as we set off to climb Clachaig Gully. The gully had turned into a waterfall. Following Chris up the Red Chimney, we became utterly drenched, to the extent that Chris worried about my contracting pneumonia from the cold. An athlete in full training is, paradoxically, less resistant to infection than the average person. Chris ordered a fellow climber to lend me dry clothes from his rucksack 'for the good of British sport'. The climber generously obliged and could later claim a little credit for protecting my health.

We climbed hard for three days, using the wrong muscles in the wrong way! There was an element of danger, too. I remember Chris falling a short way when leading a climb up a rock face depressingly named 'Jericho Wall'. Luckily, he did not hurt himself. We were both worried, lest a sprained ankle might set our training back by several weeks.

After three days our minds turned to running again. We suddenly became alarmed at the thought of taking any more risks and decided to return. We had slept little and our meals had been irregular. But when we tried to run those quarter-miles again, just three days after our return, the time came down to the magic target of 59 seconds!

It was now less than three weeks to the Oxford University v. AAA race, the first opportunity of the year for us to attack the four-minute mile in a bona fide race. Chris C joined Chris B and me in the AAA team. Chataway doubted his ability to run a ¾-mile in three minutes, but he generously offered to attempt it. I had now abandoned the severe training of the previous months and was concentrating entirely on gaining speed and freshness. I had to learn to release in four short minutes the energy I usually spent in half an hour's training. Each training session took on a special significance as the day of the Oxford race drew near. It felt a privilege each time I ran a trial on the track.

I never thought of length of stride or style, or even my judgement of pace. All this had become automatically ingrained. There was more enjoyment in my running than ever before: it was as if all my muscles were a part of a perfectly tuned machine. I felt fresh now at the end of each training session.

I had been training almost daily since the previous November and now that the test was approaching I barely knew what to do with myself. For a ¾-mile trial at Paddington there was a high wind blowing. I would have given almost anything to be able to shirk the test that would tell me with ruthless accuracy what my chances were of achieving a four-minute mile at Oxford. I felt that 2 minutes 59.9 seconds for the ¾-mile in a solo training run, without the adrenalin boost, meant 3 minutes 59.9 seconds in a mile race. A time of 3 minutes 1 second would mean 4 minutes 1 second for the mile – just the difference between success and failure. The watch recorded a time of 2 minutes 59.9 seconds! I felt a little sick afterwards with the taste of nervousness in my mouth, which I thought of as the release of adrenalin. My speedy recovery within five minutes suggested that I had been holding something back. Two days later I ran a 1-minute 54-second half-mile quite easily, after a late night, and then took five days' complete rest before the race.

The chosen day was Thursday 6 May 1954, the day of the AAA race at Oxford. The real problem that faced me was to decide if the weather conditions justified an attempt: the wind was fierce. I went into the hospital as usual and at eleven o'clock I was sharpening my spikes on a grindstone in the laboratory. Someone passing said, 'You don't really think that's going to make any difference, do you?' Then I rubbed graphite on the spikes so that the wet cinder of the track might be less likely to stick to the spikes.

I decided to travel up to Oxford alone because I wanted time to think. However, when I boarded a carriage at Paddington, there was Franz Stampfl. This was the first of two great moments of chance that day. I could not have wished for a better companion.

Franz is not the kind of coach who, Svengali-like, wishes to turn the athlete into a machine, working to his dictation. We shared a common view of athletics as a means of 're-creation' of each individual, as a result of the liberation of the latent power within him. Franz was like an artist who could see character fulfilment in human struggle and achievement. He was also a coach whom, unlike Cerutty, I could both trust and respect.

We talked, almost impersonally, about the problem I faced. In my mind I had settled this as the day when, with every ounce of strength I possessed, I would attempt to run the four-minute mile. A wind of gale force was blowing which would slow me up by a second a lap, so in order to succeed I must run not merely a four-minute mile but the equivalent of a 3-minute 56-second mile in calm weather.

I had reached my peak physically and psychologically. There might never be another opportunity like it. I had to drive myself to the limit of my power without the stimulus of competitive opposition. This was my first race for eight months and all this time I had been storing nervous energy. If I tried and failed I should be dejected and my chances would be less on any later attempt. Yet it seemed that the high wind was going to make it impossible.

I had almost decided when I entered the carriage at Paddington that unless the wind dropped soon I would postpone the attempt. Franz understood my dilemma. With his expansive personality and twinkling eye he said, 'Roger, the weather is terrible, but even if it's as bad as this, I think you are capable of running a mile in good conditions in 3.56, and that margin is still enough to enable you to succeed today. With the proper motivation, that is a good enough reason for wanting to do it. Remember, if there is only a half-good chance, you may never forgive yourself for missing it. Who knows when or if you may be given another chance, and what about John Landy, soon to race in Europe, and Wes Santee in America? If you pass it up today, you may never forgive yourself for the rest of your life. You will feel pain, but what is it? It's just pain!'

Franz had almost won his point. Racing has always been more of a mental than a physical problem to me. He went on talking about athletes and performances, but I heard no more. The dilemma was not banished from my mind, but the idea uppermost was that this might be my only chance. He stiffened my resolve. 'How would I ever forgive myself if I rejected it?' I thought, as the train arrived in Oxford. I had been wrong to think that the athlete could be self-sufficient.

I arrived at the Iffley Road track and tested two pairs of running shoes. A climbing friend, Eustace Thomas, had had a new set made specifically for me for this occasion, with the weight reduced from six to four ounces per shoe. This small alteration could mean the difference between success and failure. Watching the St George's flag stand horizontal to the flagpole of a nearby church, however, the chances of success seemed increasingly dismal.

Still undecided as to whether to give it a go, I walked to Charles Wenden's house in north Oxford for lunch (a ham salad). A lot of my early running at Oxford had been in Charles's company and I had lived in this house during my later year of research. Now, as then, I appreciated his and Eileen's calming influence as they went about their business, preparing lunch and looking after their children. The sheer normality of a house with children, who knew nothing of the significance of the event, was soothing.

Later in the afternoon, on my way to the track, I sought out Chris C at Magdalen College. He was two years younger than me and had done his National Service and so was in his last year at Oxford. The sun shone briefly and he was typically upbeat. 'The day could be a lot worse, couldn't it? The forecast says the wind may drop towards evening. Let's not decide until five o'clock.'

We arrived at the track at around 4.30 p.m. At 5.15 p.m. there was a shower of rain. Afterwards, the wind blew equally strongly, but now came in gusts. As Brasher, Chataway and I warmed up, we knew the eyes of the spectators were on us; they were hoping that the wind would drop just a little – if not enough to run a four-minute mile, enough for us to decide to make the attempt.

Failure in sport can be almost as exciting to watch as success, provided the effort is absolutely genuine and complete. But spectators fail to understand – and how can they know? – the intense mental anguish through which an athlete must pass before he can give his maximum effort.

The agony of waiting on the day of the race is almost unbearable. It is so intense that I used to say to myself, 'Why do I put myself through this? I don't want ever to do it again.' Yet in the subsequent exhilaration of winning, the agony of the period of waiting beforehand is forgotten. For some athletes this tension was too great. Lennart Strand, part of the Swedish mile record-breaking team, eventually found the strain of races more than he could bear. After helping Arne Andersson and Gunder Hägg to their records he was forced to retire and became a concert pianist, which he found much less stressful!

The strain of racing is comparable to other situations, like 'stage fright' in actors. Speakers at the Royal Institution, where Moyra and I heard many lectures, have by tradition been locked into an ante-room beside the stage before lecturing since an early speaker became so agitated that he ran away without ever giving his lecture.

At Iffley Road, I could sense that the two Chrises were becoming increasingly irritated with me when, just half an hour before the race, I still had not decided whether to make the world record attempt. They came into the changing room and with one voice pleaded, 'Come on, Roger, do make up your mind.' Their impatience was palpable and looking back I understand how difficult it was for them to get in the mood for the race if I went on shilly-shallying, keeping my eye on the flag of the church tower, using it as a wind gauge. I could see I was being unreasonable and so I said, 'Right, we'll go for it, we all know what we have to do.'

As we lined up for the start I glanced at the flag again. It fluttered more gently now and the scene from Shaw's *Saint Joan* flashed through my mind, how she, at her desperate moment, waited for the wind to change, so that her army could cross the river. This was the second moment of chance, a moment of calm, which I took as a reassuring sign that the wind was indeed dropping.

There was complete silence on the ground ... then a false start by Chris B ... I felt angry that precious moments during the lull in the wind might be slipping by. The gun fired a second time ... Brasher went into the lead and I slipped in effortlessly behind him, feeling tremendously full of running. My legs seemed to meet no resistance at all, as if propelled by some unknown force. We seemed to be going so slowly! Impatiently I shouted, 'Faster!' But Brasher kept his head and did not change the pace. I went on worrying until I heard the first lap time, 57.5 seconds. In the excitement my knowledge of pace had temporarily deserted me. After five days' rest my muscles were full of glycogen, the energy source required by the muscles to contract efficiently. Brasher could have run the first quarter in 55 seconds without my realising it, but for any faster running at such uneven pacing I would have had to pay the price later. Instead, he had made success possible.

At one and a half laps I was still worrying about the pace. A voice shouting 'relax' penetrated to me above the noise of the crowd. I learnt afterwards it was Stampfl's. Unconsciously I obeyed. If the speed was wrong it was too late to do anything about it, so why worry? I was relaxing so much that my mind seemed almost detached from my body. There was no feeling of strain.

I barely noticed the half-mile, passed in 1 minute 58 seconds, nor when, round the next bend, Chataway went into the lead. At three-quarters of a mile my effort was still barely perceptible; the time was 3 minutes 0.7 seconds and by now the crowd was roaring. Somehow I had to run that last lap in 59 seconds. Then I pounced past Chataway at the beginning of the back straight, 300 yards from the finish.

There was a moment of mixed excitement and anguish when my mind took over. It raced well ahead of my body and drew me compellingly forward. There was no pain, only a great unity of movement and aim. Time seemed to stand still, or did not exist. The only reality was the next 200 yards of track under my feet. The tape meant finality, even extinction perhaps.

I felt at that moment that it was my chance to do one thing supremely well. I drove on, impelled by a combination of fear and pride. The air filled me with the spirit of the track where I had run my first race. The noise in my ears was that of the faithful Oxford crowd. Their hope and encouragement gave me greater strength: I had now turned the last bend and there were only fifty yards more.

My body must have exhausted its energy, but it still went on running just the same. The physical overdraft came only from greater will-power. This was the crucial moment when my legs were strong enough to carry me over the last few yards, as they could not have done in previous years. With five yards to go, the finishing line seemed almost to recede. Those last few seconds seemed an eternity. The faint line of the finishing tape stood ahead as a haven of peace after the struggle. The arms of the world were waiting to receive me only if I reached the tape without slackening my speed. If I faltered now, there would be no arms to hold me and the world would seem a cold, forbidding place. I leapt at the tape like a man taking his last desperate spring to save himself from a chasm that threatens to engulf him.

Then my effort was over and I collapsed almost unconscious, with an arm on either side of me. It was only then that real pain overtook me. It was as if all my limbs were caught in an ever-tightening vice. Blood surged from my muscles to my brain and seemed to fell me. I felt like an exploded flashbulb. Vision became black and white. I existed in the most passive physical state without being quite unconscious. I knew that I had done it before I even heard the time. I was surely too close to have failed, unless my legs had played strange tricks at the finish by slowing me down and not telling my tiring brain that they had done so.

The stopwatches held the answer. The announcement came from Norris McWhirter, delivered with a dramatic, slow, clear diction: 'Result of Event Eight: One mile. First, R. G. Bannister of Exeter and Merton Colleges, in a time which, subject to ratification, is a new Track Record, British Native Record, British All-Comers Record, European Record, Commonwealth Record and World Record... Three minutes...' The rest was lost in the roar of excitement. I grabbed Brasher and Chataway and together we scampered round the track in a burst of happiness. We had done it, the three of us!

We shared a place where no man had yet ventured, secure for all time, however fast men might run miles in future. We had done it where we wanted, when we wanted, in our first attempt of the year. In the excitement my pain was forgotten and I wanted to prolong those precious moments of happiness.

I felt suddenly and gloriously free from the burden of athletic ambition that I had been carrying for years. No words could be invented for such supreme happiness, eclipsing all other feelings. I thought at that moment I could never again reach such a climax of single-mindedness. I felt bewildered and overpowered.

Looking back at the lap times, it becomes clear we had come dangerously close to missing our goal, despite each of us playing our parts as heroically as we could. The race started according to plan. Brasher rightly ignored my shouted instruction for him to run faster at a time when his pace judgement was in fact excellent. He managed the half-mile in 1 minute 58.3 seconds. Asked afterwards how he judged the pace he replied in his characteristic vernacular: 'I bloody well couldn't go any faster!' He then continued for another half-lap before Chris C took over for one lap between 2½ and 3½ laps.

Only with hindsight is it clear how close to failure we were at that point. The danger is shown by the 220-yard times, which I will list, with the full quarter-mile lap times in parentheses:

Lap 1: 28.7, 29.0 (57.7)
Lap 2: 29.8, 30.8 (60.6)
Lap 3: 31.3, 31.1 (62.4)
Lap 4: 29.7, 29.0 (58.7)
Total 3 minutes 59.4 seconds.

The fifth 220, when Chris B was tiring, was 31.3 and the sixth 220, after Chris C had taken over, was 31.1. So this pair of 220s took 62.4 seconds, which was 3.7 seconds slower than the last lap. Clearly, if this third lap had been any slower, my sprint over the last 220 yards might well not have been enough to bring us success. There had been a marked but understandable slowing of the pace, making the effort more uneven and less efficient than we had planned.

I had made no promise that I would attempt to break the four-minute mile that day but Norris McWhirter had leaked to the BBC that there could be something afoot on the Oxford track that day which they wouldn't want to miss. They put two and two together. The reason I didn't want to make any announcement of my attempt was that if the weather was hopeless, in particular too windy, I would call off any attempt and perhaps just run a 4-minute 5-second mile, which I knew would be a disappointment to the crowd. It meant that I could save myself for the next possible occasion – ten days later at the White City in London. In the event, the BBC only sent a lone cameraman, who stood on the roof of his van parked in the centre of the track and wielded a camera on a tripod. Norris had also passed the same message to the dozen or so athletic correspondents whom he knew well, who turned out in force. Enigmatically, Norris just said to them, 'You might regret it if you were not there.' We went to Vincent's Club before I was whisked off by the BBC to the studio in London to appear in a new BBC weekly sports programme with an 8 p.m. deadline. To my surprise the BBC had managed to get the whole of the black-and-white film taken in Oxford only two hours before and it was shown on television that night.

We had an evening of celebration in London, starting with dinner at the Royal Court Club in Chelsea and ending up with our girlfriends in a nightclub until the early morning. At about 2 a.m. we drove off to Fleet Street, where we expected all-night book stands might already have early editions of the papers. Chris B's driving must have been erratic because a policeman stopped us, and we thought, 'Oh no! What have we done wrong?'

When Chris wound down his window and stuck his head out, the policeman said, 'You are driving as though you had lost your way, sir,' which indeed we had. Then, glancing into the car, he recognised our faces and said, 'Oh, I recognise you, it's the three record breakers. Well done! Would you mind giving me your autographs?' This we happily did and went on our way. When we got the newspapers, we found they had gone to town. There were banner headlines and front- and back-page pieces which the newsrooms had been storing up in advance with long background stories about whether a four-minute mile, like the climbing of Everest, was possible. It was rather bad for our egos.

The next morning, my fellow students carried me into the medical school on their shoulders. We learnt later that the news had leaked through to the Oxford Union, where a member interrupted the debate to move for the adjournment of the house for 3 minutes 59.4 seconds. The new president of the Union was confused. He refused to accept the motion because 'notice had not been given'.

The press were on my trail everywhere for the next few days. To avoid their attentions I could only reach and leave my home in Harrow through the back garden, with the help of chairs and ladders over a succession of fences. I escaped to Oxford for a quiet day with my friends the Wendens. When I returned to London, I needed a suitcase to carry off my telegrams and letters. It was the beginning of a series of fan mail and of invitations to open sports centres and running tracks that has continued to this very day.

A week later, the Foreign Office passed on to me an invitation to go to America to appear on various television shows. They hoped I would accept in order to, in that well-worn phrase, strengthen Anglo-American relations. But that was only partly true. The impetus had come from a TV company in New York which had a popular weekly programme called *I've Got a Secret*. Unbeknownst to me and without my consent, I found myself being smuggled out under an assumed name. But the news of my arrival was leaked and, standing on the airport steps in New York, I was surrounded by a ring of reporters. The matter then became vastly more complicated. I was shocked to learn that a cigarette company was sponsoring the TV show. It won't surprise you to learn that even before Richard Doll's definitive research incriminating smoking in causing lung cancer, the deadly effects of smoking were well known medically. I had never smoked. The Foreign Office now took over the whole management of my tour and had by then already paid my fare and covered my expenses in New York. I made one interview after another and was presented with a colossal trophy valued at hundreds of pounds for the first person to run a four-minute mile. I suppose the donors hoped and expected it to be won by an American. I handed it back and got them to prepare a modest replica the size of an egg cup costing $25, the amount to which an amateur athlete was entitled. One day I was taken up in a New York Harbour Authority helicopter and we skirted round skyscrapers like a giant busy mosquito, slipping under bridges and buzzing the Statue of Liberty.

My trip was summed up well by a formal statement by a Foreign Office minister. Less formal was a comment made in the Oxford Union a week later: 'You can hardly give a girl a bunch of flowers nowadays without endangering her amateur status.' In 1956, Wes Santee lost his amateur status for receiving expenses above the maximum allowed, as had Gunder Hägg during the war. This shows just how careful I had to be, that it could happen almost inadvertently.

The four-minute mile was a team achievement in which all of the members – me, Chris B, Chris C and Franz Stampfl – played crucial parts, as well as the faithful McWhirters, who kept us apprised of Landy and Santee's every attempt. Without any one of us, it would not have been run on 6 May 1954, soon enough to forestall foreign rivals and bring the achievement to Britain.

Each of our relationships with Franz as a coach differed. The closest was Chris B, frustrated by his 'failure' at Helsinki, putting himself entirely in the hands of Franz Stampfl, who persuaded him that if he followed exactly the training regimes Franz would provide, he would win a gold medal in the steeplechase at Melbourne in 1956.

Chris C knew that the boredom of training alone was too much and so he joined Brasher at the Duke of York's barracks, where he was introduced to Franz, with whom he planned his training in a much more general way than Chris B. There was no British runner other than Chris Chataway who could have paced the latter part of the race.

Chris B and Chris C were very good friends, coming from the same background of Oxford and Cambridge athletics. Brasher and I had toured America in 1949 when I was captain of the combined Oxford and Cambridge team to Princeton, Harvard, Yale and Cornell. I had also beaten him when he represented Cambridge in the 7½-mile 1949 Oxford v. Cambridge cross-country race, but we were not track rivals because he was clearly better than me over longer distances. By the time Chataway went up to Oxford I had graduated and was doing research. A photograph now in the National Portrait Gallery shows my arms round the two Chrises after the race. My gratitude to them is absolutely evident. It was clear then and has been ever since.

We all had a common aim and shared the success. Chris B,

Chris C and Franz Stampfl were all very generous in the support and companionship they offered me during training. The secret, I think, was that we realised it would be a first for Britain, a national achievement, and for British athletics. It was old-fashioned patriotism in the best sense, which is less popular today.

There was another element firing me and perhaps the Chrises too. We were members of the generation that had been at school during the war. I was acutely conscious of the men only two years older than me who had fought and been killed, never having the chance to show what they could achieve both in sport and the rest of their lives. I believe this spurred me to grasp every opportunity I had, and to seek some way of showing that, had I been older, I might have perhaps displayed at least some of their spirit. Now in a civilian world the question had become – could I show this by achieving this historic target in athletics?

Chris Brasher was a year older than me and the toughest and most determined runner of the trio; the three musketeers, as some called us. However, in 1954 he was then basically a climber and a cross-country runner, not a miler. He also had the most confidence, sure that his will-power and hard work would bring him success. His father had served in the British Empire as an engineer, directing the laying of telephone cables in the Middle East in the 1930s while his children attended boarding schools in England. Chris had run at Rugby School and there, at the age of sixteen, ran in the longest schoolboys' race in Britain, the Crick Run, over ten miles. He had also taken up mountain climbing while at school. After graduating in Engineering at Cambridge, he had joined an expedition to Greenland and then started work in London for the Mobil Oil Company.

Under Franz's direction, Brasher went on to win the 1956 Olympics as a steeplechaser. After years of struggling with variable form and frustrating injuries, he finally took the gold that his efforts deserved. The victory only came after an agonising wait while a protest that he had obstructed another runner was dismissed. In a piece for the *Sunday Times* praising his victory, I wrote, 'It lifted a huge personal burden from his shoulders and, in his own words, freed him from the imprisonment he had felt in his own body.' It was also an important symbolic victory. With the Soviet Vladimir Kuts, supported entirely by his country and training up to five hours every day, winning both the 5,000m and the 10,000m, amateur runners looked in danger of extinction. That extinction may now have come about, but at the time Brasher's gold medal gave hope to a generation of athletes still simultaneously supporting separate full-time careers.

There followed a successful career as a journalist for *The Observer* and as a BBC producer. However, when the history of the twentieth century is written, it is his creation of the London Marathon for which he will be primarily remembered. Modelling it on the New York Marathon, he and co-creator John Disley, his fellow steeplechase runner, realised that London had more historic sites than New York. Capitalising on the running revolution which had started in America in the 1960s, a London Marathon would be a winner. But Chris B had to fight fierce opposition from London authorities and the police to get it off the ground. It was only because of his bull-headed tenacity that he won the day. Within a few years it became the largest marathon in the world, with 40,000 runners and many turned away each year. Sadly Chris B died of pancreatic cancer in 2003, after a brave battle.

Chris Chataway was rightly thought of as the most glamorous of the trio, having an air of nonchalance and sophistication, marked by publicly smoking an occasional cigarette. He always had immense charm. His father had worked as a pilot in the First World War, then a test pilot and finally as an overseas civil servant in the Sudan Political Service. The challenging climate had led him to early retirement. Sadly, he had returned to England with heart disease and was ill at home for several years before he eventually died in 1955. As the oldest of four children, much of the guidance and financial control fell upon Chris's shoulders, protecting his three younger siblings, who were all educated privately.

Chris had gone to Sherborne School and was more of a boxer than a runner at first, until he saw Zátopek winning the 5,000m in the 1948 Olympics. He immediately stopped buying *Boxing Weekly* to read *Athletics Weekly* instead. He then completed his National Service with the Royal Artillery, before going up to Magdalen College, Oxford, where his uncle had been president, in order to read history. While at Magdalen, he concentrated on sport and, as I had four years before, became president of the Oxford University Athletic Club.

After finals he joined Guinness as an executive trainee. At first he lived at the company's headquarters in Hanger Lane, Ealing, where the nearby playing fields were convenient for training. The executive trainees at Guinness were given the name 'brewers' and regularly lunched with the chairman, Sir Hugh Beaver. One day, when Sir Hugh had spent the weekend grouse shooting, he asked, 'Who can tell me how fast those wretched birds can fly?' Chris said he didn't know, but he knew someone who did – thinking of Norris McWhirter, whose memory was encyclopaedic. 'Bring him to lunch,' Sir Hugh Beaver said. When they met, Sir Hugh was both astonished and fascinated by how much Norris knew, apart from the speed of flight of the grouse. This was the start of the close relationship between Sir Hugh and Norris which led to the Guinness Book of Records, now published in fifty-two languages, which still has the largest annual sales of any book except the Bible.

I once visited Chris C at his home in Woking. He took me running round some of his training circuits, through its neighbouring heath and woodland. I simply could not match him. By 1952 he had become Britain's most promising three miler and 5,000m runner. But he had missed winning a medal in Helsinki, probably since, like me, he was undertrained. He tripped and fell on the last bend through fatigue, but valiantly got up and came fifth in the race which was won by Emil Zátopek. I believe this left him still fiercely ambitious for athletic fame, though he wanted to limit his running career to only a few more years.

Though the 5,000m was his best distance, he had already run a 4-minute 10-second mile and, perhaps like every middle-distance runner of our generation, hoped that the four-minute mile would sooner or later be within his own compass. He did go on to break the four-minute mile himself a year later in the Emsley Carr mile at the White City, which was won by Derek Ibbotson and Brian Hewson in a dead heat. A sub-four-minute mile was not realistic for Chris B, though he did admit after the four-minute mile was over to having a dream of completing the first half-mile and then somehow carrying on at the same pace and breaking the barrier himself. So the two Chrises, despite having their own ambitions, agreed to be pacemakers, playing the role of supporting cast, helping me to break four minutes.

Chris C defeated Vladimir Kuts and set up a new world record for 5k in a dramatic duel under floodlights, one of the most iconic races of the 1950s, and an event which earned him the BBC Sports Personality of the Year award. He ran in the Olympic 5,000m in Melbourne in 1956 but was not at his best.

He got into the final though did not manage to make the top ten and retired soon after.

Chris's handsome and debonair impression led many to underestimate his abilities on first meeting. He became the first television newscaster for ITV with Robin Day, then launched into politics. Underlying his wish to be an MP was a great idealism and compassion, which found its early fruits in his contribution towards resolving the post-war refugee problem – the distressed people swirling about Europe. For this he was awarded the rare honour of the Nansen Medal. He had two spells as a Conservative MP, first between 1959 and 1966, during which time he held the seat at Lewisham North and was briefly a junior Education Minister. He returned to be elected as MP for Chichester in 1969 and became Ted Heath's Minister for Posts and Communications in 1970. At one point he incurred the wrath of Opposition leader Harold Wilson for sacking a favoured trade unionist; political colleagues attest to his firm handling of such difficult situations. After a period in opposition he decided to retire from politics and went into banking. His final appointment was as chairman of the Airports Authority, following which he was knighted. He lent his vision and knowledge to many charities. When his son Adam started a water scheme for Ethiopia in 2010, Chris, then over seventy, ran in the Great North Run to raise funds for it. He was very much loved by his family – indeed, one son said that above all his father's achievements he will remember him as a good father. I know that after a long illness he was gallant to the end.

Franz Stampfl had been the focal point of our team. He was a handsome, debonair Viennese Rex Harrison. He started with Brasher, whom he had coached for several years since Helsinki, and then Chataway for a season, by the time I joined them in

October 1953. When Franz first came to Britain at the age of seventeen, he was a promising javelin thrower and skier in his native Austria, but he was interned at the outbreak of the war. In 1940, along with other aliens, he was bound for Australia on what amounted to a prison-ship, the *Demera Star*. After leaving Liverpool, the ship was torpedoed and Franz survived several hours in the ice-cold water before he was picked up. To us, who had missed the war, the knowledge that he had faced death and survived through courage and endurance gave his words of exhortation a unique force. But more important, he radiated charm, humour and enthusiasm, all vital in coaching, where a large part of a coach's success depends on inculcating self-confidence into his athletes, just as I was learning how important the same qualities were for a doctor. He became a freelance coach, renting the Duke of York's army barracks in Chelsea in the evenings. I went weekly with the Chrises to the sessions he ran here, usually running 400m fast and slow, totalling twenty laps, or five miles.

The need for coaching varies greatly between different sports and the different disciplines within each. Track athletes generally need less coaching than sportsmen in the more technical hurdling and field events, which had been Franz's real specialty until then. By the time Franz and I had met, I had run for eight years. But I knew to my cost I had made mistakes in planning my training for Helsinki. Franz had the measure of my character; he knew I needed to be handled on a loose rein and also had the insight to know what was needed to increase my strength and confidence for the following May.

Each week through the winter of 1953–54 he watched our interval running, noting the times we had done and judging how hard it had been to achieve them. He approved the climbing break with Chris B when we seemed to be getting 'stale'. Unlike Landy's Percy Cerutty (from whom Landy parted company) Franz never commented to the press on my progress or running plans or that a four-minute mile record attempt might soon be made. He was never authoritarian in his advice or directions. Franz was concerned with athletics as a liberating force because it is an individual pursuit: there may on occasion be records to be broken and medals to be won, but mostly there is fun in company and in attempting to better one's own performance, no matter how modest. Franz understood this and instilled this attitude of individualism among his athletes. I shall always regard the crux of his contribution that, on the day of the race, he gave me the self-belief that despite the bad weather I could break the four-minute mile, and I believed him.

Chapter 8

International Running Career: Vancouver and Bern

My four-minute mile was secure, but it was only a matter of time before John Landy or Wes Santee also achieved it. Landy had arrived in Finland in search of the record and had run 4 minutes 1.6 seconds just before my Oxford run. Santee lowered his own record to 4 minutes 1.3 seconds on 29 May, then missed out on the four-minute mark by just fractions of a second on both 4 and 11 June. He was then drafted into the US marines, prematurely ending his chances of breaking the barrier. These times by Landy and Santee show just how close we were to being forestalled in Oxford.

One day Chris surprised me by saying he had decided to go to Finland to race against John Landy. I understood his reasoning. I said I felt certain that this would provide Landy with the stimulus he was so obviously needing. Chris thought he might beat Landy, who was believed to have no finishing burst, by hanging on and sprinting past him in the final straight, perhaps breaking the four-minute mile himself.

They raced on 21 June and weather conditions were ideal. Landy led after the first lap. He glanced behind him at the bell and, seeing Chris on his heels, took fright as he had never done during his previous solo runs. For the first time, under the stimulus of real competition, Landy unleashed a tremendous finish, which at last brought him below four minutes. He set up a new world record of 3 minutes 58.0 seconds, just as I had expected. I was waiting for the news at home and heard the first announcement. For a few minutes I was stunned. The margin of 1.4 seconds by which he had broken my record was greater than I had expected. Chris came second in 4 minutes 4 seconds, beating his own time from our run in Oxford by 4 seconds.

Until this surprise I was easing off my training, feeling I had no incentive. The moment I heard this news my whole attitude changed. I commented to the press half an hour later that I was glad that Landy had broken the barrier too. I told them I had cabled him my heartiest congratulations. He had tried harder than anyone and I felt happy for him that he had joined the exclusive club of two sub-four-minute milers.

The real struggle with Landy now began. In only six weeks we were to race against each other in the Empire Games in Vancouver. The four-minute mile, however final and perfect it had seemed at Oxford, now meant little unless I could defeat Landy. The challenge of such a race engaged world attention. The American publisher Time Life decided to launch their new global sport magazine, *Sports Illustrated*, the day of the Vancouver mile. Landy had now become the favourite, so taking some of the pressure from me. We found our lives were again dissected in endless detail.

Tactical plans for big races have to be thought out long in advance. A runner must be prepared to meet several possible moves by an opponent and to retain the flexibility to modify his plan if something unexpected happens. The simpler such plans are, the better, because then the mind can be freer from worry during the race. This makes it easier to relax and so run more economically.

My plan was extremely simple. I had to try to persuade John Landy that his best chance of defeating me was to lead so fast that he killed off my sprint finish. I must reserve my own effort of will power for the moment when I would fling myself past him near the finish. Until then I would be entirely passive, thinking of nothing throughout the whole race but this final effort.

It was lucky for me that Landy had always run his best races from the front, including his recent world record. My only worry was that at the last minute he might try to run a waiting race. If he did this, then either of us might win, and the final time would be slow. The race would give no satisfaction either to us or to the spectators. To dissuade him from running this kind of race I tried to demonstrate in the AAA Championships on 10 July 1954, only three weeks before the Empire Games, what might happen if he failed to set a fast enough pace. I waited behind the field until the beginning of the back straight, 300 yards from the tape. Then I tore home with the fastest sprint I could produce. My time was only 4 minutes 7.6 seconds but I ran the last lap in 53.8 seconds. I may have had some added verve that day because I had just passed all my Oxford final exams and so qualified as a doctor the day before the race. This was a relief to all my family, but especially my worried mother, who had earlier said to me, 'I hope, Roger, all this running doesn't take time from your medicine.' Including my master's degree in physiology at Oxford, I had now been both studying medicine and also running for nearly eight years.

For some weeks beforehand, journalists had been flying between Scandinavia and England, comparing details, even of our chest measurements and stride length.

Soon after our arrival, Chris C and I were invited to go swimming by a Vancouver family who had befriended us. Driving past
the university track we saw Landy training hard. I seized on the
chance to get our first meeting over. I should have been embarrassed alone and I was grateful that Chris C, who, of course, had
met Landy recently, was with me.

I had not seen Landy for two years, since we ran in the same
heat in the Olympic Games, when we barely noticed each other.
For the last few months he had never been far from my thoughts.
I was conscious of blushing as we met, betraying my ambigu-
ous feelings for a rival. Landy faced me bare-chested, wearing
only running shorts. His dark curly hair was cut short and his
tough body bronzed by the Australian sun. He had been running
barefoot on the grass between harder bursts on the cinder track.
We exchanged a few words as two circumspect rivals might be
expected to do before a boxing prize fight. He had an attractive
personality and seemed friendly in an easy way. He then went
on with his training. We went swimming instead and it may have
been on one of these expeditions that I caught a cold.

How lucky I was to share a room with Chris C, ever the opti-
mist about his own three-mile race, and I found further comfort
in the fact that Chris B had also been picked for the mile.

John Landy did all his training in the full glare of publicity on
the main track and often in two sessions a day. Details appeared
in the newspapers and it made most disturbing reading. On one
occasion he ran a 4-minute 13-second mile just to warm up and
followed it with a ¾-mile in 2 minutes 59 seconds. He appeared
to have an insatiable appetite for interval running. Before I
arrived he had run ten quarter-miles each in 58 seconds, with
a two-minute recovery interval between each. Much later, he
confided to me that in retrospect he thought this had been too

strenuous! By then I was able to admit to him that it was incomparably superior to the best I had ever done – ten quarters in 60 seconds each with a full two minutes' interval between each. He ran twice as many 220-yard dashes as I could manage and in a much faster average time. Until this time I had no first-hand experience of the 'hard work' school of training. It made my own preparation seem most inadequate. When I felt depressed, however, I reminded myself that my training had been good enough to run a four-minute mile under far from ideal weather conditions, and the relationship between severity of training and performance is complex. I was content to leave it at that.

The great contrast in our training methods was not lost on the press. They never saw me running on a track and wondered whether I ever trained at all. One day they noticed a British sprinter, Peter Fryer, running extremely fast on the track. In build and height he looked remarkably like me and when I opened my paper next day I was delighted to read of the improvement in my powers of sprinting!

I was training mostly on a golf course nearby, away from the prying eyes of the reporters. On my last training day, on the Sunday six days before the race, when my cold was getting worse, I ran a 1-minute 54.7-second half-mile. But Landy had run three successive half-miles two days previously in as fast a time, so I felt dejected again. I wrapped myself up, did no more training and waited anxiously for the preliminary heat on the following Thursday.

Chris C's convincing victory in the three miles was an encouraging omen for my race. It had been a great season for Chris. He helped to set up two world records for the mile, mine and Landy's, and himself only just missed by a fraction of a second the two-mile record for which I had paced him. At the White City he established a new world's best time for three miles, but had to share it with the victor in that race, Freddie Green. As he broke the tape at Vancouver, Chris could feel that his day had come and a broad grin spread across his face. Chris enjoyed racing tremendously, but like the rest of us, he enjoyed it even more when he won. His defeat at Helsinki in 1952 had cast a shadow over his career, which had now been erased. Now I hoped that I could follow him in his good fortune in Vancouver.

There were two heats for the mile on the Thursday, with one day's rest before the final on the Saturday. I still had a thick cold and was worried that I might have a burst of coughing during the race. In my heat Geoffrey Warren, the Australian, led with a 59-second first quarter. I assumed that he was trying to tempt me into running a four-minute mile in the heat and so tire me for the struggle in the final with Landy. He passed the half-mile in 2 minutes, twenty yards ahead of me. Soon after he dropped out. He looked quite surprised when he saw that I had not been following him. This incident is typical of the unexpected element in races and of the need to be constantly on the alert; I might easily have been led astray into trying to keep up with Landy's countryman, but I realised in time that his pace was unnecessarily fast. I came in third in my heat, comfortably qualifying for the final, with New Zealander Murray Halberg winning. In the other heat William Baillie of New Zealand came first, with Landy third, England's Ian Boyd fourth and Chris B sixth.

It encouraged me that I could run a mile in 4 minutes 8.4 seconds so easily with a cold. After all, a good sweat, as everyone knows, can often be the best way to get over a cold. Empire Games heats may be one good a way as any of achieving a cure. The next day my cold was getting distinctly better and I was regaining the hopeful attitude that I had when I arrived in Vancouver.

I am certain that one's feelings at the last minute before a race matter most. Confidence that has been supreme until that moment can be lost quite suddenly. Twice a day I took longish walks, sometimes with Chris C, but often alone, and during these I screwed up my determination to win. I felt coolly confident. Almost for the first time in my life I could honestly say the day before the race that I was ready for it.

There were eight finalists, with Landy the only Australian and quoted as the four to one favourite. David Law and Ian Boyd, both Oxford milers, had also qualified for the final and I was fortunate to have their company.

There were rumours that Murray Halberg might set the pace for Landy for a couple of laps, but I did not take them seriously. I still believed that Landy himself would try to run me off my feet. With Law and Boyd, I had only very briefly considered the possibility of going into the lead to slow the pace a little, but dismissed it as I wanted the total time to be less than four minutes. I had to consider how great a lead I could allow Landy to establish. There were times when he had misjudged the pace and run a first lap in 56 seconds. If he were to do this and I could keep to 59 seconds, he would play into my hands. By running evenly I might have a greater reserve than him left at the finish.

On the day of the final, Saturday 7 August, the last day of the Games, the stadium was filled with one of the most enthusiastic crowds I have ever seen. The setting was perfect. The newly built stadium lay there in the sunshine, the flags of the competing countries silhouetted against the mountains of Vancouver Island.

We lined up for the start. Landy had drawn the inside place. The gun fired and Baillie of New Zealand went straight into the lead. I stayed some yards back at Landy's shoulder until he took over the lead at the 220-yard mark. Gradually he drew away and I lay second at the end of the first lap in 59.2 seconds. Landy's pace in the next lap was too fast for my own plans (58.2 seconds) and I had allowed a gap of seven yards to open up. In the second lap this lead had increased to fifteen yards. I completed the half-mile in 1 minute 59 seconds, so I was within a four-minute mile schedule.

By now I had almost lost contact with Landy. I no longer had the advantage of being pulled along by him in his slipstream. The field had split. Landy was out in front on his own and I was leading the rest, ten yards farther back. I felt complete detachment and at the half-mile I remember saying to myself, 'Only two minutes more.' The stage was set for relaxed running until my final burst, but I must somehow get back to Landy's shoulder by the bell.

My speed was now the same as Landy's. The only problem was that Landy was a long way in front and looked like staying there. I was on schedule but he was not slowing down as I had expected. This was the moment when my confidence wavered. Was he going to break the world record again, but by an even greater margin? To have any 'finish' left I must be able to follow at his shoulder throughout the early part of the last lap.

Abandoning my own schedule, I quickened my stride, trying at the same time to keep relaxed. I won back the first yard, then each succeeding yard until his lead was halved by the time we reached the back straight on the third lap. How I wished I had never allowed him to establish such a lead.

By the end of the third lap I had 'connected' myself to Landy again, though he was still five yards ahead. I was almost hypnotised by his easy shuffling stride, the most clipped and economical I have ever seen. I tried to imagine myself attached to him by some invisible cord. With each stride, I drew the cord tighter and reduced his lead. At the ¾-mile when the bell rang I was at

Landy's shoulder. The rest of the field were twenty yards back and I was so absorbed by our struggle that I heard no lap time.

The third lap had tired me. This was the lap when a runner expects to slow down a little to gather momentum for the finish and instead I had been toiling hard to win back those painful yards. Now I fixed myself to Landy like a shadow. He must have known I was at his heels because he began to quicken his stride as soon as we turned into the last back straight. It was incredible that in a race run at this speed he should start a finishing burst 300 yards from the tape. I was amused to remember that three weeks before in England I had actually considered whether I might overtake him at the 220-yard mark! Now it was all I could do to hold him. I left it as late as possible because the pace had been so fast I doubted if I could sustain my finish for more than eighty yards.

As we entered the last bend I tried to convince myself that he was tiring. With each stride now I attempted to husband a little strength for the moment at the end of the bend when I had decided to make my decisive move. I knew this would be the point where Landy would least expect it. If I failed to overtake him there the race would be his.

When the moment came, my mind would try to galvanise my body. There might be no response, but it was my only chance. This moment had occurred dozens of times before. This time the only difference was that the whole race was being run to my absolute limit.

Just before the end of the last bend I flung myself past Landy. As I did so I saw him glance inwards over his opposite shoulder, something I had trained myself never to do, as it signalled despair in a runner. This tiny act of his held great significance and gave me confidence. I interpreted it as meaning that he had already made his great effort along the back straight and could not resist the temptation to find out if he had dropped me.

All round the bend he had been unable to hear me coming behind him, the noise of the crowd was so great. He must have hoped desperately that I had fallen back. The crux of the race came when the worry of whether he had succeeded grew on Landy. His last chance to look round came at the end of the bend. Here, because of the curve of the track, he could see behind him with only half a turn of the head. He knew that to challenge now I must run wide and therefore extra distance, and he did not expect it. The moment he looked round, he was unprotected against me and so lost a valuable fraction of a second in his response to my challenge. It was my tremendous luck that these two happenings – his turning round and my final spurt – came absolutely simultaneously, so when he turned his head to the front again I was already about two yards ahead. Though I was slowing, I just managed to reach the tape, winning by five yards in 3 minutes 58.8 seconds. Once again the four-minute mile had been broken, this time by both of us in the same race. This last lap was one of the most intense and exciting moments of my running career. The first issue of *Sports Illustrated*, among many great pictures, had captured the moment when Landy turned his head and I overtook him.

After the Games, Vancouver put up an 8ft statue of this moment in bronze. Landy quipped, 'Lot's wife was turned into a pillar of salt for looking back. I'm the first person to be turned into bronze!'

After the race was over it was as if a barrier between us had lifted, and ever since we have been good friends, meeting every few years in England, Vancouver or Australia. We have the warmest feeling and respect for each other and I fervently admire his subsequent work, involved as he is in the environment, natural history and photography. The Australian press treated John Landy very harshly after his defeat in Vancouver. Australians do not like a 'loser'. He continued racing and they hoped he would win the 1,500m gold medal in the Olympics in 1956, situated in his home town, Melbourne. Sadly, for whatever reason, he did not come in the first six in his race, whereupon even more opprobrium was piled on his head. Gradually, a reassessment of his brilliance as an athlete and world-record holder was recognised by the Australian public. He was made Governor of the State of Victoria. His name now stands alongside the greatest Australian sporting figures.

There was another incident that shed further light on Landy's character. Unable to sleep the night before the race, he was walking barefoot and accidentally trod on a photographer's old flashbulb. He cut the instep of his foot and required several stitches. True to the measure of the man, he did not wish this to be taken as an excuse if he were defeated. News about it only leaked a week or so later.

My running career was now nearly over. Only the European Championships remained, which were as near as I could ever come to matching the Olympic final, for which I still felt the need to make amends. They would be in Bern, Switzerland, from 25 to 29 August. Unlike the Olympics, however, there would be only one day of heats on the Thursday, then a two-day break to rest before the final on the 29th.

Breaking the four-minute barrier for the mile was of greater public significance, but that personal record was made more enduring by the win over Landy in Vancouver. A gold medal in Bern would further underline the achievement. European medals were the most coveted in international athletics, after the

Olympics, and the 1,500m field in Bern would include most of the best runners whom I had not already beaten over the distance that year: Nielsen of Denmark was probably the best 'fighter' on the track and had a deadly finish; Jungwirth, the Czech, had beaten me over 880m earlier in the year, after my goodwill trip to America; the Hungarian Iharos had beaten Gunder Hägg's world record for the 1,500m just weeks before, but was otherwise an unknown quantity. Werner Lueg, the Berlin schoolmaster who had finished just ahead of me in Helsinki, would also be racing. The only notable exception was José Barthel who, despite being the Helsinki Olympic champion, had failed to qualify for the final. I would have loved the chance to turn the tables on him, but only if he was at his best would the victory be significant.

I did not run particularly well in the heat. Whether it was my shoes tearing during my warm up, leading me to run in a pair with spikes that were too long, or the elbow I caught on the first bend, I ended up running a frantic race, darting up and down through the field with little tactical intent. But I did qualify in third place, in the relatively easy time of 3 minutes 51.8 seconds.

I used the next two days to prepare for the final, taking long walks to find the mental calm I needed. On the morning of the race I was relaxed and my mind seemed cool and detached. I had not spent the night bathed in sweat, running the distance a dozen times over in my imagination, as I had before previous important international meetings. I was favourite for the final, but I did not mind, perhaps because I knew it would be my last race.

Eleven of us lined up on the start line, squeezed towards the inside lane and ready to fight for position going into the first corner. The gun went and the scrambling began. Fifteen yards down the track there was a crash and the Yugoslavian Mugosa fell at my feet, so I had to jump to avoid impaling his hand on my spikes. I stayed back, going around the corner in last place while the leaders fought three abreast. None of the favourites, including me, was willing to set the pace and the race slowed accordingly. If Landy had been there he would probably have led from the start. Nielsen was the runner I most respected and I knew he would prefer a slower, bunched race in order that his sprint finish could have the most possible impact.

We were all still together when the bell sounded for the last lap. I moved up to the leader Jungwirth's shoulder, guessing that he would try to break away first as his finish was not strong. He tried to stretch away at the start of the back straight but could not extend his lead more than a yard. I had decided that my burst would be most effective coming from about 200 metres, the start of the last bend. This would be when my opponents would least expect it, as I would have to run extra distance because of the bend. If I went earlier I might be caught; later and I might find myself in a flat-out race with Nielsen. Lueg and Nielsen were still with us. Iharos I did not see as I took a glimpse over my shoulder (breaking my own cardinal rule). I forced Jungwirth's pace up to the last bend, letting him know that he would have to keep his speed up if he wanted to retain the lead.

I was almost sandwiched between Jungwirth and Nielsen as we came to the bend. Before Nielsen could make his move I struck past Jungwirth with all my power, opening up a five-yard lead before the Dane had a chance to react. I later learnt that he came back up to my shoulder as we entered the home straight, but he could not sustain the sprint and fell back five yards. Never did my finishing burst serve me so well: I ran the last 220 yards in 25 seconds, which suggests a last lap of around 50 seconds. There was no longer any need to call on emotion to produce this overdraft on my energy. There had been times in other races when I felt real fear as I tore down the home straight – such was the distortion of values produced by my excitement during a race. This time I simply switched my mental lever that unleashed the well-worn channels that carried my body to the finish. I remember looking up at the clock as I came towards the line and thinking coolly, 'What a pity – no world record today. If only Boysen had been with us!' The final time was 3 minutes 43.8 seconds, a championship record and 1.4 seconds faster than the Olympic final two years before in Helsinki. If only…

That is how my ten-year running career ended. Though I had firm plans to retire in 1952 to concentrate on my medical studies, after the Helsinki debacle I felt I would never forgive myself if I retired on this negative note – a seeming dismissal of my approach to running. Fortunately, having made this decision my last two years had been successful. Crucially for my own satisfaction, my last two races were proper races, not time trials, and therefore I felt they had been a real challenge to my skills as a competitor.

My retirement was both anticipated and inevitable. It absolved me from one of the most difficult decisions sportsmen and sportswomen have to take and one which many do not get right. Though retirement made the way clear for my hospital posts and neurological training, that is not to say I took it easily. It also led to the greatest change in my life, namely love and marriage, which was interwoven into my medical career. At the time it seemed I had left sport behind, but this conclusion was premature. Fifteen years later I was appointed by the government to be chairman of the Sports Council, giving me the chance to use the experience of both my sports and medical careers, my twin tracks, and hopefully helping to play a part in setting Britain on the path that led eventually to the triumphs of the 2012 Olympics.

Chapter 9

Marriage and Parenthood

In April 1954, a Saturday loomed and I would have welcomed any party to lighten the tension before the attack on the four-minute mile, planned for two weeks later. My spirits rose when I went to a party and met a girl who caught my eye. She was prettily dressed, with dangling earrings, and was chatting to a fellow runner. I cut in and we had a vivid conversation, joking and laughing. This was Moyra, and I arranged to see her the very next day, when she had invited friends for an open-house Sunday tea.

At three o'clock the next day, I rang in the optimistic hope that Moyra would come for a walk in Kensington Gardens before the tea party. 'Oh, I am sorry, but I am far too busy getting things ready for the party – but I do have a very pretty girlfriend. I could arrange for her to come with you.' I declined the offer and put down the phone, and Moyra thought that was that. However, I found her studio address and, despite our conversational brusqueness, earlier that day I crossed a flower-filled courtyard, up steps, to her studio. Moyra later told me that that Sunday was the first and last time she knew me to be taciturn at a party – I was not used to being stood up! I was uncertain in which direction this new relationship was heading.

That summer of 1954 was for me an *annus mirabilis*. Looking back now, sixty years later, had I not been superbly fit, there was no way I could have mastered my finals, vanquished my rival John Landy in Vancouver and commanded the field in Bern, winning the European Games title. Also, the embryo of a book took shape in my mind. To say I was busy does not do justice to that year. It was not surprising that Moyra and I saw very little of each other during it.

She was then an aspiring portrait painter, having been at the Ruskin School of Fine Art in Oxford at the same time I was in Oxford. Her father, Per Jacobsson, was a Swede, and at the time was chief economist at the Bank for International Settlements in Basel. Moyra's mother had been a passionate suffragist, a captain in the Queen Alexandra's Auxiliary Corps and decorated for her services. Both parents chose Cheltenham Ladies' College, the leading girls' boarding school, for their daughters – a pioneering school dedicated to taking girls' education seriously. However, her first house mistress was a dour Scot, harsh in her ideas of discipline and grotesquely keen on rhubarb served in every meal in one way or another to 'rinse out the system'! There was a railway track at the end of the garden at Cheltenham and Moyra often stood there, longing for home. I may have been intermittently bored at home, but at least it was a haven to escape any bullying and my father's gentle humour could put life in proportion.

When Moyra was very young, the household included a German cook and a French governess. Her father, of course, sometimes spoke his native Swedish, but her mother's English was used predominantly in family conversation. It seems quite extraordinary, even to a neurologist, that a child brought up in this atmosphere was able to learn four languages by the age of six and, almost without thinking, address each person in the correct language.

Starting at the age of nearly seven, along with her two sisters who were four and six years older than her, Moyra travelled across France by train and then the Channel by ferryboat to England, to go to Cheltenham. Moyra tells me that by the time we met, she had crossed the Channel sixty-two times. Before the war, travelling to a boarding school was a massive undertaking. There had to be clothes for every occasion and sport; at one stage, each schoolgirl was required to bring thirteen different pairs of shoes. Moyra was a self-confident child and coped well with the school's social life and the various cruelties of separation from her parents in Switzerland, unreachable except by letters, which were in fact read and censored by the school before being sent. She was quite good at swimming, but soon rebelled against all sports except riding, for which special lessons were arranged. In summer she would drift away from games of cricket and rounders to read a book in the long grass.

The war obviously put paid to the three sisters jaunting across Europe from Switzerland and back. Moyra's eldest sister, Erin, never took up her scholarship to Cambridge and started at the University of Basel. The second sister, Bridgit, aged fifteen, and Moyra, just turned eleven, went to St George's School on a hill overlooking Lake Geneva and within sight of the snow-covered mountains. It was run along English lines, but more cheerful and liberal than Cheltenham. Her education was as much by then a matter of reading eclectically from her father's enormous library and joining in the jolly and wide-ranging discussions with her family and guests at the dinner table. I attribute to this her independence from received opinion. Another remarkable aspect of her education was that she read and learnt by heart great tracts of English poetry. Ever since, she has had a fund of language and wisdom on which to muse. She had already resolved to become an artist rather than read a formal academic subject at university. Just as I had been gripped by the beauty of Bath after a Harrow suburb, Moyra exulted in the ever-changing skies reflected in the lake.

We had both been liberated by the war. In this book I have already described my schooling. Moyra's included pupils of all nationalities – one was a refugee Polish princess, whose brothers had waded across a river to escape the Germans. She was a descendant of Napoleon's love affair with a Polish aristocrat. Then there was a Swiss armaments manufacturer's daughter, who was obstreperous and spoilt. There were some German and Italian girls who came after Alamein when their parents realised that, as the Allies might win, it was better to 'play safe' by putting their daughters in an English school. Another was a harmless manufacturer's daughter. The school ran on mostly happy, very liberal rules – concerts and plays both outside and in were to be had in plenty.

However, I was astonished to learn that during the war Switzerland was much more severely rationed than we were, as the Germans had completely encircled the country and could extract as much food as they wished. The menace of invasion never quite went away. The German Army had massed on the Swiss border in the spring of 1940, which necessitated the Bank for International Settlements to take to the mountains. Moyra spent one glorious summer in a medieval castle. In truth, for her it was a romantic thrill. Hitler changed his mind and said, 'Switzerland is a hard nut to crack. I will keep her for the dessert.' Thanks to the courage of the Swiss, that moment never came.

When the war ended, Moyra returned briefly to Cheltenham, but after a disastrous quarantining under the unjustified suspicion that she had contracted typhus, she left quickly to attend the Ruskin School of Fine Art in Oxford in October 1945.

By the time we met she had visited many countries, usually as her father's companion, but as early as six she had been catapulted into Cheltenham Ladies' College. True, her two older sisters had preceded her but she hardly ever saw them as they were in different houses.

It seemed to me that I worked harder in my exams, covering much more, much faster than Moyra. She had many fewer exams to pass than I did and had enriched her mind with wide reading, and every spare moment she had, there was a paintbrush in her hand.

When we returned to London I started as a house physician and was not formally allowed to leave the hospital, so Moyra had to come and visit me. One evening about two weeks after a holiday in Basel, she brought a hamper of food to my rooms in the hospital. Her male friend who drove her there was under the illusion she was being so kind as to visit a sick and elderly relative. Anyway, when she visited, at that moment I knew that my life had to change. I was about to embark on two years of residential work in hospital, then take my exams for the Royal College of Physicians, become a physician, do my two years' National Service as a doctor and then, after five years of hard training, become a consultant neurologist, and Moyra was the perfect partner. So without further ado I proposed marriage there and then and, to my everlasting good fortune, she said yes. We kissed and then she went off with her empty basket.

As I still could not leave the hospital, a little while after that, to

Moyra's embarrassment, she had to go to Garrards, the jewellers in Regent Street, and borrow from them three or four engagement rings from which I could choose one.

Since I had to get on with my hospital work, the whole machinery of the wedding in Basel – only six weeks later – was transferred to the competent administrative care of the Jacobsson family. Her oldest sister, Erin, who was living in Basel, arranged everything there. The date had to be between my hospital appointments. I was hoping to create such a positive impression during my first appointment with Professor George Pickering, the Professor of Medicine at St Mary's, that he would then recommend me for good hospital appointments afterwards. I am glad to say he did – to the Hammersmith Hospital and Royal Postgraduate Medical School.

Our engagement was officially announced on 17 May 1955, a Saturday. Just before, Moyra and her mother had moved temporarily into some rooms at the Kensington Palace Hotel, so that there would be no crush of reporters at St Albans Studios. Through the morning Moyra stayed in her room, with the press making importunate calls for her to come down and be photographed. However, she waited until I could leave the hospital, steal into the hotel through a side entrance, meet up with her and only then go downstairs for the press to take engagement pictures of us together.

Our wedding took place on 11 June. My parents flew out for it and my best man was Chris Brasher. Hilary Rubinstein was one of the few other friends from England who managed to come. The wedding coincided with the annual meeting of the Bank for International Settlements, attended by European Central Bank heads including the Governor of the Bank of England, the Lord Cobbold, so a heavy international banking presence filled the aisles. As we left the church we were met by an honour guard of Swiss athletes in tracksuits. Any groom's speech is important but at our reception this audience of eminent bankers made my effort especially challenging.

The announcement on the day of my wedding of a CBE awarded for my athletic career certainly added a gloss to the day. When Moyra saw her father clutching a sheaf of notes for his wedding speech that morning, she enjoined him to cut it by two-thirds – which he gracefully did. As to my own speech, in such distinguished company, it was, to say the least, taxing, but it must have rung true as several guests predicted I would go into politics! Before the church wedding the civil wedding took place in the town hall and the British consul made Moyra a British citizen.

Then we sped away from the wedding with our car festooned with ribbons and confetti and tin cans until we got out of town and swept the tell-tale encumbrances all away.

We drove to Lugano to start our honeymoon at the Grand Hotel there, but it was a little too grand; we drove on to northern Italy to stay in small hotels while Moyra painted the lakes and I read medical books. The plan had been to stay in Venice but my continental driving skills were too rudimentary for that city. After one night, mercilessly attacked by mosquitoes, we fled back to cooler northern Italy, at Lake Maggiore. Following a minor though alarming collision with a harvester on a winding road, we retreated to Basel and stayed in Moyra's parents' home. But no change in plan or untoward incident could dislodge our sense of contentment. I have never felt alone since my marriage and Moyra's steadier disposition has been an invaluable counterbalance to my nature. Over the years I have appreciated even more Moyra's good judgement and our shared intellectual interests.

The main aim of our marriage was to create a happy union

in which we could pursue our careers and also bring up and educate a large family. With help from our parents and our own hard work we thought we had a good chance of setting up a small home, which we could expand as my medical career progressed. My principles then were more socialist than Moyra's, but we agreed on the need to secure for our children the best education we could afford. It turned out that with the scale of my medical and outside commitments such as the Sports Council and our having four children, the labour had to be divided, with Moyra looking after the children. Unfortunately this came at the cost, for a long while, of her artistic career, though she loved bringing up the children and has no regrets.

Erin was our first child, born on 8 February 1957. Though Moyra's labour pains started early in the morning, I was not aware of them, as she let me sleep. In the morning, before breakfast, I drove her to University College Hospital (UCH) and then went on to the Brompton, where I was a senior house physician. She chose UCH as she did not wish to be in the glare of attention at St Mary's, my own hospital, and UCH was then the only hospital in London that allowed mothers to have their babies next to them during the day. I returned at eight that evening and Erin finally appeared at about ten o'clock at night. The next morning there was a full press onslaught, with pictures of Erin's perfect little feet, captioned with speculation as to whether she would be an athlete or a dancer. Erin was a delightfully precocious baby and according to family lore was able to repeat her alphabet at the age of eighteen months.

Our first home in London as a family was a rented flat in Kensington Mansions, Trebovir Road, a street of late Edwardian mansion blocks off the Earls Court Road. Our flat overlooked a garden square which gave us a patch of grass on which the children could play. The block in which we lived was filled with other young families and Moyra soon formed a set of friends for playgroups, coffee mornings and dinners.

Our elder son arrived on 28 October 1958, also at University College Hospital. We named him Clive Christopher Roger, after the two Chrises, Brasher and Chataway, and after Clive of India, the great soldier and administrator, in Moyra's thoughts as I was serving in the army at the time out in Aden. Just after he arrived, some thoughtless patient in the ward showed Moyra a newspaper carrying a picture from Aden of an explosion caused by terrorists who were trying to oust the British. Seeing it dried up her milk. Fortunately, I was able to return to England for Christmas and Clive's christening. A newsreel film of the christening showed the two Chrises, who were made godfathers, and Carol, the wife of Norris McWhirter, who was his godmother. A picture of him in Moyra's arms appeared in the newspapers and we had a very jolly christening party back at Trebovir Road. Clive received close sisterly attention from Erin. He had a voracious appetite and so became what Moyra called 'my cheerful roly-poly baby'.

Thurstan was our third child, born at home in Trebovir Road on 30 July 1960. The National Health Service regulations then decreed that if normal deliveries of one or possibly two children had taken place in hospital then further children should be born at home, to save the NHS money. I was not present for the birth, having gone to play golf fifty miles away at Frinton-on-Sea with Moyra's father, Per, not imagining a baby would appear that weekend. Fortunately, our immediate neighbour and friend Caroline Parks, Alan's wife, was a fully qualified doctor and helped Moyra with the delivery, which mercifully went well though without the benefit of any painkillers, and Alan Parks, a consultant surgeon, became Thurstan's godfather. The health service midwife, who went around the neighbourhood on a bicycle with her equipment in a leather bag strapped to the back, arrived late and, on hearing Thurstan's lusty cries as she entered the front door, remarked, 'That's the sound I like to hear when I go out on a case.'

Our fourth child, Charlotte, was born at Queen Charlotte's Hospital on 16 August 1963. She was named after Moyra's mother's favourite brother, Charles, who was killed in the First World War at Delville Wood in the Battle of the Somme on 16 August 1916. From the outset, Charlie, as we soon called her with a soft 'ch', was a small but highly energetic baby.

One has to be ever vigilant of young children's safety, as I learnt in two dramatic incidents. The first concerned Clive. Every year we were very kindly entertained by my sister Joyce, married and with her own family, who lived in a house overlooking the sea at Weston-super-Mare. There we would spend two weeks, occasionally even longer, each summer.

The seafront was very exposed to the elements, with a concrete sea wall or breaker which protected an inner pool. At low tide the water receded by about a mile, but there was always some water left in this pool for the children to use for paddling and sailing toy boats. It was a typical summer day in Weston-super-Mare: wind and rain. We went for a walk along the path atop the seawall, which becomes covered by water at high tide and so is damp and strewn with seaweed and slime. Clive got away from my hand and ran towards the two-bar railing lining the pond. One bar was at about two feet and the other at about four. He ran forward and just at the point when he might have been going to stop and look into the water, he slid on the seaweed and shot under the lower bar and disappeared into the murky, muddy water of the inner pool, which was about twelve feet deep.

Moyra, who was behind me, was frozen to the spot by fear. But I ran several yards forward to where he had slid through and leapt over the railing. He was not floating and I swam about under the water until, more by chance than anything, one hand felt a limb and I pulled him out. At first he was not breathing. He seemed to be filled with water. But by dint of tipping him and tapping him he came back to life and started breathing again. It seemed as though he had been in the water for a minute, as time passes very slowly at moments like this. Clive, revived, caterwauled for a bit, and then was unusually quiet for the remainder of the day.

A second episode, in which we thought we might lose Thurstan, occurred when we were travelling to the States in 1961. Our plane was heading for New York. Unknown to us, there had been a smallpox outbreak in Birmingham and so the airlines were asked to take particular care with anyone who showed signs of illness, so they could be quarantined. Thurstan, only a year old, seemed to stop breathing and went blue. We were not aware that he had any particular illness, respiratory or otherwise, at the time. I said to the air hostess, 'Bring an oxygen mask, quickly,' to which she said, 'Oh, he's gone to sleep, he doesn't need the oxygen.' I insisted, 'I'm a doctor, I need an oxygen mask *now*.' She replied, 'It may panic the other passengers, we're not allowed to do this without asking.' So I went up to the captain's cabin and asked for oxygen. After this she brought a mask and Thurstan appeared to recover and was breathing again but became very flushed. We took off his clothes, since he may have had a fever. We were for a while threatened with an indefinite quarantining of the whole family in New York, but in the end convinced the authorities we had not been near Birmingham and we were then allowed to continue our journey on to Washington DC, home of Moyra's parents, where Per Jacobsson was now head of the International Monetary Fund.

These were rare frightening moments amidst the many pleasures of our first becoming parents. Moyra subscribed to no harsh or arbitrary precepts of childcare. They each soon changed from delicate and serious bundles into plump and cheerful crawlers. As a chuffed father and neurologist, I was fascinated to observe their nervous systems take hold: limbs moving deliberately, senses drinking in the outside world and nerve fibres linking to interpret it all. Soon they were off on furious missions to investigate everything, in every different direction. It came as a pleasing shock how soon afterwards their strong wills and distinct characters manifested themselves.

Chapter 10

In Transition

M y first appointment as a doctor in 1954 was to the challenging post of house physician to George Pickering, Professor of Medicine at St Mary's Hospital, later knighted and coincidentally my predecessor-but-one as Master of Pembroke College, Oxford. After Moyra and I married in June 1955, I spent six months at the John Radcliffe in Oxford, doing a compulsory surgical resident appointment, then went to Hammersmith Hospital, the Royal Postgraduate Medical School and after that to the Royal Brompton Hospital, awaiting call-up for my two years of National Service. There were some press queries as to why I had not yet done National Service, especially after the cricketer, Colin Cowdrey, was found ineligible on medical grounds from serving because of flat feet. The explanation for the delay was that as I gained more senior appointments and then higher qualifications, it was in the interests of the army that my service should be legitimately deferred.

Moyra had been used to living in the centre of towns, whether abroad or in London, and, after leaving my home in Harrow, so had I. We had lived for seven years in an old-fashioned flat off the Earls Court Road, always dreaming that we would eventually own our own home. We needed a house as near to my work as possible, so that at least sometimes I could be home for bath time. At that stage it was an impossible dream, however hard we saved. Slowly, through various earnings outside medicine and with the security of my consultant posts and our parents' help in 1963, we decided to buy a house in Edwardes Square. We were stretching ourselves financially, but continued to save. We never went out for meals and our treats were only occasional trips to the cinema.

In 1955, glowing invitations to operas and dinners had to be turned down because of my resident hospital work. My book, *The First Four Minutes*, was published in 1955, of which 60,000 copies of the hardback were printed. Perhaps quixotically, I gave away half of the British royalties to the Amateur Athletic Association for their coaching scheme, still feeling that it was almost improper to benefit financially from my amateur running. Some of these royalties also went towards the building of a running track near my home in Harrow, which until then had been without any track at all. I had the book's serialisation contract with the *Sunday Times*, and to give us an extra income for seven years, I had agreed to write up to twelve articles a year and I had a leeway to choose subjects outside sport. The discipline of writing made me realise that, both in articles and for speeches, being humorous was both the most important task and the most difficult to accomplish gracefully. Sometimes fortune played into my hands. I was still being showered with fan mail and Moyra helped by answering much of it – the topic of one early article.

Because it interested me, I accepted BBC engagements to do television commentaries on athletic events, usually with Norris McWhirter. Both he and his identical twin brother Ross had photographic memories and were then professional sports journalists. I was there to provide some insight into the athletes' personalities and their likely training programmes. As I did not have the time to do any homework on athletics, this work lasted for roughly three years. It also helped financially that we holidayed in those days only in the summer, thanks to the great generosity of my sister and her husband. We stayed with them at their home in Weston-super-Mare in Somerset.

Another venture arose out of a chance meeting with the chairman of Schweppes, who had wide discretion in matters of company philanthropy, on the flight to the Rome Olympics in 1960. We also discussed various social problems and he seemed to be interested by my comments, and before the end of the flight he asked me if I would edit a book they were thinking of sponsoring, called *Prospect: The Book of The New Generation*. I was able to call on my friends, who already had careers filled with promise. One of the better-known contributors was my friend from Oxford Shirley Williams.

I also took part in a number of BBC radio programmes. The first was a brief post-war revival of *The Brains Trust*, which had almost become compulsory listening during the war. For New Year's Eve 1955, I was asked by the BBC to prepare a twenty-minute talk which expressed my views on the 'younger generation'. I was given a free hand and perhaps the result reads now as a rather idealistic and naive assessment. It was also clear that we were all worried about the conflicting philosophies of East and West and the dangers of the Cold War.

Another BBC programme which I joined was called *Frankly Speaking*. In this programme I had the chance, along with a writer and a psychologist, to interview over a year about fifteen leading figures in Britain, including actors, scientists and politicians. The interview sessions took place after we dined together and the interview with the victim lasted for some three-quarters of an hour, the producer then editing the tape down to thirty minutes. I rapidly realised that actors like Sybil Thorndyke, who in her youth had played Saint Joan in George Bernard Shaw's play, could, not surprisingly, express their thoughts and feelings in a more forceful and amusing way than other public figures, because the acting profession gave them more practice in baring their emotions. These programmes formed part of a BBC that was at its Reithian zenith, pursuing culture and disdaining trivialisation in the absence of commercial competitors and populist pressures.

My hospital work generally forced me to turn down travel and requests to join committees and speaking at meetings, but I made an exception for the National Association of Boys' Clubs (NABC). This body had a network of about a thousand boys' clubs across the country. I was impressed by their aims, which were philanthropic rather than religious (though some clubs were attached to churches) in contrast to the youth organisations run by the armed services. The clubs were engaged in 'self-improving' activities, both social and sporting. The national organisation had some paid organisers and received some funding from the Department of Education, but the bulk of the club leaders and coaches were volunteers. It was related to the Boy Scout movement and was prominent in Britain's less affluent towns after the war. I was asked to help by organising and becoming president of a fitness scheme whereby boys would be able to gain badges and certificates for proficiency at a series of athletic events to be organised, timed and measured by club leaders. This initiative was spurred on in part by evidence of declining fitness among children in Britain. The scheme was quite successful and I spent many hours signing certificates and on occasion presenting them to boys in different parts of the country.

My first introduction to higher-level sport organisations in Britain came in 1955 with a surprise invitation from the Duke of Edinburgh to join the steering group planning a scheme of youth awards, to be named after him. The invitation arose in part out of my work on the NABC's fitness scheme. The first meeting of the group was to be held at Buckingham Palace in 1954 on a weekday at 10.30 a.m., shortly after I started my post as house physician under George Pickering.

My future career in medicine depended upon Professor Pickering's view of my diligence and competence, because halfway through that post I would have to ask his advice on my next step. I hoped this would be an appointment at the Royal Postgraduate School at Hammersmith in London, for which his reference would be crucial.

Yet I was in no way inclined to turn down the invitation from the Duke of Edinburgh – indeed I took it as a royal command. But I was equally reluctant to tell my new professor, who had never shown the slightest curiosity about sport, that I had a conflicting engagement at Buckingham Palace, of all places. That morning, as usual, I had to accompany Professor Pickering round the ward, with the ward sister in attendance, to see the twenty-five patients under his personal care, starting at nine o'clock. At that stage if I put the palace before patients, I might have run the risk of ending up with a reference saying, 'He is a good doctor but I am uncertain whether in view of his sports background his priorities are now in medicine' – a damning verdict. So I decided to take the risk of being able to keep the ward round moving swiftly enough until he had finished and then leap into a taxi outside the hospital, leaving Professor Pickering unaware of my other engagement.

My worry grew that morning, because as we went round the patients, Professor Pickering seemed far more curious than usual about every single detail. It was my habit to have memorised the details of each case overnight and to present them succinctly, without reference to any notes. Was it just my imagination that this particular morning he had a surfeit of questions and helpful suggestions? With increasing but, I hoped, well-concealed impatience, I over-simplified a few cases and we finished at 10.15. He left the ward and, seconds later, so did I. I took off my white coat and shot out into the street and then, after a few precious minutes ticked by, an empty taxi arrived. Outside Buckingham Palace, I was stopped by the policemen at the gates, waved my invitation and within a few minutes was shown to the Duke of Edinburgh's small private conference room. I was ten minutes late and blurted abjectly, 'I am sorry, Your Royal Highness. I have to say that I was held up at the hospital.' It was the only half-decent explanation I could meekly apply, apologising for such *lèse-majesté*.

As I made for the one empty seat, I saw on my right Field Marshal Alexander, the wartime victor over Rommel in north Africa, who later as High Commissioner in Canada had presented me with my Empire Games medal in Vancouver the previous year. Next to him was General 'Boy' Browning, the Parachute Division commander at Arnhem, then treasurer in the office of the Duke of Edinburgh. On the other side of the Duke was Kurt Hahn, with his brooding hooded eyes and shiny bald head, who had founded Gordonstoun School in Scotland, where Prince Philip had been educated. Across the table I saw the friendly face of Colonel John Hunt, leader of the successful 1953 Everest expedition, who later became the full-time director of the Duke's award scheme. Characteristically for that time, though lack of fitness affected men and women equally, there were no women in the room.

The past history of fitness schemes in Britain was rather controversial. Before the war, when the government became aware of the general unfitness of British men, meaning, in fact, unfitness for fighting, it had promoted a national scheme. It had an unhappy echo of Germany's own 'Strength through Joy' sport and exercise movement.

The meeting at Buckingham Palace was dominated by its instigator, Kurt Hahn, from whom the Duke may have absorbed a rather rigid Germanic approach to the problem. In 1938, when Hitler barred Jews from all official posts, Hahn had been dismissed from the headmastership of Salem School in Germany and had started a similar school at Gordonstoun. When war broke out, the government attempted to intern one of his teachers who was a German Jew. It was a measure of the man that Hahn immediately went 500 miles by taxi from the school in Scotland to the Home Office with the teacher concerned and demanded an interview, saying, 'If you intern him you must intern me too, because I am also a German Jew.' The Home Office relented. At the Buckingham Palace meeting, Hahn led the discussion while the Duke of Edinburgh listened respectfully to his former headmaster. We mulled over research on fitness schemes in West Germany, East Germany, Russia and America. Hahn spoke firmly about the physical and moral decay of the nation, which only this type of universal scheme could reverse. 'Sport is the moral equivalent of war' was the phrase he used. Put bluntly, he meant that for young people the various

challenges of sport and activities like emergency rescue could
bring out qualities of self-sacrifice, courage and endurance, so
recently shown by troops during the war.

From this and other meetings, the Duke's award scheme
gradually took shape. The secret was to add to the individual-
istic trio of improvement of speed, strength and endurance an
element of social or community service through mountain and
sea rescue, as Hahn had done at Gordonstoun. This made the
scheme socially useful and more appealing to the general public
in Britain. It countered any possible criticism that the Duke of
Edinburgh, descended from the Battenbergs, was too Germanic
an influence. The Duke's scheme, under the direction of Sir
John Hunt, was a great success, but administering bronze, silver
and gold awards from five different sections including fitness,
rescue, service and expedition was so large a burden that it soon
needed public money. Over time it became a regular adjunct to
many schools' formal curricula and flourishes to this day. Many
schools took it up with enthusiasm and quite recently we were at
Windsor Castle at a dinner hosted by Prince Edward, now president of the award scheme. Students spoke of how the award had
transformed their lives. One girl in particular comes to mind.
She had a hopeless family, without any optimism for her life.
Doing the award up to gold standard had given her a self-belief
and ambition that lifted her into another sphere. Rich donors
sitting around those tables in the great St George's Hall, which
had been rebuilt after the massive fire there, could not help but
give generously when they heard her story.

In 1954 the Duke of Edinburgh, perhaps consciously copy-
ing his predecessor, Prince Albert, sought his own role to help
the Queen and his adopted country. He chose sport as an area
presumed to be removed from party politics. Though that may

have been true then, sport became quite highly politicised within a few years. At the time, the main umbrella organising body promoting both high-level and recreation-based sport was the Central Council of Physical Recreation (CCPR), set up in 1935. The Duke of Edinburgh became its president and has remained so ever since. Another body was the National Playing Fields Association, founded with the wider aim of improving sports facilities in villages and towns across Britain, and the Duke was president of this too.

Over the years after the war, British sport had benefited from the transfer of a number of training centres, previously large country houses with grounds, which were being sold off cheaply by members of the harassed British aristocracy. This became a problem until the government was able to transfer them to the independent Sports Council.

As an international athlete I was invited to the formal opening of the National Sports Centre at Lilleshall by the Queen in 1952. I was impatient to put in a bout of training while the dignitaries were being given the official tour and was in a tracksuit for a later formal presentation to the Queen. I burst through an enclave of bushes and by accident surprised the royal party. The Queen recognised me, having not long before presented me with a cup for the AAA Half-Mile at White City, and was kind enough not to ignore this sudden apparition, instead stopping to chat.

At about the same time as I worked on the Duke of Edinburgh's Award, I became involved with another scheme, a charity unrelated to sport, that brought me into contact with Winston Churchill. Ivor Bulmer-Thomas, a former Oxford athlete and at the time a junior minister, had started the Historic Churches Preservation Trust. Many fine churches in London, including those built by Wren, had been bombed and were in decay, but no public funds were available to save them because any money was needed for rebuilding houses. I took part in a relay including Chris C and Chris B, starting from Buckingham Palace and ending by delivering a cheque to 10 Downing Street. The great man received us outside No. 10. He was still Prime Minister but about to be succceded by Anthony Eden. Churchill was then far from well but as he spoke to us there was still a twinkle in his eye.

In 1957, just after the Suez Crisis, my call-up papers came for National Service as a doctor with the Royal Army Medical Corps (RAMC). For some time there had been some grumbling in sections of the press, asking why I had not yet been called up for National Service. First we had two weeks of 'square bashing' at the RAMC depot. The sergeant-major knew that however awful our marching and drill, he could not stop us being made officers at the end of this training. He was particularly angry with all such squads because, some months previously, the squad had shamed him by deliberately wheeling the wrong way and marching off into the distance, avoiding saluting the base and its senior officer altogether.

I started at the Queen Alexandra Military Hospital at Millbank in charge of the senior officers' ward, where in the course of a year I met a number of generals and field marshals responsible for winning the war, including General Auchinleck (also known as 'The Auk'), whose insistence on building up the Eighth Army led to Churchill impatiently sacking him, but would prove to be the foundation on which Montgomery's success was built. Also looming for me was a critical examination for physicians, membership of the Royal College of Physicians (MRCP). At the time there was only an 8 per cent pass rate for this exam on the first attempt. It was impossible to start specialist training as a neurologist without passing it and with such a low pass rate obviously a high element of chance was involved. There were written papers, about which I was not too worried. Then there was a two-hour clinical examination at a London teaching hospital, with a 'long case'. One had to take a history from a patient and then examine him or her and then present orally the whole case to the examiners. This could be difficult if the patient spoke no English. This was followed by a series of 'short cases', up to five or so, in which it was expected that the candidate would instantly recognise the physical signs of whichever diseases they had. This led to another question-and-answer session. Finally, on another day, there was the third stage, a viva (oral examination) in pathology at the Royal College of Physicians in which candidates were shown 'pickled' specimens of diseased organs, again with an open-ended discussion. In stages two and three, some area of ignorance could easily be uncovered and, if so, the question arose whether to admit ignorance, which I did, or rely on guesswork or 'bluff', which was dangerous.

Fortunately I passed the MRCP examination first time without having to grind away at it any longer. Passing the exam resulted in the army designating me a medical specialist and promoting me to the rank of captain, which made me liable to serve abroad.

Before this could happen, a devastating national flu epidemic occurred in 1958. I received a telegram from the guards camp at Thetford in Norfolk. Typically, the army order was tersely expressed: 'Proceed soonest Thetford. Travel voucher enclosed.' At last I thought my big moment in the British Army had come. So, imagining the 'camp' was in tents and under canvas, I donned my battledress with the CBE medal strip and my brown shoes, officer type, with my shaving kit in a small holdall hand case. To my surprise, I was met at Thetford station by the guards adjutant, wearing a well-tailored civilian suit. He looked askance at my holdall: 'Unless we are on military exercises, we always wear civilian clothes at our depot camp.' The camp was a well-structured building, with roses around the door. As the adjutant took me into the mess, for a pre-lunch drink, I received some strange looks from the guards officers, some of whom looked languid in the extreme, as their eyes focused on my battledress, which made me look so out of place. I somehow survived lunch, but afterwards I couldn't reach the phone quickly enough. I told Moyra of my predicament and asked her to send some civilian clothes soonest. She rang the postmaster general's office, explained that no post would reach me in time by any ordinary means, and persuaded the PMG's office whereby she delivered it to the Post Office HQ at St Pancras Station so that my suit and shoes arrived in time for dinner.

At the time, a British Army contingent was serving in the Aden Protectorate (now Yemen), fighting against Communist insurgents who were leading mountain tribesmen. There had recently been several deaths among the troops there, which were attributed to heat illness. In order to avoid being posted to some other far-flung trouble spot, I wrote directly to the director general of the RAMC volunteering to investigate the causes of these deaths. I was promised I would receive the money to buy necessary equipment and was under my own command, with the local commanding officer asked to provide me with all the assistance I needed. The situation reminded me of Crouchback's experiences in Evelyn Waugh's trilogy, *Men at Arms*. The deaths were clearly related in some way to the combined effect of heat exposure and exercise stress and this was a field in which I could reasonably claim to have done prior physiological research and could be expected to reach some useful conclusions. I knew that some aspect of the research there would also probably add to the Oxford University doctoral thesis on which I was working.

Aden was a strange place. The British authorities originally needed it as a coaling station for ships going through the Suez Canal and had to protect it from the tribesmen in the surrounding mountains. It was a desert studded with rocks and unforgiving hills, with hardly anything else there at all. The army had also used it in the past as a 'punishment station' for those soldiers, officers or men, who were unpopular in India, for whatever reason. There was an RAF base there, along with the port. The army sought to keep the various warring tribes nearby in some kind of control. Some of these tribes had a private army and sometimes these were led by British officers as a device to dissuade them from fighting each other. Most Yemeni men carried knives and rifles and spent their time in unending tribal conflict.

For a time I was attached to an army regiment that supplied me with 'volunteers' I could use as subjects for the experiments I designed, submitting myself and them to heat stress and salt restriction. We marched or climbed up mountains in the heat. Sometimes during these marches I submitted myself to the same condition as the men, 'pour encourager les autres'. Sometimes I would follow in an army ambulance and would take any man who collapsed into the back to revive him and study his workload, rate of sweating, weight loss, the salt content of the sweat, and skin and deep body temperature.

At one point, this regiment offered me a chance to go on a patrol. Now and again, presumably to demonstrate to the tribesmen that there were British troops around, army units would set off with the supplies needed for twenty-four or forty-eight hours and climb up the jebels. On the map there was a dotted line that indicated the boundary between Aden Protectorate and the Communist-controlled Yemen. On this occasion we went up along the line of dots and reached a point where they stopped. That was clearly where the map-maker had either given up or been killed or had died. For this expedition I was given a revolver, because, though the RAMC is not supposed to use weapons in anger, an officer is expected to defend patients if under attack. I think I had fired only forty shots with it in training and so was not very reliable. With sentries posted, we camped for a night in tents on the top of this mountain, which, as the heat of the day ebbed, got very cold. Fortunately, that night and during our return to camp we were left in peace. It was a risky episode and I chose not to tell Moyra about it at the time. But it made me feel a bit more as though I was actually part of the army.

My research showed that troops, instead of coming out by sea, had been swiftly flown out via Cyprus and were being thrown too quickly into active duty in conditions of the most extreme temperatures in the world. The heat-induced profuse sweating was ineffective in cooling the body if the humidity was also high, because sweat dripped off the skin without cooling the skin by evaporation. So troops suffered enormous losses of water and salt. This dehydration, sometimes coupled with infection, led to heat exhaustion and hyperpyrexia – a sudden rise in body temperature – and the risk of death. Back in England I did some more studies in a climatic chamber at the Institute of Hygiene and Tropical Medicine in London to confirm and extend my results from Aden, but in a properly controlled laboratory setting. In some experiments, which did not involve the army, I injected myself with a preparation of bacteria which gave me a high fever and, in a hot chamber with exercise, I proved that hyperpyrexia would occur, though I stopped the experiment when my body temperature was over 103. No army volunteer stuck the step-wise exercise twice in the hot chamber! When I reached home one day, after such an experiment, I had forgotten my key and Moyra, with my son Clive in her arms, opened the door and said I was a ghastly grey-white colour. Such self-experimentation, particularly as I was on my own without medical help, had its risks and would not be permitted today. In retrospect it was a reflection of my determination that nothing would stand in the way of my research. I wrote up my findings, including recom-mendations on how slowly the acclimatisation should take place and the appropriate provision of water and salt tablets and suit-able treatment in the field.

The army accepted the recommendations I had made and they were promulgated within the army and published in *The Lancet*, but, sadly, there are still unnecessary deaths from heat illness. In 2013 there were three deaths during army exercises on Brecon Beacons in a heatwave. Three quite unnecessary deaths.

Chapter 11

First Medical Appointments

One fascination with medicine for me is its many branches. A general practitioner needs a sensitive feeling for families and their ailments, taking them under his wing. At the other end of the scale there is a pure researcher. Some may choose early to be a specialist based on their particular skills and inclination, in the knowledge that it will take several more years of hospital training and more arduous exams. The Membership of the Royal College of Physicians is the gateway to becoming a physician. My good fortune was to make up my mind early in my career to become a neurologist. Neurology, the study of the brain, the organ of the mind, is very complex and extremely difficult, but having passed the membership examination at my first attempt, I felt confident that I would be able to achieve this.

In the autumn of 1951, with a scholarship from St Mary's Medical School, I looked forward to starting my clinical training there. St Mary's was a hospital buzzing with activity. It was famous for Alexander Fleming, who discovered penicillin while working in the laboratory of the immunologist Sir Almroth Wright in 1922, though it had to wait until the urgency of the

Second World War for Ernst Chain and Howard Florey in Oxford to develop it a stage further from which the Americans mass-produced it in the later stages of the war.

Fleming only came to St Mary's purely due to an unexpected legacy at a time when he was a shipping clerk, and knew of St Mary's because he had played water polo for his territorial regiment at the medical school. He was a clever student and won most of the prizes, but having taken his surgical fellowship exams was then unable to find a hospital appointment. The immunology department under the control of the powerful Sir Almroth Wright, usually won in the inter-hospitals annual rifle shooting competition. He heard that Fleming, a territorial, was trained as a rifle shooter and so Fleming's path was smoothed to Wright's department.

When I came to St Mary's, aged twenty-one, it was a stimulating time of discoveries that had worldwide significance. One of the surgeons, Arthur Dickson Wright, had just performed the first renal transplant in Britain, and the Professor of Immunology, Rodney Porter, had won the Nobel Prize for success in discovering the structure of antibodies. It must also be said that St Mary's had the best rugby team of all the London medical schools and the joke was that Welsh boys who could play rugby got off the train from Wales at Paddington and turned left to find St Mary's Hospital Medical School, 200 yards from Paddington Station. The dean, Lord Moran, who was Winston Churchill's physician during the war, had a belief that character could be linked with sporting endeavour. After his own First World War experiences, in the trenches, as a doctor, he had written a book, *The Anatomy of Courage*. He founded scholarships for those with both academic and sporting ability and I was offered one of those scholarships, which helped clinch my decision to choose St Mary's, and I never regretted my choice. Lord Moran's main sporting interest was rugby and it was rumoured that when interviewing potential students who declared that they played rugby, surreptitiously at the end of the interview, he picked up a rugby ball from behind his desk and flung it at the candidate. Candidates who caught the ball were 'in'. Shortly before I arrived at St Mary's, Lord Moran retired as dean. He was succeeded by a consultant neurologist to the hospital, whom I eventually followed. The then England match-winning fly-half was Nim Hall, whose speciality was executing drop goals. He was the 1944 equivalent of Jonny Wilkinson, who won the World Rugby Cup with a drop goal in 2003. Nim Hall had been at St Mary's for several years without passing any exams. Lord Moran's successor as dean warned him that unless he passed his first medical examination, at the next opportunity he would be expelled. This necessary decision to expel him when he duly failed his exams yet again, taken by the new dean, was so unpopular that students pelted the poor man with bread rolls when he came into the restaurant the next day.

It was not easy to fit into the type of undergraduate life that I had known four years earlier in Oxford. Heraclitus, the ancient philosopher, said, 'You cannot step into the same river twice', but I remember my fellow students in London with great warmth and how they carried me on their shoulders through the medical school the morning after the four-minute mile, though I wasn't even a rugby player! I remember the old-fashioned swimming pool in the basement under the library which, apart from its primary purpose of scholarship, was periodically cleared for musical concerts, the production of plays and the performance of sketches, often lampooning consultants who took it all in good part.

Do not imagine that the library, after these evening interruptions, did not speedily return to its proper use. Another annual event was a consultants' lecture given ostensibly on ethics and medicine. The lecture was given by an Irish radiologist, much given to telling humorous anecdotes. He treated each intake of students to this introductory talk. He wore a wig and moustache for this performance, which started seemingly as a serious lecture on the challenges of medicine, but gradually metamorphosed into a cynical farce. The students started off taking it very seriously and it took some time for them to twig that the rules he was laying down were nonsense. In this way this lecture set the tone for an atmosphere of continual questioning of all accepted tenets of medicine and gentle mocking of the consultants.

St Mary's Hospital had grown out of an infirmary first set up for the Irish navvies who were digging out the canal basin in the 1800s and then their successors building the railways, amidst the poverty in the mid-nineteenth-century Paddington area until 1948. The consultants at the hospital gave their services without charge and the whole hospital was a charitable operation, which was then true of all London's great teaching hospitals until 1948 and the introduction of the NHS.

Lord Beaverbrook was a friend of the dean, Lord Moran, and one day, while he was waiting to see him, decided to visit the outpatient department. This was seething with patients of every age queuing to see doctors. A lady volunteer passed him pushing a trolley with cups of tea and buns. Out of curiosity, he asked the lady what the cost of a bun was. Looking at Lord Beaverbrook's rather shabby raincoat, she said, 'One penny, but if you can't afford it you can have it for nothing.' He was so moved that when he went across the road to meet Lord Moran, who was trying to raise funds for the new medical school building with a swimming pool, library and research accommodation, he just asked

Lord Moran how much he needed and sat down and wrote out a cheque for the total sum.

One day, when at the sports ground at Teddington, I saw a painting of a destroyer. The note under the picture explained that it was the destroyer on which a St Mary's student, Peter McCrae, who had just qualified as a doctor, was serving as a surgeon lieutenant. He had great gifts and captained several sports teams at St Mary's. The destroyer was torpedoed and McCrae found himself on an overloaded raft which was in danger of sinking. He murmured, 'There are too many of us on this raft,' and he quietly slipped from the raft and, of course, drowned.

The best of the consultants at St Mary's were those who, besides a deep knowledge of medicine, had an instinct for the correct diagnosis. It was by listening to them that we clinical students hoped to absorb these secrets. Today's medical care has been changed beyond belief by a whole range of investigations like MRI scanning. Huge advances in every branch of scientific medicine have led to a reduction in the mortality from disease. 'Fortune favours the prepared mind' was Sir Almroth Wright's dictum, and this could be taken as the watchword for the alert physician.

The St Mary's student medical society had lapsed and a group of us decided to revive it. As secretary, this gave me the welcome chance to invite speakers to come and debate issues in science, medicine and public affairs. The name of the society was sufficient for us to attract such luminaries as Grey Walter, the researcher into the new field of cybernetics. Another speaker was J. B. S. Haldane, son of the Oxford physiology professor. In the First World War, Haldane junior had been an explosives officer, researching into the functions of new shells. He would take a position in the trenches and lob his special shells into the opposing enemy trenches. Just when the Germans had located the site of this unexpected activity and decided to obliterate it, Haldane would by then have moved on to a different site. His unit was not popular!

My first medical appointment was at St Mary's in September 1954, as resident house physician to Professor George Pickering on the medical unit. I was one of some twenty junior doctors in this 500-bed teaching hospital. Its wards had been built in the nineteenth century, each with twenty-four patients, twelve beds on either side, all facing the centre where the ward sister had her desk placed so that nothing untoward concerning patients, nurses or doctors could escape her astute eye. Apart from a couple of weekends and occasional nights off, I was almost continuously on call for six months. Two weeks of holiday could be taken only at the end of the appointment. My duties also included looking after the hospital's ten psychiatric beds, where I made sure no organic cause for the apparent psychiatric illness had been missed, and that patients were fit enough to receive the treatments, in particular, for depression, now less often used, of repeated electric convulsive therapy (ECT) or insulin-induced hypoglycaemic coma or sometimes barbiturate-induced coma.

As recently qualified doctors, our precious sleep, or lack of it, was in the purview of the night ward sister. Our medical education had exhorted us to keep barbiturate night sedation to a minimum as several nights of it could disturb a patient's natural sleep for weeks afterwards. But reluctance to prescribe sleeping tablets 'p.r.n.' (the abbreviation of the Latin for 'as often as needed') was soon defeated. As likely as not we would be woken at three o'clock when we had just finished some real emergency

My parents, Alice and Ralph, young and in love, sharing a deckchair.

A popular song of the day, 'I'm forever blowing bubbles'.

My sister and I finding out what it's like to be a rabbit!

Third from left in the front row in the primary school running team.

With relief, after the degree ceremony in the Sheldonian, 1950.

Vacation work in an Oxford Medical School biochemistry laboratory. © Getty

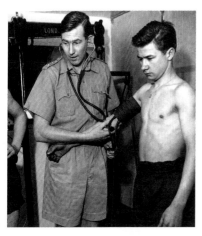

LEFT In Aden, studying heat illness with an army volunteer in 1956. © Getty

MIDDLE Trophy for the half-mile at the AAA Championships 1952, given by a smiling Queen, watched by Princess Margaret. © Press Association

BELOW The last bend, 80m from the finish of the Olympic 1,500m final in Helsinki, 1952. (The winner, José Barthel of Luxembourg, lying second; RB fourth.) © Getty

An extract from Bannister's medical student's diary for 1954, recording his training schedule. Training across the year amounted to between 35 and 53 miles per week in sessions of up to 40 minutes' duration. After five full days' rest (mistakenly labelled 3pf (sic)) rather than May), the achievement of the sub-four-minute mile is marked simply '3 59.4'. The three weeks before the race included four days' 'climbing' with Chris Brasher in Scotland. The last days of training before 6 May are recorded: on 22 April he ran 10 x 440 yards in 59 seconds each, on the 24th he completed a three-quarter mile in 3.00 and on 28 April a three-quarter mile in 2:59.9. The entries after the sub-four-minute mile are more casual and less detailed. On 15 August (sic) he says he is 'tired' and by the 20th is 'tired', but still running half a 'mixed grill' – the full 'mixed grill' was 2 x 120 yards followed by 2 x 440, 1 x 880, 2 x 440 and another 2 x 220. The last entry is for 29 August, his last race, the 1,500 metres in the European Games in Berne. Again the time – a new European record of 3.43.8 – is recorded, accompanied by the word 'Bein'. The rest of the diary reflects how Bannister's life changed after 6 May 1954 and records engagements at the BBC, an appointment at 'Buck Palace' on 14 October and a meeting with the 'Min of Educ' on 21 December, all interspersed with medical notes. (Sir Roger Bannister)

A training record written at speed in my diary in 1954.

The race programme from that windy day in May 1954.

My two friends, Brasher leading and Chataway third, seamlessly setting the pace for the four-minute mile. © Press Association

The finish of the
four-minute mile.
Thank goodness
all the stopwatches
agreed; no electronic
time-keeping then!

© Press Association

Celebrating minutes
later with Brasher and
Chataway. We had
done it! © Getty

St Mary's famously
rugby-loving students
generously acclaim
an athlete. © Getty

The very day after, stalwart medical students chair me across the medical school threshold. © Getty

Churchill beams at the Chrises and me after our charity run to rebuild the bombed London churches. © Getty

The last bend of the Vancouver Empire Games mile of 1954. John Landy looked over his left shoulder as I overtook him. © Getty

LEFT The Miracle Mile in Vancouver, a hard-fought victory. © Getty

BELOW Chris Chataway with the BBC Sports Personality of the Year trophy and RB with the Sports Illustrated Sportsman of the Year trophy. © Press Association

LEFT Climbing Finsteraarhorn, the third highest Swiss mountain. Chris Brasher and John Tyson experienced mountaineers; RB a novice climber. © John Tyson

BELOW Triumph on the peak, despite the guides and Arnold Lunn having called it a 'suicidal' expedition. © John Tyson

Swiss athletes form a guard of honour to speed us into our married life, 1 June 1955.

My mother, Moyra and I outside the gates of Buckingham Palace after I received the CBE in 1955. © Press Association

Enjoying my first experience on a motorbike outside Thetford Army Camp, Norfolk, on National Service. © Press Association

With smiling faces, Thurstan, Erin and Clive welcome Charlotte. © Press Association

A win, as *The Times* put it, 'by the width of a waistcoat button' at our sons' school.
© Getty

Taking the strain with fatherly duties: Clive, Thurstan and Erin.

Charlotte holds the insignia of knighthood outside Buckingham Palace with Moyra and Erin in 1975. © Press Association

With Moyra, meeting the Thatchers at 10 Downing Street for BBC television.
© Press Association

Our newly ordained daughter, Charlotte Bannister-Parker, outside Christ Church Cathedral with Moyra, RB, Erin, Clive and Thurstan. A great day for us all.
© Sarah Franks

A fine tally of thirteen grandchildren, with one yet to come, photographed in 2004.

Moyra and I with most of our family at Harris Manchester College.

In our lodgings garden at Pembroke College, dressed for the annual degree ceremony.

The First American Academy of Neurology Lifetime Achievement Award, presented in 2005.

Pembroke's new Thameside building with a hundred rooms and two quadrangles, built after I became Master of Pembroke.

Laughing in the sunshine with the two Chrises, still running in their seventies.

© Nick Brown

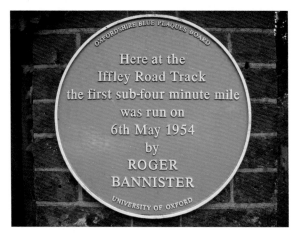

Tourist buses slow down as the guides point to this plaque by Iffley Road.

Here at the
Iffley Road Track
the first sub-four minute mile
was run on
6th May 1954
by
ROGER
BANNISTER

The trophies, books and memorabilia given to Pembroke College. Perhaps they may inspire some students.

The Queen watches as RB is handed the Commonwealth Games torch for the Manchester 2002 Commonwealth Games. © Getty

The 2012 Olympic torch was lit at dawn by RB, watched by Lord Coe; Lord Patten, the Chancellor; and Professor Andrew Hamilton, the Vice Chancellor of Oxford University. © Press Association

RB with Sir Steven Redgrave and Katherine Grainger, both Olympic gold medallists, Redgrave winning gold medals in a record five consecutive Olympic Games. © David Cotter

RB with Sir Chris Hoy, Olympic cyclist, winner of a record seven Olympic medals, and flag bearer for the 2012 London Olympics. © David Cotter

With Professor Chris Matthias, my long-term collaborator in work on the autonomic nervous system.

ABOVE Winston Churchill said, 'Do something with your hands.' A late flowering of artistic endeavours: on the left, a dolphin and on the right, an elephant.

MIDDLE Good companions: our walking group – now, for me, lunch only!

BELOW On several visits to America we met the Clintons. Once I found myself advising him on fitness!

Hillary Clinton had just made a brilliant speech without notes at the US embassy in London.

The Queen Mother, a loyal patron of the medical school, chatting to Moyra and me.

A shared joke in Buckingham Palace with Her Majesty the Queen, with Prince Philip in the background.

© Press Association

with a call from the night sister saying, 'Oh Doctor, Mrs X is very restless. Could you come and write her up for a sedative?' After a couple of weeks of this we had little option but to write every patient up for sedation at night as necessary.

We learnt an enormous amount very quickly. I was on duty in the hospital's medical casualty after 5 p.m. when the medical registrar went home. The sister in casualty undertook triage and decided whether a patient brought in was a medical or surgical emergency and then called the appropriate junior resident.

An awkward fact of hospital life was that the most junior medical staff generally saw patients in whom the consequences of errors were gravest. On one of my first nights on duty, qualified only for a matter of weeks, a patient came in with increasing face and tongue swelling, so that he was in danger of suffocation. I had never seen anything like it, but diagnosed some form of extreme allergic reaction. If so, the treatment would be adrenalin, one of the most powerful and dangerous drugs, only to be given subcutaneously or intra-muscularly. The risks of giving too large a dose included cardiac arrhythmias and even death, but given too little, the patient might suffocate or need a tracheotomy, the making of a hole in the windpipe to bypass the swelling. This was an operation I had never done. The nearest advice from our own team was my senior registrar, but he was at home, twenty-five miles away. I could have called in the surgical team in the hospital or turned to the senior doctor in residence, the medical superintendent. But all house physicians were reluctant to seek advice outside their own team too readily, as this would give the impression they were unable to cope with their new responsibilities. In fact, I gave the patient adrenalin appropriately and the swelling dramatically subsided and, to my great relief, he recovered.

One of my good friends at Oxford was at this time doing a similar residency at another London teaching hospital. The teaching hospitals are in poor parts of London where drunkenness and brawling are common, as Somerset Maugham describes in *Cakes and Ale*. On one occasion my friend working in casualty mistook an abdominal wound for a superficial cut and he sent the patient home. This was a serious error because it was in fact a deep knife wound and the patient later died of peritonitis. My friend was blamed by the coroner and the hospital was sued. The experience made him give up clinical medicine and turn to laboratory work. For the past forty years the strains under which young doctors labour have been publicised. Every now and then a real effort has been made to alleviate their workload. It is still an unresolved problem arising from the country's adherence to the European work directive stipulation of forty-eight hours a week maximum for hospital doctors. Then, we sometimes worked on call for up to 100 hours a week. Today's rotas can upset patients, who have justifiably complained that they never see the same doctor twice. I remember life in hospital during those early weeks in which we were being relentlessly tested and imagined our whole future in medicine depended on the outcome. But the pressure is still there today as it was then, to the obvious detriment of both young doctors and their patients.

The nurses needed the junior doctors as much as we needed them. Along with writing up notes on my twenty-four patients' histories and examinations, I would have to perform any practical procedures on them, which included draining abdominal fluid, called ascites, from around the heart in pericarditis or from the lungs with a pleural effusion, or taking spinal fluid by lumbar puncture. During the night I would have to trundle out a portable electrocardiogram machine if some cardiac event had occurred in one of my patients.

My professor, appointed in 1935, was only the second professor of medicine appointed to a London teaching hospital. There were then also four consultant physicians to the hospital. Most were the best of their generation of St Mary's Medical School graduates, as at the time there was little interchange of staff between different teaching hospitals. The physicians and their predecessors had not relished the idea of a less busy professor of medicine showing up some of their unscientific thought processes. But medicine in the 1950s was just becoming truly scientific. Evidence-based medicine, as it is now called, was still a vague concept and trials of new drugs with 'controls' were only just starting, even when I was still a clinical student of Professor Pickering's. After I asked a question about the use of gold injections for rheumatoid arthritis, he encouraged me to devise a small ward project on subcutaneous gold injections. The purpose was to try to shed a little scientific light on this treatment, which had been administered for a long time based really only on precedent and without understanding the mechanism of its effect. My study was to see what local skin reactions occurred to an intradermal injection among arthritic patients and a control group, hoping to discover something about patients' immune responses to gold. The outcome was inconclusive but the lesson for me was to look continuously for any ways of testing the action of drugs.

On the national scene in British medicine at that time, Professor Pickering was engaged in a battle with Professor Platt, president of the Royal College of Physicians, over whether essential (mild) hypertension was due to a disease process – probably of the kidneys – or was just part of a normal distribution of the levels of blood pressure similar to variations in height in the population. Professor Pickering's scientific approach extended to querying all existing treatments, which was excellent training for me, reinforcing my Oxford-based research training. Sometimes he carried this to lengths I found extreme. He believed stomach ulcers would eventually stop bleeding if the patient were transfused after each blood loss. This was, he maintained, safer than the 1 per cent mortality and even higher morbidity of surgical gastrectomy as then practised. To one woman patient I gave fifty pints of blood intravenously over several weeks, until I was barely able to get a canula into her veins. Meanwhile she still went on bleeding. Then I had a phone call from the blood transfusion laboratory. They were not known for querying requests but the pathologist rang to say that the patient had a very rare blood group, that despite scouring the country there were only a few pints of blood of her group left in Britain and would we please reconsider the management? She had surgery the next day and survived.

Professor Pickering made it clear to me when I started the residency that if there was any emergency at night on one of his twenty-four patients, he should himself be telephoned. For half of each year he managed the patients in this way without any intervening registrar and I therefore had the rare privilege of hearing his views directly. The practical effect of this was that I would not dare to ring him at home at night unless it was a genuine emergency and so I had to make many difficult decisions on my own as many young doctors learn to do. This was an invaluable training experience. The situation was different when I took my turn in the hospital's casualty department as the patient had often not been seen by a doctor and, at that stage, had not even been admitted to the hospital.

After some four months of this grinding work, with just

occasionally a few hours out of the hospital, when the other overworked house physicians covered for me, I got an infected thumb (whitlow) which needed minor surgery. I still bear the mark of the hasty operation. Professor Pickering thought I was 'run-down' and told me to go away for my first weekend. But by then he had clearly made up his mind about me and backed me for my next medical appointment.

In June 1955, within weeks of my marrying Moyra, I went to Oxford for six months for the statutory regulation surgical pre-registration post. At the time the only accommodation we could afford in Oxford was such a slum we actually had to put a bucket to catch water leaking from the ceiling when it rained, so Moyra returned to her London studio. I took hospital accommodation in a room opposite the Radcliffe Infirmary. It was an unfortunate start to married life. Although the main hospital was a large and elegant building, there lurked behind it a maze of semi-permanent huts thrown up during the war for patients and laboratories. In the raw damp of Oxford's winter I was lucky that by being so busy rushing about, I kept warm.

My senior registrar had the ambitious idea of clearing our firm's lengthy surgical waiting list by setting a faster schedule for operations and placing the extra beds needed in the corridors. Near the end of six months our waiting list fell, only to be restored quickly by the administrators transferring patients from other lists to ours. We realised we had overdone it when our surgical consultant, Arthur Elliot Smith, the genial son of the distinguished anatomist and anthropologist Grafton Elliott Smith, was so tired after a day's operating that, as we helped him to his car, he had difficulty in raising his foot even the nine inches or so needed to get into the front seat. But he was a great surgeon: nearly all his patients, whatever the massive operation he undertook, seemed to get better. As his house surgeon I was in a unique position to know this.

The thrill of extracting my first appendix, unsupervised, is a moment that lodges itself in my memory. The Radcliffe Infirmary where I worked was then a mere district general hospital, a distant ancestor to the massive modern blocks on Headington Hill outside Oxford, now one of the biggest research and specialist hospitals in the country, and where my son-in-law Alain, the Professor of Immunology, now works.

My next hospital, Hammersmith, had consultants, who were generally left-wing and were determined to make the health service a leading example for world medicine. The hospital was the training ground for many of the academic physicians of the next generation. The junior posts were half as busy as at St Mary's, to allow time for study and attendance at lectures on the postgraduate courses which were run largely for foreign medical graduates. Many foreign doctors were welcomed to Hammersmith, and the consultants – quite a few of whom were originally from abroad themselves – were very keen to give them a fair start in Britain. A good portion, from Australia, New Zealand, South Africa and America, had already proved their ability in their home countries. While I was there, Dr Milne treated the first case of primary aldosteronism and published some features of the disorder. A month or two later, an American doctor, Dr Conn, published a fuller description with further evidence which led to the disease being described ever after as Conn's Syndrome. This was a very frustrating experience for Dr Milne and showed me how research medicine could be a fiercely competitive career.

Though the Hammersmith Hospital had the justified reputation of having the highest scientific standards, from the patients' point of view it might not have been a wholly comfortable experience, as the level of investigation including controlled trials of various kinds led to extra stress for the patients. Also, when indicated, liver, kidney and lungs were biopsied using techniques which were just being introduced into medicine in Britain. At that early stage, some of these procedures could be painful and involved a small risk to the patient, such as bleeding after the biopsy.

My first residency in my chosen field of neurology was at the National Hospital, Queen Square, starting in March 1959 on my return from National Service. The National was the first exclusively neurological hospital in the world, founded in 1859 by some charitable ladies who held collections among their friends and knitted purses which they sold to raise funds for the first building. They persuaded the Duke of Albemarle, one of Queen Victoria's sons, to open the hospital. The first consultant was a Dr Brown-Sequard, the son of a French sea captain and a Jamaican lady. His name is attached to the first description of the effects of compression of the spinal cord. He was a wanderlust character and a few years after left for Paris. The first successful removal of a spinal cord tumour was undertaken at the National Hospital in 1870, and by the turn of the century the hospital was established as a training centre for neurologists from all over the world, ahead of the Salpêtrière Hospital in Paris.

I was trained by the last of the pre-scientific neurologists: William Goody and Denis Williams. The competition for training posts was great, and in their day the dedication was such that unmarried candidates were preferred. As the average age of applicants was thirty, this was a tall order. In any event they were expected to be continuously resident during the whole week, available on the telephone at any time when the consultant chose to call to query the state of any patient. Their lot improved when a phone line was extended from the hospital switchboard to the local pub across the square, where the publican was trained to reply to queries, 'Just a moment. I'll see if I can find Dr X for you, sir...' After the pub noise was hushed, he then passed the phone to the doctor.

On one occasion, after the resident had given his report to the consultant and awaited further instructions, he felt the line had gone dead and said, rather too audibly, 'The old b****r has hung up on me!' After a few moments, the consultant's voice reappeared: 'The old b****r has not hung up on you, he's thinking.'

When I worked there, no accommodation was provided for married house officers and Moyra used to bring Erin and Clive across London from our flat in Earls Court at weekends to introduce them to their father! My residency was a happy one but in order to add to my qualifications the desirable but unofficial letters BTA (Been to America), I had to resign from it. With the help of the Radcliffe Travelling Fellowship from Oxford University, I spent a year at the Harvard Medical School doing some animal research under the guidance of Dr Denny-Brown who, though born in New Zealand and trained in Oxford, was then America's leading neurologist.

We were in Boston during the Cuban missile crisis, which caused real terror among civilians. This was worsened by constant television warnings and absurdly inadequate advice on dealing with nuclear attacks and fallout. We stayed in a tiny apartment in Cambridge, Massachusetts, in difficult circumstances with three small children and little money, bracing ourselves against the unfamiliar extremes of Boston's steamy summer and snowy winter. Several American friends helped greatly by sharing their 'yards' and toys with us and inviting us for meals. Our stay was occasionally relieved by visits to Moyra's parents in Washington, DC. Her father entertained us there with his characteristic ebullient generosity and we saw a little of the Washington scene – prominent politicians, editors and writers at dinner parties in Georgetown – and we attended Jack Kennedy's inaugural ball.

I returned to England in the summer of 1962 at my own expense to be interviewed for a consultant post at the National. Just before the selection interview I was taken aside by the senior physician who chaired the committee, who asked me to join him for a walk around Queen Square, immediately in front of the hospital. He told me, 'We think you're the best candidate but you may not be successful this time. There are other competent candidates senior to you who may be appointed. But,' he added, 'your turn will come.' The news that I would not be appointed hit me like a blow in the solar plexus. I had the embarrassment of having made a fruitless journey and of now returning to America empty-handed to face my colleagues there. I became extremely worried about achieving my goal of a consultant post at the National, realising how arbitrary some elements of the selection might be.

But some months later I applied for an appointment as a senior registrar at the National Hospital, Queens Square, one stage below a consultancy. Eight months later, in December 1963, I was appointed to the consultant staff, at the age of thirty-four and with only four years of specialist neurological training behind me. Appointed along with me was Ralph Ross Russell, who had been Sir George Pickering's registrar in Oxford, and who became a lifelong colleague and friend.

The National Hospital, as the only specialist neurological

hospital in the country, took precedence in obtaining grants from the government for the newest forms of equipment, intensive care apparatus, stereotactic equipment and scanning devices, such as computer tomography (CT) and magnetic resonance imaging (MRI). For several years I was the consultant in charge of the Batten Intensive Care Ward, to which patients with breathing difficulties following myasthenia gravis were admitted. Their lives were saved by machines invented by an anaesthetist on the staff. These delivered intermittent positive-pressure breathing and replaced 'iron lungs'.

In June 1964 I was also appointed as consultant neurologist to St Mary's Hospital. At that time it was considered the perfect balance for a London neurologist to have one appointment at the hospital dedicated to his specialty, in my case the National Hospital, Queen Square, and a second at a general hospital, which in London was likely to be a teaching hospital. With the inpatient and outpatient duties at two hospitals, teaching post-graduate students at the National and medical students at St Mary's, and trying to keep some time for research, life became incredibly busy. One senior consultant in a relaxed moment turned to me and said, 'Of course, Roger, life as a consultant neurologist at two hospitals is like being a juggler trying to keep as many balls in the air as possible!' Since my training in physiology at Oxford, my plan had been to combine clinical work with research. Caring for patients is certainly very satisfying. Each one has something unique in their background or symptoms. To reach the right diagnosis requires academic knowledge, wide experience of patients, skill at eliciting signs which would confirm a suspicion and finally something extra, the indefinable gift of clinical acumen and the ability to convey compassion.

For twenty-five years until I returned to Oxford, I worked at both the National Hospital and St Mary's, conducting outpatient clinics and ward rounds at each twice a week. The two appointments were a welcome culmination of almost eighteen years of training in Oxford and London. I count myself lucky to have found appointments which enabled me not only to do clinical work but also research, lecture and publish medical papers and books.

Chapter 12

The Sports Council

Imagine Britain after the war, with half a million houses annihilated by the Blitz, and more than half a million people needing rehousing. We were all feeling grey and tired. It has been often said that the wartime diet was healthy, but I remember the queues for rationed foods, the powdered milk and eggs and snoek, the euphemistic name for whale meat. One reason that children were better fed than in peacetime, when some were fed on tea, bread, margarine and jam, was that in wartime many automatically bought the nutritious foods, using their ration books. In peacetime, a mother had to manage on whatever proportion of the husband's earnings he decided to give her. Three-quarters of mothers in Britain had no idea how much their husbands earned. Women doing war work then received their own wages and could spend the money on what they liked, particularly on food for their children.

Before the war there were pockets of valiant people and organisations keeping the flame of sport alive, like the CCPR. This organisation had been created in the 1930s when the 'Strength through Joy' movement started in Germany. It was blazingly obvious that the German youth were fitter than ours. We had

Boy Scouts and Girl Guides and school sports, ironically a fuller
school competitive programme than today, but many inner-city
slum districts were untouched by these social improvements, and
the truth is that whenever social benefits are provided, it is the
middle class who always reap more benefit from them, rather
than the very poor, who have more social inhibitions.

After my own athletic career ended in 1954, I took an undi-
minished interest in issues concerning sport in Britain. This was
partly out of a general concern as a doctor for promoting health
and fitness and partly from a sense of how much pleasure sports
could bring to each individual, based on my own earlier experiences. My early training as a physiologist also meant my curiosity
was whetted by the fact that for many records of performance,
scientific limiting factors could be defined.

I had enjoyed my training sessions, races and matches and also
friendships with other athletes before I had become an international athlete. Beyond these satisfactions, sport had helped to
serve as a counterbalance to academic work. It was my impression from my medical work and my links with the NABC and
the Duke of Edinburgh's Award scheme that many people were
needlessly denied the chance I had enjoyed, through lack of
training facilities. For some time I had started to feel there was a
major public interest, little recognised until now, in ensuring both
children and adults had greater opportunities to pursue sport.

The bomb sites which were part of the tragedy of war had
become adventure playgrounds for so many children. These
were slowly disappearing as housing programmes got under
way. Some changes after the war favoured increased sporting
activity. The economy revived; income and disposable income
rose, and the number of hours in the average working week fell.
Also, fewer were engaged in physically exhausting daily work.

All of these increased the time available for sport and the need for better facilities. However, there were many other changes which militated against a wider role for sport. Television was consuming on average four hours of every child's and adult's day. A higher portion of children were beginning to suffer from obesity, which, by deterring them from exercise, created a vicious circle. As towns and cities expanded, developers were building on open land once available for play. Car ownership kept rising and so streets in which children had played scratch games of cricket and soccer were now lined with parked cars and made even more dangerous by moving traffic. Shamefully, schools and their groundsmen refused to allow children or anyone else to use their facilities after their normal hours or during weekends and holidays. Even Mrs Thatcher, when Minister for Education, was unable to revise this policy, though as chairman of the Sports Council I asked directly that she should do so.

Capital investment and regular spending in relation to sport hardly appeared in the budgets of post-war administrations apart from some money from the Department of Education for the Central Council for Physical Recreation (CCPR). After the war, few thought that physical recreation should have any priority, given that there were so many urgent problems, including the need to replace homes destroyed by bombing, the shortage of food and the need to revive our industries. Sport had been crowded off the canvas until the economic situation had taken an upturn, and outside bodies began to prod the government, and it was realised that some kind of improvement in national organisations would be needed to meet the demand for active leisure and improving health.

Fortunately, Harold Macmillan, who in terms of his own sporting career was most often seen shooting grouse, on becoming

Prime Minister in 1957 started to pay attention to sport as a legitimate policy issue, eligible for the use of public funds. He commissioned a government inquiry into the subject, which was chaired by Lord Wolfenden. His report recommended the setting up of an advisory sports council, which it was hoped would galvanise the reluctant government and civil service into making better provision for sport.

Though Macmillan had started the process, it fell to Harold Wilson, who became Prime Minister in October 1964, to implement the Wolfenden committee's recommendations. Wilson came from Huddersfield Grammar School and had won a half-blue for cross-country running when at Oxford during the war. He had an amazingly clear memory and when I first met him that year he described with pride detailed incidents and individual players from his Huddersfield Football Club. He already knew that he wanted a sports council and he understood what sport meant to ordinary people better than his Conservative predecessors.

Denis Howell, the first ever Minister for Sport, a trade union Member of Parliament, came from the hurly-burly of Birmingham Labour politics with corresponding self-confidence. He was quite capable of standing up to a powerful establishment body like the MCC, that all-powerful governing body of cricket. At the height of apartheid, it was an enormous step for the MCC to tell the South African government that unless they accepted D'Oliveira, a non-white cricketer, as a member of the MCC touring team, the MCC would cancel the tour. This outraged all cricket lovers in South Africa and was one of the factors that eventually led to the boycott of South Africa by all sporting world bodies, including the Olympic Games. This lasted more than twenty years. For a sports-obsessed nation, it brought home to South Africans that the rest for the world had a revulsion to apartheid and would go on expressing it until the regime changed. I was several times invited to visit South Africa, before and after my running days were over, but declined because I would not lend my name in any way to any sporting events until apartheid was over.

Harold Wilson invited Denis Howell to be the first Minister for Sport in part because he had been a football referee and in part because David Munrow, director of physical education at Birmingham University, and the real architect of the Wolfenden committee's report, was Denis's close friend in Birmingham. Denis enjoyed telling the story of how he was called to Downing Street two days after the election in which Harold Wilson had ushered in the 'white heat' of the technological revolution. Wilson told Howell that he had appointed him to take up the post of a new Minister for Sport. Howell asked, 'What do I do?' To which Wilson replied, 'You're the minister, you decide what to do.' Howell had the presence of mind then to ask, 'How much money do I have?' Wilson countered, 'How much money do you want?' Howell stabbed in the air and produced the figure 'half a million pounds' – and got it. This seemingly trivial sum can be contrasted with the funding fifty years later of the sports councils, through which £100 million of Treasury funding and £200 million lottery funding is channelled annually.

Denis Howell, after seeing the PM, was then driven in his new ministerial car to the Department of Education. He was bemused, after an apparently confidential meeting, to find his driver knew exactly where to go and the doorman greeting him respectfully as 'Minister'. Led along corridors to his office, he found Sir John Lang, the principal adviser on sport, greeting him likewise. Sir John had unusually worked his way up from the clerical grade to Permanent Secretary and was a true British civil servant, warning of all the dangers in a given course of action, but ultimately there to serve his political masters. Sir John Lang brought out a file from his briefcase and said, 'Minister, may I explain to you the reasons why a sports council is a bad idea?' Like all civil servants, he generally opposed a further drain on the Treasury. After listening to Lang's list of reasons, Denis Howell said, 'Thank you, Sir John. I still want to have a sports council.' Sir John then brought out another file and, ever the deferential civil servant, replied, 'Very well, Minister, these are the steps I recommend you take to create a sports council.'

Soon, sport threw up some major controversies. In previous governments, international sporting issues would have been dealt with by the Foreign Office and often adroitly ducked, shelved, or obfuscated. Now they had to be faced boldly by the new Labour government. Though Denis Howell, a secretary of state, was not by any means a senior minister, his own national profile was high and he had some clout.

The advisory sports council work was divided into three sections: first, advice to the governing bodies of the various sports; second, development of large capital projects, such as the Holme Pierrepont Rowing Centre in Nottingham and the Crystal Palace athletics track in London; and third, research and planning, to be conducted by a committee of which I was made chairman. Our task as I saw it was to draw up plans for the whole of Britain to remedy the certain deficiencies in sports facilities in comparison with other European countries, particularly

East and West Germany. It was obvious that people could not participate in sports without the right facilities.

We chose to do a study of three kinds of facilities: swimming pools, because they are popular and costly to build; golf courses, because they require so much land; and, most important, indoor sports centres, because these appeared to be the right kind of facility for our mainly urban population in a country with frequently poor weather. It was Byron who commented, 'The English winter – ending in July to recommence in August.'

Although this was classic socialist planning to fight the poverty of facilities, it was still, though not intentionally, the middle classes who benefited most, try as we might to draw in other people. Even when the centres were built in very deprived cities such as Belfast and Glasgow, it was difficult to show a fall in juvenile delinquency or drug-taking or other socially related problems. While sports provision may have been a positive factor, it was not enough in itself to measurably affect the social ills facing these cities. But ''twas ever thus' and it should not have surprised me.

After the war, high-level sport had changed in Europe with the creation of East Germany, which combined Communist planning with the legacy of the Nazi regime's ruthless efficiency and soon led to their winning many times more Olympic gold medals per capita than the United States. British athletes and other sportsmen were left far behind. But a start had been made in Britain with the building of our new multipurpose indoor centres, which provided for both recreational and elite sport.

As chairman of the research committee and a doctor with research experience, I led the council's permanent staff in amassing information about existing facilities and devising a rational formula for determining where the worst deficiencies across the country were, with the general population in mind.

The formula helped us to propose a full national programme of public spending.

A senior civil servant sat in at all the meetings of our research committee for two years, presumably to see that we did not get up to too much mischief and to report to the minister how we were progressing. When our work was complete, as chairman of our committee I proposed the publication of our findings, and he warned me, 'I'm afraid that you cannot possibly expect the minister to allow that. It would embarrass him to be seen to be proposing such a large expenditure and it would embarrass his government colleagues too.' After nearly three years of work on these plans, I was appalled. We were being used as a dogsbody to prepare information which the minister could then ignore for political reasons. I maintained that these deficiencies needed to be made public, so that local authorities, who would have to bear the main burden of the cost, could start planning, with our support and using our arguments for making good the deficiencies. But these words were not the last on this subject.

In 1970, when the Conservatives formed a new government, most of the members of the advisory sports council were serving in their fifth year. Having accumulated a wide experience of sports problems, they were asked to continue for the time being. We all wondered what would happen next. The original Conservative view had been against the idea of any sports council at all, possibly because the Conservatives had felt it their duty to oppose Labour's setting one up, but probably also because it was general Conservative policy to restrict government to vital core spheres of action, of which sport was not one. Eldon Griffiths, the new Minister for Sport, took a different view. His objection was to the creation of party political capital out of sport, of which he felt Denis Howell had been guilty.

By chance, Griffiths as shadow minister had been in the audience at a speech I had given at a conference. He congratulated me on it afterwards. By then he had probably already made up his mind that he wanted to see an independent sports council under an impartial chairman who was not a politician. He thought, firstly, that such a structure would fit well with the Conservative view that direct government involvement in sporting decisions was inappropriate. Secondly, he felt that the practical means of setting up such a council would be to follow the line of the Arts Council, which was an executive council set up by royal charter. It was a political device used for legislation which was supposed to be uncontroversial in a party political sense and had to be supported by the leaders of the major political parties. He had probably also decided that if I could be persuaded to do so, I would be able to handle the chairmanship of this independent council. It was well known that I was not aligned with any political party but simply wanted to get the best possible government support for sport.

A debate was set up for the council and I was chosen by Griffiths to give the arguments for an independent sports council, with which I had real sympathy. Howell was vocal in support of no change and was spoiling for a fight, with no love lost between him and Eldon Griffiths.

The advisory council at any rate had a chance to hear why I favoured an independent council. The principal argument was the need for the council to state publicly the national requirements for sport without being gagged by a minister, so that local

authorities knew what they should aim to build without committing central government to financing them.

The minister left the meeting and soon afterwards concluded
that he wished to create an independent sports council. Before
any announcement was made, he wanted my agreement that I
would become the first independent chairman. I thought hard
about this, especially about its effect on my neurological work,
now well established in the eight years since I had become a
consultant at St Mary's and the National Hospital, and on the
research projects I had underway. How could I possibly take on
this additional load without it damaging my medical work or
greatly diminishing my time with my family? I sensed from the
experience of the previous six years that there would be major
issues in sport in the public domain. My views on everything
around the periphery of sport – soccer hooliganism; the ethics
of boxing and of tobacco company sponsorship of cricket and
motor racing; the politics of apartheid – would be sought, publicised and challenged.

I went to see Eldon Griffiths, asked about the conditions,
status, assistance and government support, and he gave me
guarantees which seemed reasonable, so I said yes, thinking that
Eldon Griffiths was a man of his word, as he proved to be.

In the next few weeks, frantic activity followed and the independent council structure was set up. For the next four years
I attended sporting events several evenings a week and nearly
the whole of the weekend was devoted to the Sports Council.
My status was the same as that of the minister – in civil service
terms, a deputy Permanent Secretary.

I was assured by Griffiths of my freedom to speak out for sport
on public matters, uncensored by the minister or the government. Clearly the government and ministers would have the

right to say 'no' to my demands. Naturally, I explained that my first act would be to publish the shelved reports from my research advisory committee of the advisory sports council on the deficiencies in Britain's sporting facilities, and I would also expect an increase in government grant. The Sports Council's direct grant went up from the original advisory council's grant of £500,000 to £2.5 million (around £35 million in today's terms), and this sum was further increased later.

Legislation creating the independent sports council under royal charter was passed by a majority vote in Parliament. For a few splendid days, we actually had the royal charter in our Edwardes Square home, with its six-inch seal and brilliant calligraphy.

Among my first tasks was the need to appoint full-time administrators to support me. I stuck out in the planning for two equal senior executives, with myself as chairman able to take advice from either and hold the balance between them. The first was Walter Winterbottom (the full-time paid director of the previous advisory sports council) as director, with the second, a civil servant, yet to be chosen, acting as chief financial officer. The government department had its own ways of searching for a suitable civil servant and a candidate soon emerged, whose credentials I was asked to approve. When I met him I liked him immediately. Without him, my task would have been impossible. He was utterly trustworthy and very hard-working. I can remember many times when, faced with some seemingly insoluble crisis, I would have to choose between two courses of action, and I would say to him, 'Please write down the consequences of these two courses as you would predict them.' The next day he would have done so and my mind could then be made up.

He reminded me, as my contact with other senior civil servants has confirmed, that in Britain we probably have the most efficient and honourable public service – a service in which my own father had played his small part.

My second major task was to select members of the new council. My vice-chairman was Sir Jack Longland, formerly a CCPR vice-chairman, whose sporting credentials were as a Cambridge University pole vaulter and a member of the failed 1936 attempt on Everest. He was director of education for Norfolk and host of a famous BBC radio game called *My Word!* As a long-term member of the CCPR he was ideal to help heal the breach between that body and the Sports Council. Among the other twenty-four first members was my friend Norris McWhirter, who had been a sprinter at Oxford and incidentally the sole time-keeper at my unofficial 2-minute 52.9-second ¾-mile at Motspur Park in 1952 just before the Helsinki Olympics.

On my first day, after the announcement of my chairmanship had been made, I went to my office to meet my senior staff and we started work. Soon the new independent sports council launched into its programmes. We chose to develop several existing campaigns and created a logo for a new one of our own: Sport for All, a public awareness campaign designed to encourage exercise and recreation by everyone, not only talented young athletes. I also released all the documents prepared by the research committee of the advisory sports council, with the immediate target of the £120 million worth of sports facilities urgently needed in Britain and the ultimate target of 1,000 sports centres and 500 swimming pools. I frequently declared that the government should pay more for sport and that the total cost of the programme would be over £1 billion. As my press officer said, 'Don't ever consider any press release with a figure of less than £1 million!' I negotiated with other ministers whose interests were holding up our development. In particular, I recall my meeting with Margaret Thatcher, then Minister of Education. Nearly fifteen minutes passed before she stopped unnecessarily recounting to me her impressive understanding of various education and recreation problems. Eventually, I was able to get a word in edgeways about schools' failure to open their playing fields for general use, which was the object of my visit. Sadly, like her predecessors and successors she seemed unable to overcome the combined objections of teachers, trade unions, caretakers and groundsmen – a sad waste of costly facilities.

The regional sports councils, now all executive councils influencing major local authorities quite effectively, continued the advances made by Denis Howell when he set up their basic structure. Local authorities now readily took on the idea of the Sport for All campaign as their own and included plans for swimming pools, golf courses and sports centres in their sports facilities building programmes. I began to wonder whether I might have overdone it when I heard that Hillingdon had built no fewer than two artificial ski slopes and was advertising for a basketball coach who spoke Urdu. The fact of the matter was that local authorities were only too anxious to spend money on sports facilities, which were universally popular. It was only necessary for the Sports Council to give a token 10 per cent of financial support for facilities which included a national or regional or specialist sporting element going beyond local needs. When the Sports Council was formed, there were only four multipurpose sports centres in the country. In 1974, when I retired as chairman of the independent sports council, there were 400 in planning, and ten years later there were 1,000. This was truly a revolution in sport, taken together with the major increase in funding; I was excited by these challenges and felt I was part of a revolution in meeting ordinary people's hopes of a fairer chance in sport.

Over the next fifty years, British amateur sport and recreation facilities were as much transformed as health had been by the creation of the National Health Service in 1948. The crowning result of this was seen eventually in the triumph of the teams in the London Olympics of 2012.

Another task of the Sports Council was more delicate – to persuade the eighty governing bodies of amateur sports to reform themselves and modernise. The overall aim was for them to become more efficient so that they could increase participation rates and avoid discouraging younger people with arbitrary rules and bureaucratic procedures. The easiest way of doing this was to offer each body financial help to appoint a professional administrator, so long as they drafted a five-year plan for our approval. Such administrators would replace some of the well-meaning but sometimes inefficient voluntary officials who tended to remain in place, if not for life, for too many years.

Strictly speaking, the voluntary governing bodies were autonomous, with their own constitutions and rules usually dating back to the Victorian foundations of their sports. Most thought themselves quite competent to deal with any complaints and disputes. They were never going to allow the Sports Council to intervene in the precise conduct of their affairs. Most wished that the Sports Council would just award them funds and leave their administration untouched. I can remember a long feud with two rival governing bodies of judo, each espousing slightly different judo styles. For several years they preferred to have no Sports Council grant at all rather than to submerge their differences and combine for the better interest of their sport as a whole, as we asked them to do. And more than forty years later, some were still divided.

Another problem was sponsorship. Under my aegis, the Sports

Council set up and promoted corporate sponsorship to help sports, but I made it clear there would never be any contact with tobacco companies, then the principal sponsors of cricket and several other major sports including motor racing. One of my earliest medical appointments had been at the Royal Brompton Hospital and its specialist centre for diseases of the lung. Richard Doll had shown the unequivocal connection between smoking and lung cancer and I decided to have nothing to do with the tobacco industry promoting death and disease in Britain. Later, when asked to be on a body financing health research which was tobacco-linked, I refused point-blank.

In the meantime, almost every evening there would be dinners to attend and speeches to be made in London and the regions promoting the Sports Council's policies. My aim was also to keep up a civilised dialogue with Denis Howell, with whom I was the joint chief guest at many national sports occasions such as the FA Cup Final and Twickenham Rugby internationals. This was in part because sooner or later the chairman of the independent sports council might have to work with him as minister.

With journalists, my style was not exactly 'hail fellow well met', dropping quotes to spice up their copy. However, my objective was to give them access to me and to dispense facts rather than gossip. It took several years to establish good relationships with individual correspondents. At all times I tried to maintain a non-party political stance, never linking myself with specific Conservative or Labour policies or having favourites among the press. In the end I think the press learnt to trust my statements.

One sport that nearly trapped me in a crisis was my own, athletics, which used to be one of the most reactionary governing bodies and was at that time still ruled by Harold Abrahams. The advisory sports council had commissioned the Byers Report on athletics because of the perpetual rebellion of athletes at loggerheads with the governing body. The report pointed out, as the athletes themselves had done, that as treasurer of their governing body, Harold Abrahams, then the leading BBC athletics commentator, was negotiating with the BBC on the fees for televising athletics, so he had a conflict of interest. Harold Abrahams then resigned as treasurer but re-emerged shortly after in a newly created office of chairman. The Byers Report recommended a full-time director of athletics in Britain but at that time this was rejected by the governing body. Apart from this there continued to be confusion among the Amateur Athletic Associations of England, Scotland, Wales and Northern Ireland and separate women's governing bodies.

In 1972 when I was at the annual meeting of the Coca-Cola International Athletes Club (IAC) at Crystal Palace, its chairman Derek Johnson, a thirty-year-old Olympic 800m silver medallist, challenged the Sports Council by handing me an 'open letter' demanding action from me, as the chairman of the Sports Council, on these major items of reform. I had not experienced before the 'open letter' technique of getting publicity before, but the press, who had also received the letter, asked me that very night what I was going to do about it. I read the letter and sympathised with the plight of young athletes against a reactionary governing body. So I said I would discuss it at the Sports Council's next meeting, which happened to be the following week. This was unwise because the IAC was a revolutionary movement split from the governing body. One can imagine the confusion if we had responded to the demands of every splinter group in every sport. Nevertheless, the following week the Sports Council backed a statement I made endorsing the Byers Report and, indirectly, its recommendations. Harold Abrahams, with whom I had been on friendly terms since my running days, threatened to sue me for defamation over my implicitly agreeing to the charge in the Byers Report that he had a conflict of interest. After this, hardly any amateur athletics officials were on speaking terms with me for several years. This incident taught me that if the Sports Council chose to take issue with a governing body it was not wise to choose a sport that had a lawyer as chairman.

The many events I attended tend to blend into one at such a distance of time, but there are a few that stand out. On one occasion, we were unable to find a taxi to take us up the high street to the Annual Cyclists' Ball in Derry and Tom's. Theirs was an enthusiastic governing body and there were exhibits emphasising how cycling had been an active sport in Britain for more than a hundred years, particularly in the north-west of England. At one point, there came a moment during the dancing when the MC asked the ladies to pluck the longest hair they could find from their partners chest and bring it to the MC, who would judge the winner. Moyra caught my eye and we decided the moment had come for us to retire gracefully.

On one occasion I visited the championships of the Amateur Gliding Association. After the lunch, the president came up to me and asked, 'Are you ready yet?' I said, 'For what?' and he replied, 'Well, to come up and have a glide.' I confess I had some trepidation, but barely ten minutes later I was perched in a glider with an instructor behind me and we were catapulted into the sky. After showing me the controls, he said, 'Right, over to you now,' and I found myself silently sweeping the skies with the alarming feeling of slipping sideways, until my instructor took over to get us back on a level flight again.

I admire those who find speech-making easy. I have lectured

on neurology all over the world, but to engage with an audience who really only want a stand-up comedian is quite a different matter. I blush to remember an occasion when I made a journey to Cardiff, expecting to make an after-dinner speech rallying the enthusiasts to the cause. When I reached the civic hall I found a mass of guests, but there was no dinner, worse still, no wine, and worst of all, no microphone, because of some catastrophic error. So, to a cold, disappointed and drink-less assembly, I stood on a curve of the staircase above the hall and did my valiant best to salvage something of the evening.

Moyra's support was invaluable on these occasions. I remember one particular moment when I was speaking from the platform and she was sitting near me. In a slip of the tongue, I dropped a nought from one of the statistics I was quoting, so 30,000 became 3,000. Moyra knew my speech almost as well as I knew it myself, and her attention had lapsed until she heard my mistake. Roused from her musing, she was unable to restrain herself from saying, 'No, he means 30,000.' The audience laughed and said afterwards, 'That was the best part of the evening.'

One night, our absent neighbours' burglar alarm made a loud insistent wailing for a long time – until an intrepid friend took a hammer down the area steps and smashed it into silence. Thanks to the uproar, we overslept the next morning, when we were due to drive 200 miles up the M1 to Stanhope, a town next to Burghley House, for the annual horse trials. We found that there was a block on the motorway and eventually we turned into the grounds of Burghley House an hour late. As we walked in, to our horror we heard the Tannoy system asking that if we were in the grounds, could we please make our way to the lunch tent. When we found the tent, the guests had already finished the first course, and Moyra was shown to her place opposite the

Duke of Edinburgh. A kindly aide-de-camp, seeing our extreme discomfort, murmured to the Duke that there had been a severe road block on the motorway and the Duke remarked somewhat dryly, 'One has heard of these things happening, but they have not happened to one.' Precisely.

Later that afternoon, Moyra was sitting next to the Duke in the show area. Though she had ridden as a child, Moyra knew nothing about equestrian competitions, but was conscious of my battle to keep drugs out of sport. She ventured to ask about whether there were any drugs taken in the equestrian events and the Duke's reply was a brisk 'Certainly not.' Moments later, a horse came in so violently out of control that one felt it may well have been given drugs. After it kicked over the electronic score board, it looked in danger of attacking the crowd, but the rider managed to catch it and it had to be led away from the competition.

It was a miserable afternoon for us and not much fun for the Duke either to be next to someone so unknowledgeable about his favourite sport. We had so hoped to be able to see the fabled treasures at Burghley House, home of the *Chariots of Fire* low hurdler, David Burghley. He was played by Nigel Havers and anonymised at his request in the film. His butler was shown having laid nearly full glasses of champagne on each hurdle. On an occasion when I met one of Lord Burghley's daughters when she visited Leeds Castle, she told me that in fact matchboxes had been used, but David Putnam, the producer, said that would be insufficiently dramatic. After a long and tiring day, we returned to find the children in a less than joyful mood, so we set about feeding them and trying to jolly them up with our adventurous day. They were very forgiving of our absences.

There was a marked contrast by the time I completed my

three-year term as chairman of the Sports Council. Despite our occasional disagreements, at a farewell reception for me, Prince Philip made a presentation of a silver tray that was so heavy I almost had difficulty holding it. He said in making the presentation that despite our differences he had never doubted my sincerity and that I had made a great contribution to the development of governing bodies in sport as well as increasing the opportunities for Sport for All.

Fifty years after I retired from the independent sports council, the organisation has been split into Sport England, the body concerned with the Sport for All programme and community sport, and Sport UK, the body that is concerned with elite grants. Both remain outside direct political control.

I look back with some pride at what the Sports Council achieved. My colleagues over the years were extremely supportive and many of them became good friends. The battle for better sporting facilities is not yet won and the percentage of children who give up sport on leaving school is still lamentably high. But governments deserve credit for the steady increase in the size of grants to the sports councils, now £300 million in total, and credit for the inclusion for sport among the causes supported by the National Lottery goes to John Major.

At the end of my three years as chairman of the independent sports council, Heath's government fell over the miners' strike and the issue of 'Who governs the country?' I can remember during that strike speaking in candlelight to the British Yachting Association's annual banquet at the Dorchester Hotel. Harold Wilson returned to power in February 1974 with a tiny margin of only four seats over the Conservatives, so he went to the country again in October and was returned with a workable majority. After the first election, he gave Denis Howell back his previous job as Minister for Sport, and Howell soon made clear he wanted the Sports Council to revert to its advisory role, but fortunately the royal charter had been carefully devised to prevent this and was, intentionally, almost impossible to revoke.

He leaked to the press his prediction that I would soon step down as chairman. Since he had disagreed with so many of the Sports Council's policies while in opposition, he would certainly want a chairman more amenable to his views and it was obvious he was not keen to have me continue. He asked me if I would accept £1 million for building a new spectator stand at the Crystal Palace athletic track. I presumed he thought that as a former athlete I would be unable to refuse such a sum of money, even with strings attached as to how it should be spent. As this struck at the heart of the relationship between a minister and the independent sports council, I had to tell him that I would welcome the gift of £1 million to the Sports Council but that it was up to the council to decide whether its use for a new stand was a higher priority than other needs. The outcome was that I left it to the Sports Council to make the decision whether this sum would be best spent at Crystal Palace. In the event, they voted that it would and in due course the stand was built. But I think this was the point at which Denis Howell realised that in the future he would not be able to dictate to the independent sports council.

In November 1974, the Permanent Secretary of the Department of Environment, Denis Howell's most senior civil servant, invited me out to lunch, clearly having been asked by Howell to try to find out whether I was likely to take the break clause that existed in my contract and was coming up at the end of the year, or whether I wanted to continue for another two years.

Once I saw that the independent sports council and the royal

charter were safe, honour was satisfied. I had kept the flag flying
for its independence in the teeth of several assaults. It would be
difficult to work with Denis Howell, so I decided I would not seek
reappointment at the end of my third year, in December 1974.

My time as chairman was certainly marred on occasion by
Howell's interventions. To be fair to him, he saw it as his duty to
oppose much of what the Conservative government had done
and I happened to be chairman at the time and so was in the
firing line. He had first appointed me to the advisory sports
council and was unhappy with my taking it further from its
undoubted original success under his aegis into an independent role. Chris Chataway and Shirley Williams, both friends,
were junior ministers in Conservative and Labour governments
respectively, and they had sympathy for me when they realised
that I was having a difficult time.

I still find it difficult to imagine how for ten years I could have
devoted so much time to the Sports Council and yet continued
my commitment to the NHS. It was only possible because my
two hospitals, St Mary's and the National, were both in central
London and only minutes away from each other. As chairman I
could set the times of all meetings to suit myself, except for those
with the minister. I gave up completely the small amount of
private practice I had previously done, ceding it to my St Mary's
colleagues, though during this time I did also edit the third and
fourth editions of *Brain's Clinical Neurology*. Undoubtedly my
family bore the strain of the worry I was caused. In truth I can
say I was relieved to make an honourable exit when I did.

On my departure from the independent sports council, many
members of the governing bodies and other officials were generous in their praise of my work. Later, in recognition of the service
I had given to the Sports Council, I was awarded a knighthood

and in the following spring went with Moyra, Erin (then seventeen) and Charlotte (aged eleven) to receive the insignia from the Queen at Buckingham Palace. How could the girls fail to thrill at seeing the Queen among the glitter and the gold?

The precedents set by the independent sports council were good ones which have lasted ever since. The sound basic principles of grant aid for improving the administration of many governing bodies by professionals remain to this day. There was for me in the role of chairman the satisfaction of being in control of a staff of about 500 and of seeing tangible and widespread results: new sports halls echoing with the shouts and footfalls of children and adults engrossed in games and competitions. To this role I brought a passion that extended around the country among people whose interest I had first won by my running so many years before.

The London Olympics of 2012 were the proof that we could face the world with our prowess. The Union Jack was raised many times and the exhilaration of that glorious summer infected spectators and sportsmen alike. It flooded me with gratitude that I had been given the chance many years before to have helped. The good work must go on.

Chapter 13

Family Life

Imagine our exhilaration when we secured a six-bedroom house on Edwardes Square. We counted ourselves extremely fortunate that Moyra's parents and mine made this possible. We had had seven happy years in our Earls Court flat but we now felt more than ready to find a house which we could buy freehold. There is a four-acre garden in the middle of the square which was extremely enticing and well cared for by a resident gardener who lived in a mock Palladian cottage in the gardens, and we looked forward to learning the rich history that surrounded us.

In the house next door to us, Leigh Hunt had entertained Keats, Byron and many other literary luminaries of the day. The early-nineteenth-century houses had a pleasing uniformity. They appeared modest but through many generations all sorts of extensions had been added at the back. In the centre of the square on a plinth rested a large cannonball from the Crimean War. There were two grass tennis courts which we could foresee could give our children many happy hours of play. Settling in was utterly hilarious as Charlie was only one and a half and danced about as the removers juggled crates full of our belongings. We painted most of the walls ourselves and Moyra made our curtains, which must have given our rather wealthy neighbours a surprise. At last there was a semblance of order. It was an elastic house with six bedrooms where we could have friends to stay and entertain informally. Moyra had been brought up in a house where there was room to entertain visitors, which is what we ourselves did. Despite some later cash-flow problems, we have never stinted on our entertaining. Most occasions called for the signing of our large guestbook decorated by Moyra. We look back feeling that whatever vicissitudes the future holds we do not regret a single moment because we had so many friends and acquaintances and our children were always entertaining their own friends. There was a very large long terrace facing Kensington High Street and three of the houses were owned by the Russian Embassy. It transpired that one of the residents was Gordievsky, the most successful double agent we ever had, from 1974–85. We like to think that the benign influence of the beauty of the square convinced him that our lives here were happier than those in Moscow and this led him to join our side!

One winter when the snows were very heavy, snowmen were built. Our children were horrified to find that the Russian children had filled their snowballs with stones.

The Earls Court Road had a police station a stone's throw from the square and picture the astonished look on the sergeant's face when Moyra, carrying two shopping bags, approached him and said that she had noted two large recording dishes on the roofs of the Russians' houses. I think the police may have thought at first that Moyra was suffering from either paranoid delusions, or that perhaps it was a jest!

At the corner of the square was a public house, the Coach and Horses, even more ancient than the square. At outdoor tables on

summer evenings there sat a cross-section of London's jeunesse
dorée.

Is there anyone at all who has been at a dinner table when yet
another conversation on education has failed to crop up? Many
of our like-minded friends longed for a Britain where neither
grammar nor public schools sifted out many of the cleverest
children. We were all prepared to embrace comprehensives.
There was no fiercer advocate of this than Tony Benn and his
American wife. We ourselves took an early decision to try and
give our children the best education from London's most prestigious schools. I have already related that I myself had been at a
comprehensive school in Bath, though the word comprehensive
was not then used; secondary modern was the official name. My
winning a county scholarship to a direct grant school, University
College School in Hampstead, greatly enriched my life. We had
many friends who decided to send their children to Holland
Park Comprehensive School, but who were disappointed with
their lack of progress. Indeed, it was rumoured that many
children there had to be given private tutoring when they were
slipping behind.

At the time, along with many friends, though not overtly
political, we had a belief not only in the vigour and justice of a
state health service, in which I was working, but also in a state
education service, both of these aiming to provide equally and
effectively for all. Though Holland Park no doubt had many
gifted and idealistic teachers, its early policy of complete non-
streaming despite many foreign children, when starting there,
unable to read any English, made it almost impossible to teach
the more advanced English children to a high standard in a
peaceful atmosphere.

The house in Edwardes Square proved a happy foundation to

our lives, a peaceful and comfortable home for bringing up our children. Sometimes we could not believe our luck. The back garden could fit in a climbing frame, sandpit and even a small above-ground swimming pool during the summer. In those days from quite a young age the children could play and cycle in the square unsupervised, and on rainy days under Moyra's tutelage they would become engrossed in drawings and crafts on our large dining room table in the basement.

Moyra's aim was to impart to our children her own love and knowledge of the arts and give them the skills and interest to pursue them later in life, either as a pastime or vocation. She chose their books with immense care and read to them every evening when they were young. On buses and in taxis she sallied forth with them to the Victoria and Albert Museum, the National Gallery, the National Portrait Gallery and to plays in the West End, like *The Winslow Boy* and *Journey's End*. It was a subtle task to instil an enduring excitement about culture without overdoing it and putting them off. They did sometimes rebel, groaning, 'Not today…'

My role on the other hand was to inculcate a love of sport and exercise in to our children and we would play tennis and run slowly with shorts bursts of sprinting on the lawns in the square just as I had done in my running career. Often on Saturday and Sunday mornings, partly to give Moyra a much-needed and deserved lie-in, I would take them to the swimming pool at St Mary's Hospital Medical School, or running in Kensington Gardens by the Round Pound, where Ronnie Williams, a friend from university running days, then also a doctor in London, would on occasion meet us. Then we would return to the kitchen at No. 31 and I would make a breakfast of fried everything – eggs, bacon, mushrooms and bread, as one of the children brought Moyra a restorative cup of Earl Grey tea in bed. Later, as they grew older, I would go on cross-country runs with Clive and Thurstan around Wimbledon Common and Richmond Park.

Our Christmas celebrations usually started with our going to Gilbert and Sullivan productions at St Mary's Hospital Medical School. These were remarkably well done, sometimes distinguished by an exceptional voice, but became more and more raucous towards their conclusion on the last night. After the interval, when the cast probably had had more to drink than they should, great liberties were taken with the script, any reference to rain in the last act prompting the tipping of beer from the lighting scaffolds onto the hapless actors below. The cast always added a few verses to the final solo to satirise professors and medical school policies.

The hospital was decorated, even if only with cheerful paper chains. It was my duty as consultant in the three wards in which I had patients to carve the turkey. We would emanate as much good cheer as possible. The nurses, in their smart uniforms with a silver buckle at the waist and starched caps and red capes, sang carols in the well of the main stairs and then walked from ward to ward. We would take our children, and on one occasion my six-year-old daughter was given a rather marvellous doll by a kindly nurse. Charlotte's older brother Thurstan, aged nine, told Charlotte, 'You must give the doll back at once. It is meant for the poor children.' These old traditions ended with this great climax of Christmas. Our children were given so many sweet biscuits and tiny cakes there that when we got home they were quite unable to eat any more. Some patients who were lonely, with no family to provide yuletide cheer, longed to stay in hospital and enjoy the festivities.

At No. 31 our children's schooling started in earnest. Erin was six years old by the time we moved in. She had been to an American nursery school in Cambridge and then the Lycée

Français in London. After that we sent her to Bute House, the junior school of St Paul's Girls' School.

Erin's school career was one of constant praise from her teachers and particularly at the junior school they loved her and appreciated her artistic and other talents. At the senior school some teachers were more abrasive but their teaching standards were very high: they reviewed her sixth-form essays with the same rigour as would university tutors. She also took on many other pursuits: acting in plays, both at St Paul's and at Westminster School, playing the guitar and piano and dancing. For her last year of A levels she chose to go to a tutorial college in Oxford, no longer at ease in the formal atmosphere of St Paul's School. There she finally decided to pursue art at university and, owing to the excellence of her portfolio, was accepted without having to complete a foundation course elsewhere to the Ruskin School of Drawing and Fine Art. She flourished at Oxford and soon had a wide circle of friends. She was asked to design many posters to publicise undergraduate plays. She led a successful student effort to make the Ruskin a full part of the university. At the end of her time there, she won a place at the Royal Academy Schools, the leading graduate school in England for figurative painting.

Clive and Thurstan started off together at small schools in central London: first Wetherby's in south Kensington and then Sussex House Preparatory School in Cadogan Square. Thurstan was rather overwhelmed upon arriving at Sussex House, partly because an older boy had told him there was beating at the school. Moyra and I were very proud to hear of Clive, aged only nine, taking Thurstan on his own initiative directly to the head-master, who explained that beating did not occur.

At breakfast before a Wetherby's sports day, Thurstan, then aged eight and an apprehensive participant, developed a convincing and convenient limp. My boys told me there was a fathers' race in which I 'must' run. I warned them that as the fathers' race was a short eighty-yard sprint, I would hardly be able to get moving. I did not propose to take part in it. Their faces dropped and the ignominy for the boys was not to be borne. We arrived that morning at the playing fields, which were filled with eager parents. As we crowded onto the pitch, I viewed with some dismay the healthy-looking fathers of rugby-playing vintage with whom I had to race. I took off my jacket at the beginning of the race, to reveal my waistcoat, then de rigueur for a consultant, and reluctantly lined up for the start. To my horror, I saw some of the rugger fathers quietly exchanging £10 notes, clearly betting so they could boast of winning a race against a sub-four-minute miler. In the event, using absolutely every ounce of energy I possessed, I just managed to win. Next day, in *The Times*, the fourth leader was headed 'Bannister Wins by the Width of a Waistcoat Button' and there was a photo of me breasting the tape. The gist of the article was how I had spared the feelings of the other competitors and made it look as though I was really trying. Little did they know! But two little boys' honour had been satisfied.

The sequel was a phone call from the headmistress the next day. She apologised that the press had found out about the race, though she was probably quite pleased with the publicity. She then said that the night after the race a father had a heart attack. To my relief, he had survived. I suggested that fathers' races were not a good idea and an egg-and-spoon race might be a suitable substitute.

Clive was affected by a streak of dyslexia in Moyra's family. One of her Swedish uncles who was dyslexic had run away to sea, fearing he had not passed his examinations. He eventually returned to become a very successful inventor and head of his own company. Many dyslexic children become highly innovative by dint of having to seek ways around problems others usually solve conventionally by recognising words and sounds easily. An example of this in Clive's case was that he soon learnt to build aeroplane and other models though he was unable to read the instructions. This started him on the road to a lifelong pastime of building wooden ship models and inlaid furniture. He built a two-man wooden kayak in his bedroom at No. 31, cheerfully blocking the door and removing the possibility of tidying his room.

Dyslexia was not nearly as well understood in the 1960s as it is now, but we found a special teacher for Clive and did extra English with him at home. He worked very hard despite the frustration this extra burden often caused. It was difficult for us to judge whether we had pushed him too severely. But he was self-confident and popular at Sussex House and was made head boy. He went on to my old school, University College School, in Hampstead. He was then physically strong, eventually playing at number eight for the school's rugby first XV. He won the school's annual cross-country race in his last year and was also made a prefect. A highlight of his outside activities was securing for the political society a visit by Harold Wilson, then the Prime Minister, whom he chaperoned around the school.

Thurstan proved to be a serious scholarly boy. From an early age he displayed an unusual bent for detached, lateral thinking and could spend much of his time alone reading books and thinking. His strengths at school were English and art. After Sussex House, we decided he should strike out separately from Clive, to St Paul's School. In his second term he took up cross-country running and enjoyed the training runs along the Thames tow-paths at Barnes and ran in school teams every year until leaving. He started to take science A levels, intending eventually to become a doctor, but it did not really appeal and after three weeks he turned to arts subjects. He was most fulfilled absorbing the first-rate English teaching St Paul's provided, forming and running school societies and editing and writing articles for the school magazine.

One Sunday evening I vividly remember a tired father saying of Charlotte, 'I'm returning your human dynamo.' At a huge charity tea party at Grosvenor House the master of ceremonies called for a child to sing. The only one to seize the microphone was our Charlie, then four years old, who treated the audience to a very fair rendering of 'Away in a Manger'. A delighted *Tatler* photographer caught that moment. When her turn to start schooling came, she followed Erin to Bute House. After Bute House, she went to Queen's College, Harley Street, distinguished for its music and drama teaching, which she loved. The first headmistress in Victorian times was Miss Buss, about whom – along with a Miss Beale who was headmistress of Cheltenham College – was written the verse:

Miss Buss and Miss Beale, Cupids darts do not feel,
how different from us, are Miss Beale and Miss Buss.

For the sixth form she went away to Marlborough College, a few years after the school had started to take girls. Here she continued her interest in plays, musical productions and sport.

On top of all her work at home, in 1964 Moyra accepted an invitation to join a royal commission to review British primary education – that is, from nursery school level to the age of eleven – chaired by Lady Plowden. Moyra was appointed because she was a young mother, had impressed several politicians by advising on selection with her original views and was not tied to any faction in the politics of education.

She worried that her disappearance for a couple of days each month to work for the commission, besides an enormous reading workload, was unsettling Charlotte and keeping her in the lowest 10 per cent by weight for her age. Moyra took her, aged two, to the Professor of Paediatrics at St Mary's, where Charlie's fluent speech and great energy, manifested by her somersaulting across his office, made him look at Moyra in astonishment and, after a cursory examination, say, 'Mrs Bannister, there is *nothing* wrong with your child.'

The professionals on the committee wanted to recommend a national scheme of nursery schools for all from the age of three. Lady Plowden accepted this recommendation, though much of the evidence showed the overwhelming role the mother played in children's education. Moyra's view was that besides being unaffordable, nursery schools were the wrong solution. She believed then and has ever since, notwithstanding the tide of women into the workforce, that for mothers of children under the age of five to work full-time is harmful, though such harm may not be apparent at the time. Besides, the turnover of nursery assistants was high, particularly in London, where the average stay for an assistant in each post was three months, so talk of 'mother substitutes' sounded a shade thin. As a result, Moyra ended up writing a minority report. Her report recommended, instead of nursery schools, a national scheme of pre-school playgroups run by mothers, albeit with the guidance of trained and experienced nursery supervisors. Other effects of the scheme which she envisaged were ending the loneliness facing many mothers in cities and enabling them to learn about childcare from each other. When Moyra refused to toe the committee line, Lady Plowden

was as disconcerted as the rest of the commission. It took a lot
of courage for Moyra to make herself unpopular in this way and
she knew it was likely to prejudice her further involvement in
such committees.

In the event there never were nursery schools for all. A short
time after the commission reported, Lady Plowden herself
became chair of the existing National Playgroup Association,
just the kind of organisation Moyra had recommended, which
proved a signal success and spread across the country. However,
there was much in the main report with which Moyra had
concurred, with its stress on treating children with dignity, hence
no corporal punishment, and on encouraging creativity with less
emphasis on rote learning, but still inspiring high standards.

The report, published in 1967, caused a furore. 'Plowden says
stop caning' read the headlines. Moyra had felt utter revulsion – as
had all her colleagues but one – when she learnt how rife physical
punishment was in schools. Research showed its uselessness, as
the same set of children got caned again and again. The practice
had long been banned all over Europe and in the United States.
As the distinguished head of the best-known teacher training
college exclaimed, 'What's the matter with British children that
they need hitting?' It took the government another twenty years
to ban corporal punishment in state schools, though shamefully
it lingered on in public schools, where even prefects were allowed
to wallop smaller boys.

After her rebellion, Moyra thought she had queered her pitch,
but to her surprise Keith Joseph, then Secretary of State for
Social Services, invited her to join another government council
on child health from birth to age eighteen. Chaired by Professor
Donald Court, a kindly Quaker, it proved another enthralling
but gruelling four years of work. Again, Moyra developed some

views of her own which at one point she condensed to a single
sheet of paper and circulated to the committee. The emphasis
of the report was very much on early childhood ills, and Moyra
felt it too meagre on teenage problems. She drew attention to
some of the more controversial problems of adolescent health,
which the committee seemed reluctant to tackle. These included
accidents, contraception, abortion, smoking, drugs and deafness
from noise levels at discos. All these were serious health problems and she felt that if they were addressed on a statistical basis
this would have more impact than if considered as problems of
morality. The chairman regarded her paper as a potential diversion that might open up dissension in the committee. Moyra
for her part felt she lacked full access to the research needed to
back her views. After the injuries she sustained in a serious car
accident we suffered in 1975, she decided that it would be best to
resign quietly on health grounds rather than fight an uphill battle
without the research she needed.

As our children reached adolescence, my relationship with
them, my sons in particular, became strained at times, as had
my own parents' relationship with me before I left for Oxford.
In all previous centuries, before life expectancy lengthened
and the process of education became so extended, people had
generally reached adulthood and gained their independence at
sixteen or even earlier. So, in a sense, for parents and adolescents
to remain together as long as they do now is an unnatural state.
One way of alleviating the problem is for children to go away
to school in the sixth form, if it is affordable, as both Erin and
Charlotte did, or to go to university early, as I had done. The
cultural upheaval of the 1970s, our financial strains and the scale
of my work commitments together compounded the original
difficulty. All I can say now is that this awkward period passed,

pleasant communication was restored, and during the difficult chapter our children never, as far as I knew, seriously risked their health or academic prospects by taking drugs, as they might have done.

In 1975, owing to the high inflation rates affecting private school fees in particular, we chose to sell No. 31 Edwardes Square and moved across the square to No. 16. We raised a new mortgage against this house and realised a capital gain on No. 31, which relieved our cash strains and allowed us to keep our country cottage. By now we loved the square and our immediate neighbourhood and did not wish to stray further afield. No. 16 was smaller and needed some fixing up. The basement when we arrived still held a concrete air-raid shelter that had never been dismantled. But Moyra with her design sense and ingenuity and our now much-loved paintings and furniture soon recreated the aura of our home, as No. 16 became for the following decade. While here, Clive, Thurstan and Charlotte completed their school days. Here my sons received in turn the news that they had each been accepted by Exeter College, Oxford, to read Politics, Philosophy and Economics (PPE) and from here Charlie departed to Durham University to read Politics and Anthropology. Erin returned from Oxford to live here while studying at the Royal Academy Schools. Here I would give drinks parties now and again for my graduate students at St Mary's once they had completed their tours of duty in the neurology department and on one of these occasions Erin and Alain first met.

In 1966, three years after we had settled into No. 31, we began looking for a country cottage for weekends. We wanted one

within two hours' drive of London in real countryside. On one
occasion I tried to interest Moyra in a dilapidated woodman's
cottage in thick forest at the end of a lane near Guildford. As our
own car got stuck in the mud, Moyra exclaimed, 'How on earth
would a milkman ever get here?'

We had almost given up the search when one of Moyra's
friends from the Ruskin School of Art telephoned us to say there
was a cottage for sale very near her in the village of Lyminster
in West Sussex, a few miles from Arundel. We drove down to see
it on a rainy day with my car's windscreen wipers not working
properly for some reason. By the time we reached the cottage,
Moyra was so out of sorts that she could not bring herself to
look at the place. However, her friend, Rosemary Mosley, had
asked us to tea in their large house almost next door. The rain
stopped and, in that way so many watery English evenings end,
the sun slanted out across the fields and we went back to look
at the cottage. We fell in love with it and knew that we would
find a happy life there with the children. It had belonged to a
Shakespearean scholar and his wife, whose daughter had been
at Cheltenham in Moyra's sister's class. When he passed away
it had been put up for sale, but his widow loved the place so
much that she had not accepted any offer for it for two years,
by which time the agents had lost patience. Even our offer was
at first accepted and then rejected. Feeling that we should never
find a cottage, I took Moyra out to the theatre in London to
console her. We decided to give up hunting for one and join the
Hurlingham Club instead and make the best of a London life.
But evidently the agents were so exasperated by the owner's
vacillation that they finally prevailed on her to sell.

It was the beginning of a cheerful twenty-year saga of cottage
owning. Lyminster was a typical Sussex village with a Saxon

church on a knoll sixty yards away from us. Nearby was a pool called Knucker Hole, occupied by a dragon according to Anglo-Saxon legend, 'knucker' being the Anglo-Saxon word for dragon. The imprint of the supposed dragon's ribs were on a stone in the church, the record stating a John Pulk slew it in 1215. The pond was so deep, legend also had it, that a coach and horses had been pulled backwards into it and disappeared, and that by dropping a rope with a large stone attached no one had ever found the bottom of it.

The property was called Church Field. It had been built in the late nineteenth century, in the style of a workman's cottage on an acre of land on the Duke of Norfolk's estate, whose name appeared on the deeds. The cost was £7,500, of which Moyra's mother contributed £6,000. It had electricity but the water was pumped from a deep well in the kitchen by an unreliable electric motor. We employed a London architect to supervise renovations, but would have been better advised to have used a sensible local builder. Over the years, as family finances improved, we gradually renovated it, until eventually, with its annexe, it had seven bedrooms and two bathrooms, but it was never more than a holiday or weekend cottage.

We tended to arrive there to find the dampness from Knucker Hole had made all the clothes and bedding sodden, so even when we had central heating we had to drag mattresses up to the radiators to dry them out. Often these preparations on arrival were completed by Moyra while the four children insisted on being taken to the beach a mile and a half away to lark about. Drawbacks included an erratic electricity supply, the lack of any local cleaners, the failure of the frost-stat and the occasional burglary by inmates straying from Ford Open Prison nearby.

But despite all this it was tremendous fun and none of the

problems dented our enthusiasm for it. We valued the freedom it gave us almost every weekend and school holiday. In the summer we had a large above-ground swimming pool which cost all of £50 from Harrods, then quite a considerable sum. It provided great jollity and was particularly useful while Charlotte was still small. There was a continuous war on the nettles in the orchard which we never won. We made good friends with the Dickins family who lived nearby. Bill, the father, was a Scotsman and owner of a fine art gallery who understood garden improvement and we always sought his advice and valiantly tried to carry it out. One suggestion he made was to plant rows of beech hedge cuttings, but they never quite 'took'. Breakfasts were invariably enlivened by watching the rabbit families using our back lawn for their own breakfast and as a play-pen for their young. Our children learnt to race up and down this lawn, once used as a tennis court, on top of some discarded water butts they found – quite a balancing act. It was a friendly place where teenage children congregated in a moment with no embarrassment. Many afternoons when the weather closed in they spent trying out new crafts around the dining room table.

Through the years we had many visitors: my parents and sister and her family, the Chataways, the Rubinsteins, the Glennies, not to speak of all the high-spirited teas held at our home as the climax of our orienteering meetings, of which more later. The hard work was alleviated by a series of au pair girls. One of them, a memorable beauty though utterly wordless, attracted a clutch of young men who hovered with unrequited desire around the cottage. Moyra urged them into the garden with large scythes and set them to work on our ever-present nettles.

Charlotte absolutely loved every aspect of cottage life. In the mid-1970s when our finances were stretched, we had a family conference to decide whether to sell the cottage to raise the money needed or to sell No. 31 Edwardes Square and move to a smaller house. Charlotte voted to keep the cottage and so we moved to No. 16.

Because we already had close friends in the Lyminster neighbourhood we were included in many social events, and one highlight of the year was the Red Cross Ball at Arundel Castle, home of the Duke of Norfolk, in front of log fires, with the family portraits reviewing our antics distastefully from the walls, alongside full suits of medieval armour. Dancing ended at three or four o'clock with a breakfast of eggs and bacon or kedgeree. We were far enough from London for there to be a completely independent social life there. Our neighbours entertained us and we tried to reciprocate. The largest house, a quarter of a mile away, was a Georgian manor with many acres of grounds where the owner and his wife gave parties, held cricket matches and organised the village fête. For some years I was president of the Sussex Youth Clubs which widened our acquaintanceship. The first year we moved to Lyminster I opened the village fete and three years later I was so much accepted that I ran the guinea-pig races, while the vicar, his neck and arms held in wooden stocks, was bombarded with wet sponges, especially by gleeful members of the choir!

A great advantage was having good friends nearby in the village: Nicholas and Rosemary Mosley and another friend of Moyra's from art school, Joy Woolley, and her husband, Edward. For several years furious discussions enlivened our Lyminster visits. Nicholas Mosley was the infamous Oswald Mosley's son but shared none of his views. Their hospitality was generous and frequent. We shared almost every Christmas with the Dickins family, Madge Dickins providing the turkey and Moyra the pudding. Christians in deed as well as word, they also shared their Christmases with a number of stranded Commonwealth students.

All kinds of village activities existed and made the quality of life so different from London. Sometimes we did not see the children from dawn until dusk. In the evening in the summer there might be an expedition to the beach to run and play games in the dunes. Alongside the beach there was a small golf club. I started playing golf again, occasionally with Colin Cowdrey, or Tim Raison, the MP for Aylesbury, or Peter Hordern, the MP for Horsham, who lived nearby.

One contribution we were able to make to local life was to introduce orienteering. This is a kind of cross-country sport in which the planner selects a series of small local landmarks on public land, for example a holly, beech or oak tree, a stile, a water-trough or a ditch. Near each of these he places a 'flag' which can only be seen from a few yards away. Each competitor is given a copy of the local 2 ½ inch to the mile British Ordnance Survey map, grid coordinates for the flags' locations and a set of crossword puzzle type clues, as, for example, 'Christmas needs you' (holly), 'Charles sought you' (oak), or 'as pants the hart' (stream). At the start, each team, usually a family or group of children, takes ten minutes or so to mark the flag locations on its own copy of the map and to decide on the most efficient route to find them all. The teams' maps are stamped at each flag to prove the team reached it. These events were organised about four times a year, usually on holidays, either on the Duke of Norfolk's land or nearby Forestry Commission land. Some of the most dramatic events were held in the snow on Boxing Day or New Year's Day, young children being dragged on toboggans by their parents. The participants, usually ten or more families, perhaps sixty people in all, then returned to one of their homes for an enormous tea to which everyone contributed cakes. There, with much hilarity, competitors complained to the organisers about 'unfair clues'. The winners' prize was that, having shown their prowess, they were given the task of setting the next orienteer.

Orienteering was then becoming a serious national sport, introduced from Scandinavia by my friends Chris Brasher, John Disley and Gordon Pirie. For a time it was christened the 'thinking man's sport' because it required not only fast running but accurate route plotting by compass. The skills needed included the ability to interpret the map and to count your strides as you ran or walked and as a result know exactly where you were. Sometimes an inexperienced team did get lost in the forest. Once, on a bitterly cold and snowy Boxing Day when darkness fell at three, one team had failed to return. Their leader was a neighbour in London who had been in the Scots Guards, a regiment where it is rumoured that the officers may sometimes leave the map-reading to the sergeants. I had to drive my car to the top of the course on a neighbouring hill and turn on my headlights until we finally saw a tired and frightened family emerge from the forest. After this we allowed only ninety minutes for the course, with points lost for lateness, and an earlier start in winter.

Though it is now twenty-five years since we sold the cottage because it was too far from Oxford, we still get a phone call from friends after each orienteer telling us who attended, who won and which part of the forest was used. In 1990 we returned for a twenty-fifth anniversary celebration and invited along Chris B and his son.

To our bafflement and surprise, three marriages of good friends in Lyminster ended. You could say the village imploded under the strain. But the Dickinses remained faithful stalwarts of the village and Lyminster Church. Though they later moved to Warning Camp, a village a few miles away, they still remain friends and are the lynchpin of the orienteering events. Nostalgia for this happy time in our lives is tinged with relief that we did leave, as things have now so changed, many of our closest friends have moved away and the charm Lyminster once had for us is lost.

Our lives changed drastically as the result of a car accident in June 1974. As I was knocked unconscious by the impact, it is best to let Moyra take up the story described in a letter to her sister, written in 1975, after the accident:

> The police said we would have both been killed, had we not been driving a Volvo, and wearing our seatbelts.
>
> Imagine a straight road. We were coming towards the archetypal village, the sort where you and I once stopped halfway to London. It boasts five pubs. I saw the oncoming car. There was something between a bang, a crunch, and an explosion … and then silence.
>
> Roger was gently groaning beside me, 'Oh, my leg, my leg!', and then I sensed he fell unconscious. With relief I saw Clive by the side. I heard myself whispering, 'Tell the children that I love them.' He briskly said, 'None of that mother, none of that.' You won't believe it but, the next thought I had was, 'My God, men do this on purpose to each other in war!' The first ambulance took Roger, he was so obviously massively hurt. I found myself in an ambulance with a man laid out beside me on a bunk. I kept confusedly insisting that he was my husband. The paramedic

looked down at me in puzzlement. No, the other man was the driver who had driven into us … Now I have learnt that he has crashed into other cars twice before.

To cut it short, Roger had a gash down his forehead and seven broken ribs, but by far most serious of all was the crushed ankle, that was purple with blood.

The next hours, a kaleidoscope. I can remember each scene clearly but I might get the sequence wrong.

I was on a trolley and they cut my clothes off gently. I kept asking for Roger and something to kill the pain.

A neurological colleague of Roger's – a dear friend – came and took the three children to his home in Wimbledon.

I was moved to have an X-ray, where the technician told me there were only four broken ribs. At last, they prescribed painkillers to ease the pain.

Curiously, I couldn't sleep till the early dawn, anxiety I suppose. The next day I found myself in a high-ceilinged ward. The matron refused to let me see Roger, on the men's ward, on the grounds that it 'Might upset him'! Imagine my fury on learning that friends from Lyminster who had learnt of the crash from the BBC, could visit. Still, I give the matron credit for smart deflection of photographers and reporters who tried to sneak in on him. When at last I could see him – well – my heart shrank inside me. That swollen purple face and fearful bruising of his torso, and it was as well I could not see his legs, as they were encased in plaster.

Redhill was a respectable provincial hospital. Nevertheless, Roger's colleagues clamoured for him to be looked after in St Mary's. After a week I was driven home. Seat belts were not then compulsory in England. Roger has had a letter in *The Times* strongly advocating their use. I hope it sets the trend. Typical of him to have made his mind up early on evidence, just the same way years ago he forced me never to offer a cigarette again in our house. It was hard twenty years ago. No one stepped over the threshold without you offering them coffee or a drink, and a cigarette. It was seemingly just a way to ease social life, but one of his first jobs as a house physician was at the Brompton Hospital [for diseases of the lung]. Need I say more.

I rattled across London to St Mary's, and my broken ribs ground against each other with every bounce of the vehicle. [Medical policy in those days was that ribs should not be strapped.] I found Roger propped up, and almost lost amid medical tomes. 'Mrs Bannister, could you please ask him to stop asking our librarian for even more books?' How could I? None of these kindly colleagues, who were now massively concerned about his blood clot, realised it was Roger's way of blotting out his slow realisation that he might never run again.

You understand what it means to him. Many think that his days as a champion being over, and that was that. Since his glory days he has run every day he possibly could. The children came with him, almost as soon as they could walk. Clive would make a marvellous long-distance runner, but he doesn't like being lonely and would rather play rugby.

As I write, Roger is now stretched out on the white sofa in a bay window, lying with his plaster laden leg up, falling asleep more often than he cares to admit. Erin, at only seventeen, has been heroic beyond praise, ministering to us. Had we not such terrible cash-flow problems, we would have hired a nurse, but our finances could probably not have stood it.

Most of our friends had been so concerned, and kind and understanding. But one or two had no insight at all. I was shocked to be told briskly, 'We have a relation whose car accident ended in paraplegia', as though Roger were wallowing in self-pity, instead of being quietly courageous; as though telling us of the worst cases would somehow cheer us up.

Roger would need several operations, with no guarantee of success, but a guarantee of more pain. Forgive this sorry tale, I hope for better news in my next.

Much love to the family, and keep some for you.

I tried many times to run again, wearing orthopaedic supports, very soft shoes and always on soft grass; the ankle injury never healed into what might have been a pain-free fusion of the damaged bones. Even in my sixties I remember trying a Kenyan Masai-type shoe, originally based on a section of a rubber motor-car tyre, so that a runner could follow the curve. Alas, it proved disappointing, and I never solved the problem. My running days were – definitively – at an end.

The second sport we took up in Sussex was sailing. A few years before we arrived, some families had clubbed together to form a new sailing club in Littlehampton. They leased a length of fore-shore by the River Arun and built a club headquarters. The club represented English local enthusiasm at its best: a serious sailing programme combined with dances and other social events for every age group. Two of the senior figures had been in the Navy and they arranged classes to teach basic sailing theory in the winter and then each spring a flotilla of tiny sailing boats with a 'safety' boat headed down the Arun to the sea. The Arun is one of England's fastest rivers, running at 6 knots at full tide, with a large rise and fall adding to the hazards. Out at sea races were held for each group – novices, children and seniors. I bought a wooden 10-ft 6-in. Cadet dinghy for £50 from a local doctor whose children had outgrown it and then bought a half-share in a 14-ft wooden Enterprise. Our children learnt to sail in the Cadet but then graduated to the Enterprise.

Racing at sea had the thrill of danger since it required using the highest possible sail area and the Channel's gusty winds and choppy seas resulted in frequent capsizing. We used to practise capsizing the boat in the river, letting it turn turtle and right-ing it again. Erin, who had been captivated by all the Arthur Ransome novels set on boats in the Lake District, was quickly a very proficient sailor. Thurstan as her first crew took to it as well, Clive less so. Unfortunately, during one of Charlotte's first races out at sea with a novice helm she capsized. The mainsheet (rope) got tangled round her neck and she had the terror of remain-ing trapped under the boat and feeling she might drown. She remained unkeen on sailing after that, turning her attention to other sports.

Dinghy sailing was exciting but also wet, cold and uncom-fortable. In those days, wetsuits were not worn and so we called it frostbite sailing. My sailing ambitions grew and I bought a second-hand 25-ft Westerley with twin bilge keels and a 6-horsepower outboard that could be swung into the water. This gave some security to get us at any rate out of the River Arun, though it could make no progress against a full tide. At first we went out just for the day, perhaps fishing to catch mackerel. Next, as we could sleep five on board, I was keen to go further afield to Chichester and Portsmouth for the week-end. On such occasions Erin, Clive and Thurstan would come along and I would also invite one of my friends who had been in the Navy – Ross or Norris McWhirter or Ronnie Williams – as I was uncertain of my own navigational skills. Their well-ingrained instincts could keep us safe without our having to embark on laborious navigation exercises. The only pieces of navigational equipment on the boat were a compass, an echo sounder, binoculars and a pair of dividers. Later I got a hand-held direction finder that could, with luck, pick up some radio beacons.

There were some dangerous moments, usually when a storm came up and we were in danger of being blown onto a lee shore. The twin bilge keels made trying to sail to windward very inefficient, although they were useful when we had to stand on the shingle or sand at low tide.

After five years, sensing that my navigation skills were still inadequate, I spent an evening each week through the winter at Pimlico Comprehensive School, attending a navigation class arranged by the Royal Yacht Association (RYA). Along with straight navigation, we had to learn Morse code and how to draw weather charts, but I stopped short of celestial navigation. After the exam I was awarded my Master's Offshore Certificate, elementary but enough to induce much more caution than I had exercised before. I was very proud of that certificate, my first exam since my higher medical examinations taken several decades earlier!

I chose to buy a new boat – a 26-ft, second-hand Westerley Centaur with six berths and an inboard 13-horsepower Volvo diesel engine which gave the boat ample power. Now my ambition was to cross the Channel, trips on which Moyra wisely decreed that the children should not accompany me. I looked for other suitable companions. This led to a friendship with Peter

West, a trained engineer and then local authority architect, who at that point did not have a boat of his own.

On one of our voyages to France, the wind dropped and we were using the engine, edging our way through the world's busiest shipping lane in thick fog. I then clumsily tripped coming out of the hatchway and disconnected the engine gear cable. We donned our life jackets and while Peter tried to mend the cable I sat on the deck alternately blowing a hand-held hooter powered by a can of compressed air and hitting a frying pan with a wooden spoon. These were the only measures I could take, insubstantial though they were. I hoped without much confidence that our 9-in. radar reflector at the mast-top might register on the radar screens of any passing oil tankers, each a quarter of a mile long and charging down the Channel at 15 knots. After half an hour Peter succeeded in connecting the engine again and unscathed we continued on our way to France.

Gradually I was coming to learn that there was a world of difference between doing a navigation problem in my Pimlico night class on a stable school desk and doing a real 'plot' on a small yacht in a Force 5 wind, feeling mildly sick and tired out from loss of sleep. I had a second sailing partner at this time, William Hague (no relation to the Conservative Party leader), an accountant aged thirty who had sailed dinghies all his life and passed several navigation courses. He was frustrated working as an account executive with American Express at Brighton and had ambitions to become a professional yacht skipper in the Caribbean instead. So he wanted to get as much sea experience as possible under difficult if not hazardous conditions. In the summer of 1985 I was eager to get as far west along the English coast as possible and back during a week's holiday. The plan was to sail with each favourable westerly tide, which meant a considerable amount of night sailing and seldom more than six consecutive hours of sleep.

After three days we reached Helford Harbour beyond Plymouth, about 175 miles from Littlehampton, and the next day nearly reached Lizard Point before we had to turn back because of bad weather. We then had a day at Helford waiting for the weather to improve. On the way back I began to realise that at fifty-six my stamina was less than William's at thirty and I was in danger of making mistakes. My sailing reflexes were not deeply rooted enough from childhood to guarantee the right responses as my fatigue grew. The weather was deteriorating but we still wanted to get back to Littlehampton in time. This was a danger-ous frame of mind. We had a continuous sail from Weymouth and with a Force 4–5 north-east wind we were trying to tack up past the Needles – the treacherous western tip of the Isle of Wight – into the Solent. William had taken the burden of the helm through the day and while he got some sleep my task was to keep the course and reach the safety of Yarmouth Harbour.

I realised as I struggled at the helm with darkness approaching that I was close to my absolute limit of sailing endurance. I had begun to fear for the safety of the boat as we approached the Needles, though I do not think William was at his limit. Without him I am sure I would have been in severe trouble. Physical strength and endurance play a very large part in this type of small boat sailing and were we to have capsized, admittedly very unlikely, my arm and general body strength might well have failed me. In sailing there is a conflict at a certain point between wanting to sail further and test difficult conditions and the fear of beginning to take unacceptable risks. Of course the challenge and the excitement lie in having one's own boat and being free, with the advice of one's crew, to decide to sail from one point to another and to attempt it in a certain time with favourable tides but under uncertain weather conditions. The only other time I have experienced comparable feelings of fear was during mountain climbing many years earlier. As an inexperienced climber the danger of the situation and one's perfectly rational sense of fear are strangely exhilarating: it is the thrill of living at the edge.

At two o'clock in the morning, after a ten-hour sail, we finally entered Yarmouth Harbour, which was unfamiliar to me, and found somewhere to anchor in the dark. After a six-hour sleep my strength was restored and now in more familiar waters we sailed back through the Solent past Chichester, round Selsey Bill, through the Looe channel, back safely to Littlehampton with no little feeling, certainly on my part, of achievement. But the risks we had taken, reconsidered over the following week, had not been sensible.

Later that year I accepted the post of Master of Pembroke, which required my presence in the college at weekends. Oxford is at the centre of England, further away from the sea than almost any other city. So I sold my boat and now look back on these sailing experiences, mostly happy, a few hair-raising, from the comfort of a home set well inland.

From time to time, various charitable and religious bodies have wished to enlist my help for their particular causes. It has been difficult to refuse these sometimes heartrending pleas, but if I was to complete the medical and research demands on my time, I clearly could not also give my time and expertise to these other causes. I therefore made it a rule to decline them. I have also made it a rule of not allowing my name to be linked with any commercial activity in this way, no matter how laudable its aims.

When first married, when possible we went to All Souls, Langham Place, where John Stott, formerly the Cambridge University Evangelist, had a church which was humming with enthusiasm. It was there that I was baptised and confirmed with Chris C and Chris B standing in as my 'godparents'. When we lived in Kensington, nearer to our home was a large, rather gloomy, and very ill-attended church. We were intensely sorry for the vicar, an honourable man who had given up a peaceful country parish to try to rally support for this church. We persisted, largely because the vicar had a gift for enlisting children's attention.

Eventually, most weekends found us in our beloved but ramshackle cottage 'Church Field', near Arundel in Sussex – so named as a muddy path wound from the bottom of our garden to a Saxon church of simple beauty. It drew the Lyminster village together and the vicar, an ex-naval officer, might, on occasion from the pulpit, startle us with a nautical allusion or a comment criticising the government's policy, say in relation to aircraft carriers. It may have been lost on many of his listeners. Charlotte, from four onwards was an enthusiast. And so it was not really a surprise to us after being involved in a number of charitable works, she decided, with a family of four sons, to become an ordained priest in the Church of England. She has for ten years been associate priest at the University Church of St Mary's, in the High Street, Oxford, and is now the adviser to the Bishop of Oxford on special projects. Our other children and grandchildren hold various beliefs, in which we are glad to support them.

Chapter 14

Later Work in Sport

One of England's best middle-distance runners early this century was Philip Noel-Baker. He had been a finalist in the 1,500m in the 1912 Olympics and then won a silver medal in the same event at the age of thirty-one at the 1920 Games held in Antwerp. He was a Quaker and a pacifist. He had worked at the Versailles Peace Conference and at the League of Nations, as had both of Moyra's parents, and after the Second World War he helped lead the popular movement for nuclear disarmament. He had become a Labour Member of Parliament and also Minister for the Commonwealth. In 1960 he was awarded the Nobel Peace Prize. He believed sport could engender moral responsibility in individuals and by bringing countries into greater contact help prevent another war, the consequences of which in the nuclear age were unthinkable.

Among his many commitments, he had become the first president of an organisation called the International Council of Sport and Physical Education (or ICSPE) started in 1960 with the aim of advancing these ideals, and, in a more practical way, researching issues related to sport, disseminating conclusions and helping to put them into practice. The members of

ICSPE were national sports bodies like the Sports Council, some private sports organisations and academic institutes whose focus was sport science. ICSPE was linked to the United Nations by taking on research commissions on sports issues for two of its subsidiary groups: the United Nations Educational Scientific and Cultural Organisation (UNESCO) and the World Health Organisation (WHO).

In 1975, Philip Noel-Baker, whom I had known and respected for a long time, asked me to succeed him as president of ICSPE. He was by then eighty-six years old and had served in that office for fifteen years. His own position at the time was quite difficult, irrespective of his age, because ICSPE had funding difficulties, he was in open battle with its next most senior officer, the secretary-general, and its research and exchange of ideas were hampered by conflict between representatives of the Western and Communist blocs on its various boards and committees.

I accepted because I felt ICSPE was promulgating at an international level much of what the UK Sports Council had been doing – encouraging mass participation in sport as a means of fostering individual physical and mental well-being. I also did not want Philip Noel-Baker's project to founder and it struck me in particular as a terrible waste for research and valuable practices and policies not to be shared more generally. My own background in national sports administration gave me the authority to take a lead across the range of the organisation's activities.

However, I insisted on certain conditions to ensure I could be productive: having a secretary-general of my own choosing and having my administrative offices, the secretariat, based in London and assured of adequate funding. These were agreed to: John Coghlan, a colleague in the UK Sports Council whom

I knew and liked, became secretary-general, and the Sports Council also provided the necessary offices and funding.

I started my new role in England's hot, dry summer of 1976. Crucial in my view was bringing the organisation back into a more efficient pursuit of its main aims. I felt it should focus more on serving the UN bodies well with research and communications of real value. This would require improving the quality of scientific research ICSPE produced, disseminating it better, and reducing the counterproductive influences of internal disputes and ideological conflicts. I also wanted to improve relations with several national and international sports organisations, including the International Olympic Committee (IOC).

As an example of the kind of research work undertaken, we looked at the dietary requirements of elite athletes. The training for many sports clearly required extraordinary energy intakes relative to developing countries' typical subsistence diets. With funding from the IOC, we sent experts out to advise these countries on programmes for their elite athletes.

To help select, edit and distribute more generally better research, we launched a new academic publication. It led to an instance of how the conflict with the Communist bloc countries was then being played out. The first edition was all set to be printed in Berlin, on the East German side. However, my East German colleagues, upon receiving the typescript of my first editorial, baulked at simply printing it, suggesting instead it might need editing. Having anticipated this, I explained that some London printers were ready to do a production run immediately and I would telephone them to go ahead. They then looked alarmed and suggested that nothing be done hastily and said they would consider the issue overnight. The next morning they had backed down and the first issue went ahead without alteration.

The work also involved a lot of travelling to international conferences. Moyra had been reluctant to leave the children at home while they were younger, thinking it wrong to leave them in another's care for any length of time before their late teens, but now they were older she was free to accompany me more often on these trips. On one occasion I was due to speak at an event in Sydney alongside the Prime Minister of Australia, Bob Hawke, a former Rhodes Scholar. One of Hawke's claims to fame, according to the *Guinness Book of Records*, was his drinking a yard of ale in the shortest ever time of 11.4 seconds, apparently achieved in the Turf Tavern pub during his time as a student in Oxford. As I'd been lecturing in America previously, we decided to spend a couple of days in Hawaii on our way to Australia. As we relaxed in our hotel room after a day's swimming, I looked at my air ticket to check the departure times the next day. Suddenly I realised that we were on the wrong side of the International Date Line; we'd lost a whole day and the plane was due to depart in three hours, not twenty-seven! We hurriedly gathered our belongings and jumped in a taxi to the airport.

We managed to get to Honolulu Airport with two hours to spare but then the check-in desk asked us for our visa for admission to Australia. In my simple-minded British way I had no idea a visa was needed for a Commonwealth country. The Australian embassy was closed as it was a Sunday. I asked around and managed to find the ambassador's number and thankfully he agreed to meet me at the embassy in half an hour's time. With enormous kindness he let me into the shut embassy and provided me with our visas, and we caught the plane in the nick of time. I am sure it was only the fact that I was speaking alongside his

Prime Minister that made him behave as he did – otherwise we may have been stranded.

In the end my speech ran smoothly. I had become quite used to public speaking and had a stock of several easy openers to settle the audience. Among these was one particular line that Moyra had to endure on several occasions. It was a family joke that she had never opened the sports pages and I would some-times introduce her by saying, 'My wife knew absolutely nothing about sport until we met, but I am glad to deny the rumour that when we first met she thought I'd run four miles in a minute … and wasn't even impressed by that!' This never failed to produce a laugh. When grandchildren arrived, I was able to relieve her of the advantage I had taken over the years. I changed the joke to a four-year-old grandson who was heard boasting to another child in the playground that his grandpa had run a mile in four seconds. He again was suitably unimpressed.

Less humorous were some of our visits to the Eastern bloc. One that stands out was a visit to Sofia on the invitation of the Bulgarian Sports Minister. The night we arrived, we were ushered up a bleak staircase garnished with preposterously grand chandeliers. At the meeting, there was a Cabinet minister and two pretty female interpreters who accompanied us for much of our stay. First, there were the obligatory toasts involving an evil-looking fluid, which we had to drink as there was no plant pot within reach into which we could pour it. When we asked a question about health issues in Bulgaria, the interpreters were rather taken aback and eventually a rather wintry smile creased the features of the Cabinet minister. When I pursued a line of questioning about the difficulties with lack of participation in sports, the minister simply replied that there were no such diffi-culties in his country. Eventually Moyra dredged up enough of her German so that she could talk to our hosts, eliminating the interpreters and yielding a little more information.

The next day we were asked to lunch by Giles Bullard, the British ambassador, at his embassy. There were just the three of us and we were served a plain meal by a stumpy Bulgarian cook-cum-housekeeper. When Moyra asked a potentially indiscreet question, our host pointed upwards to the small chandelier and I realised he was warning us that the room was bugged. He suggested after lunch that we should drive to a hill outside Sofia and there we were able to talk freely without fear of being overheard. I was given a true picture of the repression and misery of life in Bulgaria. When I walked, my ankle was painful, as it had been since my car accident in 1974. Giles told us that there was a bakery in a nearby village which sold very good bread. I sat on a wall resting and watched curiously as the British ambassador queued up for bread, but when he reached the head of the queue the embarrassed baker said that the bread had run out and so we were turned away with many other disappointed queuing customers.

We were staying in a glossy, newly built Japanese hotel, but it was impossible to find any Western newspapers or magazines, or even *Time* magazine. The Sports Minister informed us that there was no call for such newspapers in Bulgaria. There appeared to be only one shop which sold Western books and the whole shop was no larger than my office at home.

One day we were driven at speed to see a Roman settlement which housed some golden Roman necklaces of intricate design and great beauty. This had been a long, hot and dusty drive and the roads were littered seemingly with the corpses of dead dogs. Our relationship with the Minister for Sport had eased and he became friendly and quite jolly as he and Moyra got on well. His wife also joined in, though we continued to doubt much of what we were told. He also took us to see some curious monasteries, surprising in such a Communist country, where we saw a few tired-looking monks keeping the sacred flame alive. We assumed that these places were kept and had not been destroyed because they were a tourist attraction. Another memorable day we were taken to a mountain resort, again after a terrible drive along bumpy roads. This was a kind of picnic centre where there was a pool, full of fish. I confessed that I had never fished seriously in my life before. A look of anticipatory glee came over their faces, until, can you believe it, the gods were on my side, and I pulled out the first fish. Our companions continued to cast their rods, but were unsuccessful. Luckily they had taken the precaution of bringing spare fish in the car and we had a picnic, roasting the fish over a fire. You could not help but be wary of their eager attempts at kindness and hospitality, never forgetting the pervasive propaganda and fear in which the population was held. We look back with some disgust at the realisation that our sitting room and bedroom would doubtless also have been bugged. It was naive of us, but it was a curious and very illuminating episode.

On another occasion, I found myself in a restaurant with my colleagues up a mountain near Tbilisi in Georgia. There was a fine view over the city and the Black Sea. Our group cheerfully looked forward to lunch, and our host ordered some bottles of local champagne, only to be informed by the waiter that they had run out. Our host was deeply embarrassed and quietly told me that shortages of this kind were very common and if I wished to protest he could call for the complaints book. Were we to do this, he said, after about six weeks he would be called by the police to appear in court to give evidence of what had transpired. It seemed such an appalling rigmarole that it wasn't worth it. I admired his frankness, but realised the sheer cumbersome inefficiency of their command economy.

These visits were really hard on the stomach. In no way could we refuse the strong beverages and fatty foods offered, lest we hurt the feelings of our hosts. I was once seriously ill after a visit to what was then Leningrad. It took some weeks before I was diagnosed and six weeks before a treatment cured me. Anyone who thinks that we were just on a jolly spree should know the hazards of travel in the USSR at the time and understand the serious diplomatic work that was the focus of each trip. I felt a duty never to let my colleagues down and to continue with the research discussions in hand no matter how difficult the situation.

The era of the Cold War is already fading from memory and perhaps becoming hard to imagine. It may already seem bizarre that the USSR and East Germany should have led such systematic and expensive athletic programmes, usually involving steroid use, to produce top athletes as a means of demonstrating to the West the supposed success of a political system already so manifestly failing. But in the late 1970s, the Eastern bloc representatives were still working to grim Leninist principles. It was both frustrating and rather eerie that some of our colleagues in an innocent civilian cause of fostering sporting activity could be stopped from meeting us abroad, owing to the danger of defections, and were accompanied everywhere by 'translators', even though our hosts' English was fluent. I could not tell whether a particular colleague was a willing apparatchik, or an essentially decent individual, cowed by a system that could easily ruin him and his family the moment he fell out of line. Certainly we could see the bleak strictures of their lives, for all the papering-over that went on during our conferences held in Eastern Europe. Much of my work I carried on at home in my study at No. 16. Moyra and I worked in tandem and could help each other over her council and committee work, speeches and writing. I kept my eye on the traffic of memos and research papers. John Coghlan, my assistant, and I saw things in a similar light.

My time as president of ICSPE ended in the summer of 1982 – I had made clear at the outset I would serve for only six years, so that no political storm could blow up over my possibly extending my term. By then the council had taken an upturn from its difficulties in the mid-1970s. The central administration was running more smoothly; funding had improved and it had sponsored some impressive research, especially that produced by universities in the USA, West Germany, Australia and the UK, I am glad to say. It was back on course and still flourishes today. The wider results of our work at the time – as with any long-term and complicated project – were less tangible. Ours was one voice, along with others, set against this period's domestic social upheaval and East–West conflict, speaking up in the cause which my friend Philip Noel-Baker had bravely first espoused, of fostering individual well-being and international cooperation through sport. For six years I had done my best to carry the torch.

❧

Over Christmas and the New Year of 1979–80, when the rest of the world was on holiday, Russia, finally losing patience with their rebellious neighbour, invaded Afghanistan. President Carter was understandably unwilling to stop the Russian invasion by force and the United Nations protested to no avail. Carter looked around for a possible reprisal and chose the Olympic Games to be held in Moscow in July 1980. This looked perfect. The Russians by now saw their sporting success – as we now know fuelled by illicit drugs – as a vital way of demonstrating the superiority of the Russian political system over that of the free world. Moscow had captured the Games with the help of Antonio Samaranch, Spanish Ambassador to Russia. In return they supported his bid for the presidency of the IOC when Lord Killanin retired just before the Games.

The US could not stop the Moscow Olympics from happening, but if they boycotted them and persuaded their allies to do the same, the Games would collapse as a truly international contest. One argument that remains for the IOC's self-perpetuating oligarchy is that few of its members from the West can be told what to do by their governments. It did not matter that the IOC members representing Communist countries were in the pocket of their masters, because they all supported the Olympic Games in Moscow anyway. But the attitude of Britain and the Commonwealth countries to the boycott was critical to fulfilling America's aims.

The American government did not care if a predominantly Communist Olympic Games were damaged by a boycott, but the next Olympic site, Los Angeles, was already picked and this would almost certainly be boycotted in return by the Russians and east Europe. There was a real danger that the concept of five interlocking rings on the Olympic flag representing the continents, would disappear, let alone the ancient notion of furthering peace by a truce during the Games. After the Russian attempt to subdue Afghanistan had failed, the United States, Britain and United Nations attempted something similar, but these forces have not devised an effective exit strategy. As the war still rumbles on, as always, the women and children continue to suffer.

Mrs Thatcher at this time greatly wished to promote Britain's 'special relationship' with America and this meant securing frequent personal access to President Carter. Continental Europe was more important to America as a trade partner than Britain, and America made no secret of the fact. The special relationship also meant close links through the NATO Alliance, the United Nations, the IMF and the World Bank. All these bodies were critical to Britain's place in the world, at a time when Britain's economic state was precarious, after the three-day week and a spate of strikes and opposition from the unions. We still struggled unconvincingly to be a world nuclear force with the vastly expensive US Trident submarines and other American defence equipment.

President Carter's spokesman was Lloyd Cutler, a lawyer and White House special counsel. In February it was announced that Lloyd Cutler was going on a selective world tour to persuade as many countries as possible to join the American boycott. He told countries that to go to Moscow would be a disloyal act for the West which no Western power or its athletes should contemplate.

By then sports politics in the United Kingdom were very fraught. The Conservative government of Mrs Thatcher echoed the American view that for teams to go to the Moscow Olympics showed an irresponsible attitude by sport. The issue went well beyond the authority of the Sports Minister Colin Moynihan and was being handled directly by Mrs Thatcher and her parliamentary private secretary Ian Gow, a right-wing Conservative and her custodian of party loyalty. Denis Howell was then shadow Minister of Sport, as he was to remain for the rest of his House of Commons career, and from this position was vocally opposed to the boycott. As chairman of the CCPR, its independence remained sacrosanct to him in providing a forum to promote British sport. The staunchest spokesman against the boycott was Denis Follows, then chairman of the British Olympic Association, the umbrella body for the twenty-two Olympic sports. He had been a trade union adviser to the Airline Pilots' Association and was thought to be, by inclination, a Conservative. Comparable bodies in the United States and Canada had buckled under their governments' political pressure and agreed not to send teams to Moscow. The boycott front was not absolutely united and a group of Canadian rowers slipped out of Canada and were massively welcomed by the Russians.

The members of Denis Follows's various Olympic sports committees had debated the issues, some consulting the athletes themselves. The fencing and equestrian teams, which had a strong military basis and usually sided with the government, decided their teams should go to Moscow, against the British government's will. Sebastian Coe spoke forcefully on behalf of the athletes in favour of Moscow, where he was the favourite to win gold medals at both the 800m and 1,500m. If it was reason-able for senior athletes like Sebastian Coe to be expected to comment, it seemed wrong that teenage sportsmen and women such as gymnasts should be called upon to judge the international political significance of the Russian invasion of Afghanistan. Nor could they be expected to abandon lightly their sporting hopes after at least four years of intense training, perhaps never have the chance of entering another Olympics. But for a Prime Minister it was easy to argue in favour of a boycott.

At that time, six years after I had retired from the Sports Council, I was still chairman of ICSPE which, in general, supported sporting exchanges and their separation from politics. I held no UK post that required me to make any public state-ment on the British position and I did not do so. The Sports Council, as a government grant-aided body, with its chairman, remained neutral, passing the buck to the individual sports governing bodies to make their final decision. My stance was, 'If they want to go, let them.'

Then, to my surprise, I received an invitation from the United States Ambassador to his lavish residence in Regent's Park, the former home of Barbara Hutton, the Woolworth heiress, where I would meet Lloyd Cutler. There I found myself confronted by the Ambassador and Lloyd Cutler, along with some other senior British sporting figures who were perhaps expected to be sympathetic to the government, and of course excluding Denis Howell. I immediately knew the score, that, in Ian Gow's presence, I was expected to support the government's position.

Lloyd Cutler presented us with some opening arguments. I was then invited to be the first to respond and felt I had no option but to attack the American view. It seemed to me Lloyd Cutler had vastly exaggerated when he claimed that if British athletes went to Moscow it would lead to the 'collapse of the Western world as we know it'. I had discovered that there was that very week in Moscow a delegation of businessmen from the British chemical industry, including Imperial Chemical Industries (ICI). I said it looked as though the government thought it suitable to use sportsmen as pawns in the boycott battle, because they were individuals with no power. They had dreams of success which could be sacrificed. But serious and important people involved in the economic business of the country could proceed freely and their business would not be jeopardised. I felt that it was a massive hypocrisy to ban athletes while at the same time permitting or encouraging a trade delegation. It stuck in my throat as a gross injustice. The athletes saw their hopes come crashing down after years, if not a decade, of exhausting training, in order to realise their hopes of winning Olympic glory for their own country. Olympic competition is not a purely selfish act but has effects that eddy out to athletes' families, clubs, hometowns and countries. I ended by saying the sportsmen should be free to choose to go to Moscow and that if I were in their position, I would elect to go.

As I spoke I could see Ian Gow scowl and his jaw drop; clearly he was shaken. Others spoke, but at the end of the meeting, those representing sport thanked us for our defence. Afterwards neither Lloyd Cutler nor the Ambassador nor Ian Gow said a word to me. That meeting must have convinced Lloyd Cutler he was wasting his time in Britain, and though he went on with his European tour, the stuffing had gone out of the Carter/Cutler plan.

The Moscow Games were a success in sporting terms. The British team did well: Steve Ovett and Sebastian Coe won gold medals though not at the expected distances. Ovett first won the 800m, considered Coe's natural event, but Coe ran a surprisingly ill-judged race, and then Coe responded by taking the 1,500m, at which Ovett had held the world record. What an irony that Coe, a future Conservative MP, made his sporting name at the Games which the Conservative government wanted to boycott! In the event there was not an entirely Russian or Communist bloc walkover in the Los Angeles Games of 1984, as had been expected, and in my view the world was enriched by the mix of victories from different countries which ignored the boycott.

I feel certain that however strong the boycott it would not have deflected the Russians from their Afghan adventure. I doubt if sporting boycotts have ever worked, with one possible exception – South Africa. While the economic boycott did not prevent the South Africans from getting oil elsewhere, their exclusion from world sport hit a uniquely sensitive chord and played a significant part in the eventual end of apartheid. South Africa finally returned to international competition at the Commonwealth Games in Victoria, British Columbia in 1994 and the Olympic Games in Atlanta in 1996, marked by one of its athletes winning the marathon. The latest rejection of boycotts came in August 2013. Putin, the Russian President, fulminated against homosexuals saying they would not be welcome at the Sochi Winter Olympics. Not surprisingly this sparked many voices to ask for a boycott. This would be totally unjust. It's just a little too convenient to ask our Olympians who have spent years of their lives in preparation for their big moment to make the sacrifice while everyone else carries on regardless.

John Major had a very different attitude to sport to his predecessor. His schooling ended when he was seventeen, but cricket was his main sporting interest. Sadly his own cricket career after leaving school was ended by a severe leg injury sustained in a car accident. As Prime Minister from 1990 to 1997 he consistently and vigorously promoted school sport with pleas that team games and competitive sport should be encouraged. School sport in state schools had been in rapid decline over the previous thirty years. In the 1980s, teachers had gone on strike and suspended their usual supervision of out-of-school activities, though they gained very little. After this experience, much of the profession lost any enthusiasm for standing on a sports field in the rain, blowing a whistle, especially out of hours on weekdays or at weekends. Competitive and team school sport and valuable expertise in coaching were allowed to wither away. Also, new, more liberal concepts of setting the school curriculum had practical consequences which had been disastrous for sport.

Some social scientists and psychologists had recommended that the 'concept of failure' be abolished. Competitive sport, by supposedly demoralising the less able, came to be viewed as educationally unsound. Recently, when I was talking to a group of teachers about sport, one said quite bluntly: 'It isn't our job to teach *any* skills related to particular sports or games. We are here to encourage exercise and health in a happy, non-stressful school PE (physical education) environment.' He then added something about showing approval of a 'right attitude' to what he called 'ball skills' and skill at 'balancing'.

John Major's government strengthened the focus on sport in schools and moved sports administration to the new National Heritage ministry, which among other responsibilities handled the lottery funding for the arts and sport. This proved a brilliant boon and quickly doubled the Sports Council's funding. The Conservative Sports Minister, Ian Sproat, used expert advisers from the Sports Council to produce a plan called Raising the Game, which proposed a variety of incentives for school sport and a plea for more competition and team sport. This needed a larger department to feed expert ideas back to the minister and government. In my days the Sports Council would have happily and competently undertaken a task like this, but it now has a formidable staff of nearly forty, who produced a brochure for the new plan, launched by the Prime Minister at a breakfast party at 10 Downing Street. By a kind of reverse takeover, the Sports Council was again more under the influence of government, without losing its essential independence. They work in harmony together.

In 1996, John Major and Iain Sproat asked me to chair a working group on sports scholarships for universities. My previous experience of government had made me wary of agreeing to work on a report if the government had no clear plans or possibility of implementing it. There was little point in my chairing a report asking for more money from general taxation. I did not accept the chairmanship until the minister assured me that capital expenditures could be funded from the successful National Lottery. So it looked as though any spending we might recommend had a good chance of being financed through this fresh source of finance.

I felt the wheel had come full circle since the distancing of the Sports Council from the government after the Moscow Olympics boycott. My interest in university sport was aroused by the fact that I had just finished eight years as the Master of Pembroke College, Oxford. It was evident that many elite sportsmen and women, among the 33 per cent of 18–25-year-olds now at the 120 British universities, needed some scheme to enable them to keep training at the level required for international competition. We concluded that universities clearly had to be encouraged to allow student-athletes in special cases of Olympic possibilities to take an extra year to complete their degrees. The student-athletes also needed scholarships. There was evidence that financial and academic problems had led many athletes to abandon their sports careers leading to a great waste of rare sporting talent, which the country can ill afford to lose.

It was a happy task which in its course led me to look at the American and German sports scholarship systems. The American system acts as an effective screening process for sporting talent. But unlike the proposed English system, the academic qualifications for sportsmen and women in many American universities are minimal, and at some American universities the graduation rate for sports scholars is shockingly low, under 20 per cent. Attempts are now being made in America to withhold the right to give sports scholarships at universities which fail to ensure those on sports scholarships graduate. We concluded that we should neither go down this route nor the German one of funding through town sports clubs but rather devise our own scheme. This was to be funded by the sports councils from lottery funds, coordinated by the United Kingdom sports council, and linked to the proposed national academy of sport. The main plank of what we recommended was that scholars should gain acceptance to a university solely on academic grounds and only then negotiate a sports scholarship with their university and the governing body of their sport, but not dependent on loans. Given that their university tuition and maintenance were already provided, we recommended scholarships worth some £10,000 per year (£15,000 in today's values), depending on the training and equipment needs of their given sport. The government changed in 1997 before these recommendations could be implemented, but the new Labour administration launched its own scheme of incentives for younger athletes which incorporated many features of my own committee's approach.

These different roles and my medical background have given me a chance to observe sport's influence in Britain and abroad for more than sixty years. Some commentators fear sport is in decline, and some have dismissed it as essentially trivial.

My view is that sport has proved a strong and enduring force for good. In most countries it has helped free women from the confines of dress and custom that before prevented them from realising their full potential as individuals and contributors to their societies. A dramatic moment came in 1919 when Suzanne

Lenglen, abandoning the corset, wore a long skirt to play in the final at Wimbledon, and won with her skill and strength. Now the Olympics include a 3,000m steeplechase event and a marathon for women, which in the past were thought to be too strenuous and would in some ill-defined way damage their bodies.

Sport has changed our concept of disability, as serious athletes competed in the Paralympics taking place alongside the Olympic Games in 2012. These individuals show everyone how successfully they have defied and overcome terrible setbacks and can inspire others with similar disabilities to do the same.

I believe sport has also reduced ethnic and social divisions. Sporting events draw people together to celebrate strength, skill and speed and leave aside other distinctions. Young people from all countries and levels of wealth, run and play soccer and other games, many without expensive training or facilities, and the best finally meet as equals in international competition.

Sport has contributed to many academic disciplines, though this is rarely acknowledged. Attempts to climb Everest opened a whole new field of altitude physiology and medicine. Studying athletes at extremes of exertion has both helped them improve and added to our understanding of patients' response to the stress of severe illness. A resurgence in human physiology has analysed athletes' sudden release of energy and the changes to electrolytes and fluids in their muscles and whole new spheres of physics and biomechanics have emerged from studying competitors in field events.

Finally, in societies where sport is prevalent at all ages and levels, health improves, the diseases of affluence are fought and youthful aggression is healthily diverted. Those in government and the intellectuals who influence them should realise this, provide adequate funds for sport and avoid the kind of destructive neglect which lets schools sell playing fields and discard exercise as part of every pupil's day.

Chapter 15

Medical Work: St Mary's and the National

For twenty-five years until I returned to Oxford I worked at both the National Hospital and St Mary's, conducting outpatient clinics and ward rounds at each twice a week. The two appointments were a welcome culmination of almost seventeen years of training in Oxford and London. I count myself lucky to have found appointments which enabled me not only to do clinical work but also to research, lecture and publish medical papers and books. Along with my commitments at the National at St Mary's, I provided a weekly clinic at the Western Ophthalmic Hospital in the Marylebone Road. In the human embryo, the retina arises as an extrusion from the fore-brain, and so when some brain diseases occur, changes seen in the retina mirror what is happening to the blood vessels of the brain itself.

St Mary's holds a special affection for me not only as the hospital where I studied and worked since I was twenty-one, but also because it has mirrored almost every development in British medicine over the last 150 years. The hospital came into existence by virtue of Victorian private philanthropy. In the 1820s the wealthy citizens of Bayswater were appalled by the tented camps of the navvies digging the Grand Union Canal's basin and later constructing the railway terminus at Paddington. First there was a mere dispensary for the sick and then the main hospital was gradually built, with its large, high-ceilinged wards, which it was hoped would help prevent the spread of infectious disease from patient to patient.

Gradually, over the last century, Victorian medicine gave way to a more scientific approach, prompted by the founding of the medical school. It had a stuttering start in 1850 as a breakaway school from St George's, after a lecturer there was involved in a quarrel. For many years the school struggled to survive. Women students were accepted briefly in the 1920s, but then they were excluded again until the Second World War, rather shamefully because the male students objected.

The sportsmen of St Mary's included Arthur Porritt, a Rhodes Scholar from New Zealand who won a bronze medal in the 100m in the Paris Olympics of 1924 and was portrayed in *Chariots of Fire*. In the 1930s, Porritt (later Lord Porritt) became one of the hospital's three consultant surgeons. He was followed at St Mary's by another New Zealand Rhodes Scholar, Jack Lovelock, who won the Olympic 1,500m final in Berlin during his time at the hospital.

In the post-war days, our most famous rugby player was J. P. R. Williams, the fullback who became a Lions player and captain of Wales. He had won a scholarship to Millfield School before coming to St Mary's. It was a measure of his sporting versatility that he could equally well have been a professional tennis player. His career was as an orthopaedic surgeon in charge of a sports injury clinic in Wales.

The full-time dean of St Mary's Hospital Medical School for sixteen years until 1995 was Professor Peter Richards. Under his guidance the school received more applicants for each student place than any other medical school in the United Kingdom. It also won more London University gold medals than any other London medical school.

The medical school has a worldwide reputation for immunology since Alexander Fleming's discovery of penicillin. The immunologist Professor Rodney Porter won a Nobel Prize in 1972 for determining the chemical structure of antibodies. Sir George Pinker added a different distinction as the royal obstetrician, supervising royal births in the hospital's private Lindo Wing. Most recently, in 2013, under the care of George Pinker's successor, the Duchess of Cambridge gave birth to her son Prince George Alexander Louis, fourth in line to the throne.

I have witnessed many transformations in the National Health Service. My first medical committee meeting was at St Mary's Hospital in 1964. The hospital management was in the hands of a retired wartime colonel with an MC, the house governor, who sat unobtrusively and mostly silent, only speaking when asked questions of fact. The then chairman hardly ever deferred to him for his contribution to the discussion. I was frankly shocked by the discourtesy of one my senior colleagues, who adopted a condescending tone and seemed to regard the administrator as 'the enemy'. The management functions of St Mary's Hospital were entrusted to a small team consisting of the house governor and a few secretaries, supplemented by heads of departments such as the chief finance officer. Clearly, in the 1960s, hospitals were still largely run by consultants for consultants. The days of consultant dominance are now well and truly over. A problem today is that consultants unfortunately are increasingly busy and are less willing to devote enough time to helping the administrators.

For my first fifteen years as a consultant we all had lunch together, which enabled us to discuss difficulties in diagnosis of patients and the appropriate investigation and treatment advice without the necessity of asking for a written formal consultation from each other. I probably learnt more during those lunches than from any textbooks or journals. Sadly this privilege was clearly regarded as elitist and therefore divisive by the hospital management and was abolished in a fit of egalitarianism. Patients suffered because it was clearly improper and impossible to engage in any conversation about patients in a common dining area in the company of a variety of health service staff, doctors, nurses, management and porters.

My views on the management of the health service may be biased as they rest on my observations as a consultant. First I should make it clear that I have always regarded myself as a firm supporter of the National Health Service. It is the best, cheapest health service in the world and if seriously ill there is no doubt that I would wish to be treated in a health service bed in Britain.

I was elected to serve a term as chairman of the medical committee at St Mary's Hospital between 1983 and 1985, and the experience gave me fresh insights into the problems of administration. I appreciated the immense difficulty in the management of the NHS. It is not a business and cannot be run as one. The response to changes by management is frequently unpredictable.

My experience of hospital administration was enlarged by serving for five years on the management committee of the King's Fund for London hospitals. This organisation was founded in 1897, by Edward, then Prince of Wales. At present it has a research staff of some 200 experts engaged in the study of the functioning of London hospitals but also reaching conclusions relevant to other hospitals around the country. Later I remained on the council. As the medical trustee of Leeds Castle I was able to organise conferences in collaboration with the Kings Fund directed towards problems facing the health service. The King's Fund was able to embark on research which was critical of government directives, even if on occasion the government had itself contributed to the funding of the research. The King's Fund has rightly always valued its independence from government.

One frustrating aspect of committee work at St Mary's was the difficulty of planning a much-needed new hospital wing. We had prepared, from our own private trust funds, plans for the new hospital, but owing to recurrent national financial crises they were turned down, even though the cost of the new wing would be borne at least in part by releasing the site of the old Paddington General Hospital. Finally, at the end of one financial year, the house governor received a phone call from the department asking, 'Do you have plans ready and can you start building immediately?' The answer was 'yes' and the building was started, which became the new Queen Mary Elizabeth, Queen Mother Wing.

By the time I retired almost all new hospital building projects were undertaken by the mechanism of the Private Funding Initiative (PFI). This was a device to keep the capital expenditure 'off the balance sheet'. These deals, whereby the private sector provided finance, were supposed to leave the financiers as the lender of last resort. In practice, hospitals could not be allowed to become bankrupt so this function still lay with the government. The new hospitals were certainly built 'on budget and on time' but high charges were levied by the promoting consortium. The annual charges were set for a thirty-year term and the rates were set so high that a number of PFI schemes have led the hospitals into bankruptcy. After thirty years, when the hospital reverts to the ownership of the National Health Service, hospital needs and procedures will have changed so much that the buildings will be of doubtful value. The department is now attempting to renegotiate some of these schemes.

Another change which affected the hospital experience, both for doctors and patients, was the introduction of the so-called 'internal market' by the minister Kenneth Clarke under the Thatcher government. Under their Bill, a separation was created between purchasers and providers. An 'internal market' approach to health care resulted in the tendency for health-care professionals to be valued for the income which they could generate. This was completely at odds with the previous spirit of the NHS in general and of St Mary's in particular. In relation to the blanket introduction of the 'internal market', surely it would have been wiser to start a pilot scheme first before intro-ducing a nationwide scheme which proved to be both costly and divisive and which the next government changed. The problem of introducing reforms with a pilot scheme, as every administrator knows, is that a pilot scheme is potent at arousing the opposition to change, which may stifle a scheme which on a national scale might otherwise be desirable. Scotland followed suit in implementing the purchaser/provider scheme in the 1990s, but reverted to the old principle of a single health board for each area after devolution.

We have come a long way since the founding of the health service in 1948 when some – including its founder, Aneurin Bevan – naively believed that as a result of management improvements and better early treatment, the cost of the service might even fall. Those of us who were consultants in the '70s and '80s were doing our best to sustain the original optimism with which we had entered the National Health Service. But we found ourselves reeling under each fresh reorganisation, without having a chance to absorb the shock of the previous one. Some, less kindly, used the term 'disreorganisation'. For example, Sir Keith Joseph, who was perhaps the most 'open' Health Minister of the 1970s, made an attempt to impose on the health service a three-tier reorganisation similar to their system of local government. Sir Keith later had the grace to say that it had been a mistake. A fine time to tell us! Eventually the attempt was abandoned. Once I heard a very senior administrator of the NHS comment on his major reform, the introduction of fundholding for general practitioners, that he would be 'very interested to see if fundholding worked'. Any attempts at reform were hardly helped by the feeling that successive ministers were 'birds of passage'. Of the twelve consecutive ministers in the 1970s and '80s, only two stayed longer than two years.

Hospital relations in the 1980s were riven by trouble with the trade unions. At some stages it looked as though the hospital porters' trade union was determining the hospital's work. An acquaintance who was a professor of surgery at another teaching hospital, when told the unions were refusing to bring a patient up to the operating theatre, took off his mask and gown, went down to the ward, put the patient on a trolley, took the patient to the operating theatre, operated, then took him back again.

When I was chairman of the medical committee at St Mary's, the hospital porters were refusing to wear uniforms, using the excuse that they had 'lost' them. They appeared in all manner of sloppy clothing without any name badges. I discussed what might be done with our general manager Barbara Young. She sent the porters a letter saying that if they did not find their uniforms and wear them, the cost of the clothing would be deducted from their next week's pay. Surprise, surprise, the next day they appeared in their uniforms. I felt this was a major triumph.

Another instance of union action struck closer to home. A close friend of Moyra's was dying in the hospital. Moyra was speaking to her on the telephone when the switchboard operator interrupted to say, 'This does not seem to be a strictly medical call and so I'm cutting you off.'

Over the last twenty years all governments have been concerned about the cost of the NHS. I remember seeing a TV interview with Prime Minister Blair in which his interrogator asked him whether he knew that the expenditure on the National Health Service in Britain was in fact lower than most major European countries. Blair seemed surprised and promised that the UK expenditure on health would at least be brought up to the European average, then 7 per cent of GDP. When the Chancellor of the Exchequer Gordon Brown heard of this 'promise' he commented that the PM had not made a promise, only an 'aspiration'. Brown's expenditure was of course much smaller than America's, which was some 15 per cent of GDP. In America a large section of the spending, perhaps as much as a quarter, was eaten up by the administrative costs of insurance companies and private health maintenance organisations. This high American spending level is even more remarkable in that 30 million Americans (more than 10 per cent of the population) are still left without effective health care other than emergency treatment, and the quality of medical care outside major cities is uneven. President Obama's beleaguered health-care Bill eventually came into effect at the beginning of 2014.

The supposed deficiencies of the National Health Service are held up as a warning in America. One major difference is that in the UK, within the health service, patients do not usually choose individual consultants to treat them, as is the case in the United States. In my view this is not a significant disadvantage and applying this principle adds considerably to the expense of the American system.

From the 1980s and '90s the health services faced rising patient expectations, especially as expensive new treatments became available, and an increasing immigrant population. Also, the increased longevity of the population led to increasing demand for hip and other joint replacements, coronary bypasses and treatment of abdominal and cerebral aneurysms. Improvements in anaesthesia enabled surgeons to tackle more difficult, lengthy and potentially dangerous operations, leading to an increased demand. The pattern of care also changed. For example, patients with massive heart attacks would have been allowed to die peacefully in my early days as a house physician. These patients were now given intravenous drugs, and 'cardioversion' was used to restart their hearts. On the other side of the equation, as a house physician I had patients with peptic ulcers who previously would have remained on a milk drip for six weeks. Nowadays, the treatment, given on an outpatient basis, is an antibiotic to kill the *Helicobacter pylori*, which is now thought to be the cause of peptic ulcers in most patients. Nearly all patients now pass through the hospital more quickly than the leisurely pace that prevailed in the 1960s.

In recent years, St Mary's has been in danger of losing some of its special character as it has been merged with other hospitals, on the grounds that larger groupings are more efficient and can deliver better care at a lower cost. St Mary's Hospital

Medical School has joined a group of institutions led by Imperial College, along with Charing Cross and Westminster Hospitals and Medical Schools and the Royal Postgraduate Medical School and the Hammersmith Hospital. This group, named the Imperial College of Science, Technology and Medicine, is now one of the largest medical schools in Britain and is one of the largest combined medical and scientific institutions in the world, rivalling the Massachusetts Institute of Technology and Medicine in Boston. Along with Oxford and Cambridge, Imperial College has the highest ratings for medical research in the UK.

One feature of St Mary's Hospital which increases my confidence in its future is that has always been the least parochial of the London hospitals. It welcomes outside applicants for its consultant posts so that during my career there, most of my colleagues were not St Mary's-trained. This liberal outlook will sensibly benefit what may well be difficult years ahead.

While doing my clinical training at St Mary's I was busy writing up papers for the *Journal of Physiology* on the control of breathing, based on my MSc thesis. The research done in Aden was continued in a climatic heat chamber at the London Hospital for Hygiene and Tropical Medicine in Bloomsbury, the grim effects of which I described earlier. The results were published in *The Lancet*. I showed that heat illness associated with cessation of sweating, hyperpyrexia and possible death could be due to an infection raising the setting of the brain thermostat.

Until 1970 I collaborated with a number of colleagues at the National Hospital in a number of different fields – cerebrovascular disease, neuroradiology, neurochemistry and neurophysiology

– in order to increase my understanding of these specialties. This experience served me in good stead in my neurological teaching and also when preparing new editions of *Brain's Clinical Neurology*. I accepted the editorship and revision of this major textbook at Lord Brain's request. *Brain's Clinical Neurology* in its two editions under Lord Brain had become a small but well-favoured text for candidates for membership of the Royal College of Physicians. It was meant to be easily readable but much fuller than the neurological sections of general medical textbooks. I enjoyed revising it and it gave me the stimulus to keep up to date in different fields of neurology beyond those in which I was actually researching. Most weekends I would gather the medical and neurological journals published during the week and keep a file index of papers of interest, so that every five years or so, when the time came for the next revision, my task was made easier.

The pictures I gathered for the book were added to my collection of slides needed for giving lectures. Despite my specialisation in the autonomic nervous system I was happy to lecture on other common neurological topics in which I had formed a strong interest, particularly the dementias, eye disease in neurology and Parkinson's disease. It is a strange irony that I myself now have Parkinson's disease.

Despite my efforts to control the size of the book, which was later retitled *Brain and Bannister's Clinical Neurology*, it has grown steadily over the years from 400 to 800 pages. By 1992 when I edited the seventh edition, the task had become too great for a single author, so that became the last edition. The book had sold well over the years, with editions in many languages including Spanish and Polish. It was particularly popular in Scandinavia and America and also in India, where special low-cost editions were published.

These projects were interludes while I began to establish the laboratory for an autonomic investigation unit in a room, at first little larger than a broom cupboard, at the National Hospital in 1968. I could now embark on what became my lifelong research interest into the autonomic nervous system. My intention was to follow Claude Bernard's dictum: 'Disease represents an experiment of nature from which the physician may profit.' I hired a physiological technician and offered a testing service for my colleagues' patients. This grew rapidly in a few years, as it was the only such laboratory in the UK at that time. By the time I retired, patients were referred from all parts of this country and abroad.

I had first become interested in this field of research in 1948 while I was a student in Oxford. I had visited Stoke Mandeville and had seen the problems arising in paraplegic patients in which the sympathetic nervous output was cut off by transection of the spinal cord. It was my quite deliberate choice of a relatively neglected field that lay at the interface of neurology with general medicine. This made the autonomic nervous system very suitable for a research programme, by comparison with neurological diseases like multiple sclerosis and Parkinsonism, which already attracted large and better-financed research teams at the National Hospital.

What is the autonomic nervous system? It is the parts of the brain, spinal cord and the peripheral nervous system which innervate the whole body – that is, supply the body with special nerves. As the American physiologist Walter Cannon described it, 'It is that part of the nervous system which Providence in its wisdom decided should be outside the range of voluntary control.' In man and other mammals, there are two balancing systems: the sympathetic and the parasympathetic. The sympathetic system is required for the body's response to risk, the so-called 'fight or flight' system. Counterbalancing this is the parasympathetic system, which is concerned with the restorative functions of the body, like digestion. The dual parasympathetic–sympathetic systems innervate every organ of the body. Everyone is aware that their heartbeat is strengthened as muscles prepare for vigorous contraction, the fight or flight impulse. Incidentally, it was of course the system on which I relied for my races as an athlete, with the sympathetic nervous system going into overdrive during the last part of the race.

The fact that the autonomic nervous system innervates every organ in the body means that it provides a fertile source for our investigation of patients. The immediate presenting symptom we were concerned with, postural hypotension (a fall in blood pressure on standing), was like the tip of an iceberg with much deeper underlying abnormalities. We studied cerebral circulation, the eye and pupil, the lungs, the digestive system, the heart, the bladder and the urinary function. For each of these functions investigative techniques were devised and, where appropriate, treatment developed.

This may be the point at which I should make a comment about the common emotional disturbance of fainting. Its purpose is still not properly understood, but emotional stresses, like the sight of blood, or even the sight of a hypodermic needle, may cause a student nurse or medical student to faint on their first exposure to the wards. Everyone knows there is a link between emotion and heart rate. As Wordsworth wrote, 'My heart leaps up when I behold / a rainbow in the sky,' and many a lover will have the same sensation if they so much as think of their beloved. In addition to this psychological input, the Victorian fashion for wickedly tight corsetry, even in pregnancy, contributed, though smelling salts were always conveniently available to Victorian ladies. For centuries, there have been 'epidemics' of fainting and feelings of weakness in institutions, in which no unequivocal medical basic defect has ever been detected. One of the most remarkable of these started in 1955 and was labelled the 'Royal Free Disease'. Lassitude and weakness affected a large number of the staff at that hospital. In due course most of the sufferers recovered. No cause was ever found. The 'chronic fatigue syndrome' may prove to be another example of this. Some physicians still believe that these diseases have an organic entity, but the jury is still out.

Fainting in an institution has a high element of suggestibility. In the 1940s at a famous girls' school, an escalating number of girls 'fainted' on successive days when they stood for hymns in the morning assembly. The powerful headmistress then announced at prayers, 'There will be no more fainting.' Next day, only a few girls fainted, and the 'epidemic' was over.

The starting point of my research was a report from America in 1960 on two patients in whom postural hypotension was a leading feature, and in whom, after their deaths, it was found that there was a degeneration of particular cells of the spinal cord. These cells are the final pathway of the sympathetic neurones, and if destroyed, the patient's capacity to constrict the blood vessels in the leg on standing led to postural hypotension. By 1967 I had published a paper on a number of patients with the same symptoms but with different neurological lesions.

In simple terms, I realised that what was needed was a form of stress test for the autonomic nervous system which would simplify the methods of finding out which part of the system might be failing. By luck, one day at the National Hospital I saw that the neighbouring Great Ormond Street hospital was replacing an old motorised paediatric tilt table used for radiography. It was exactly what I wanted in order to tilt patients safely into the upright position while measuring blood pressure and other cardiac functions. An electric motor gave a standard rate of tilt. This tilt table is still in use in our department nearly fifty years later. The tilt table had a strap which was placed round the patient's chest like a seatbelt, to prevent any falling. Over the years we included monitoring blood pressure through non-invasive means, with an inflatable finger cuff, and together with measurements of cardiac function, this enabled us to build up a picture of any patient's autonomic stability.

In 1970, I was asked to give the Savile Lecture at the West End Hospital for Nervous Diseases and I chose the subject 'Autonomic Failure and Disorders of the Autonomic Nervous System'. This was a chance to review the whole scene of autonomic disorders and was published in *The Lancet* in 1972.

My first collaborator at St Mary's in the 1970s was Dr Peter Sever, the Professor of Pharmacology who had mastered the technique for measuring plasma noradrenalin not hitherto possible. Not surprisingly, we found this reduced in patients with autonomic failure, but the degree of reduction varied depending on whether the patient was lying or standing, and this threw some light on the site of the lesion. This research was submitted for publication in *Brain* in 1977, but owing to the delay for refereeing, an American group published this important result ahead of us. This was one of my earlier introductions to the competitive nature of clinical research.

All clinical research involves collaboration but for me the most enduring and rewarding collaboration has been with my colleague Chris Mathias, an Oxford Rhodes Scholar from India.

His PhD research thesis involved some studies of disturbances of cardiovascular function in spinal cord-injured patients with autonomic defects. I was his examiner and quickly realised his unusual ability. He continued his training at St Mary's Hospital. We worked closely together for nearly twenty years, until my retirement in 1993. He was appointed to a personal chair of neurovascular medicine at St Mary's Hospital, in recognition of his distinction. He took over the direction of the Autonomic Investigation Unit at the National Hospital, Queen Square, when I retired in 1993, and it is a source of great pleasure to me that it has expanded in a remarkable way under his direction.

The partnership was an ideal one in that Professor Mathias's expertise in cardiovascular medicine neatly complemented my own training as a physiologist and neurologist. Our intention was to apply to the whole range of autonomic disorders highly focused investigations of different organs of the body. The first paper in which he was a co-author was published in 1980 and together we published some eighty research papers. Of course, there is no particular merit in the number of papers written but this is an indication of the wide range of opportunities presented by this new field of study.

A number of observations were made linking up what were previously termed 'medically unexplained symptoms' and, in many cases, forming a firm basis for treatment. For example, some patients presented with postural hypotension only after meals. This was found to be due to abnormalities of gut and other peptides. After treatment with a drug, octreotide, which prevents the release of vasoactive peptides, their symptoms improved. This disability had revealed the early stages of chronic autonomic failure. This is a collection of several neurological abnormalities which indicate a definite clinical entity, though as yet we have been unable to discover the cause.

Another instance of early diagnosis of chronic autonomic failure was the observation of postural hypotension after exercise. One patient was a fireman who complained of dizziness after climbing ladders, a handicap which naturally made it impossible to do his job. He was one of a number of patients complaining of dizziness during and after exercise. This proved to be due to the increase in blood flow in active muscles during exercise, not counteracted by an appropriate increase in sympathetic activity. The postural hypotension after exercise in these patients unmasked the early stages of chronic autonomic failure. In the case of the fireman, his symptoms may have been aggravated by the heat of a fire.

Our particular study was of 'fainting' which patients also described as 'blackouts' and 'funny turns'. Attacks were occasionally found to be due to the well-recognised syndrome of hypersensitivity of nerve receptors in the wall of the carotid artery stimulated by the patient wearing a tight collar or looking upwards. When the carotid sinus was surgically denervated, the attacks ceased. These patients are now described under the heading of 'autonomically mediated syncope'.

One patient had had more than 400 visits to A&E departments before he was referred to us and a diagnosis could be made, and appropriate treatment prevented the attacks. In some patients in whom attacks involved both a fall in blood pressure and slowing of the heart, cardiac pacemakers were inserted, but these patients occurred less often if the autonomic defect was properly investigated.

Our work also led to the recognition of some exceedingly rare disorders. For example, one patient with postural hypotension proved to have dopamine beta hydroxylase deficiency, of which only fourteen cases in the world have been described. Though rare, such diseases often offer disproportionately promising research opportunities. Our first patient was a young man in his twenties, itself unusual as most patients with postural hypotension were over fifty. He had no detectable noradrenalin or adrenalin in the blood, but high levels of dopamine. This led to the diagnosis of a deficiency of the enzyme converting dopamine to noradrenalin and adrenalin, and hence the high levels of dopamine. The patient's sister also had a similar defect. They were the first affected siblings reported and Professor Mathias has been treating them with the drug L-DOPS, which bypasses the missing enzyme. For more than twenty years they have been able to lead full lives.

In the last decade since I retired, Professor Mathias and his team have continued to define a number of previously unrecognised or misdiagnosed disorders and contributed substantially to improving their treatment. One of these is the disorder known as postural orthostatic tachycardia syndrome (POTS), when the patient's heart rate rises excessively while standing, causing dizziness, palpitations and in some cases loss of consciousness. It is common among young people. In some patients there are links with other medical disorders and they are referred to numerous specialists and have unnecessary investigations, usually without adequate treatment. The condition now accounts for 40 per cent of new referrals to the autonomic unit. The Autonomic Investigation Unit and the St Mary's Hospital Unit have increased much in size. There are now eleven clinical autonomic scientists with three consultants, in addition to academic staff and research fellows from different parts of the world. There are a number of junior, intermediate and senior clinical support staff, who are kept busy with the ever increasing demand for autonomic services. The number of autonomic tests undertaken in the past year exceeded 2,400. Recently, the University College and Middlesex Hospitals Trust have been discussing a major grant to the Autonomic Investigation Unit.

It is difficult to express the pleasure this collaboration with Professor Mathias has given me. When I received the American Academy of Neurology's first Lifetime Achievement Award in 2005, it was a reflection of our joint cooperative work. This is now evidenced by the recent edition of our textbook titled *Autonomic Failure: A Textbook of the Disorders of the Autonomic Nervous System*, of which Professor Mathias is now the senior editor. The book now costs more than £200 and is 2,000 pages long – hardly a students' vade mecum, but a necessary reference book for medical libraries around the world. A British autonomic research society I established in 1982 now has counterparts in many countries, including America, Canada, Australia, France, Italy and Japan. Professor Mathias is now himself about to retire, with justified satisfaction that the autonomic nervous system is no longer a neglected area of medicine, lying forgotten between neurology, cardiology and general medicine.

꽃

The National Hospital, where I served a term as chairman of the medical committee in the 1980s, put itself forward with proposals to become an independent trust. Though we were financially viable, the political tide favouring trusts had turned against us and our proposals were twice turned down by the Health Minister.

As a merger was required, the only valid option was to merge with University College and the Middlesex Hospitals. This complex was undergoing major rebuilding on Gower Street. We had worries about the financing of this change but these were unfounded and the National Hospital with its unique research and clinical skills has continued to flourish. Today, it seems that the University College and Middlesex Trust regards the National Hospital as a jewel in its crown.

There are moves in the NHS to group some specialist services at regional or national centres in order to save money and increase efficiency. We are making a case for our units at the National and at St Mary's Hospital combining at the National Hospital and undertaking autonomic investigations of referred patients who have suffered from faints and falls seeking help in Accident and Emergency departments. Such patients form one-third of the non-traumatic patients attending A&E departments. These conditions understandably cause alarm among GPs, who fear they may be missing a serious disorder such as a brain tumour. In practice, many of these patients do not have any life-threatening condition but if seen by inexperienced doctors in A&E may be over-investigated, causing the patients inconvenience and the National Health Service unnecessary expense. Our proposal would include creating an algorithm for A&E departments consisting of a series of questions and simple tests which can establish a basis for either reassuring the patient and returning them to the GP, or on the other hand referring them to our own special unit.

It is only human to be grateful that our efforts are recognised, even though I have stressed that this whole area of autonomic disorders is but a very small part of the spectrum of medical disease. It happens to be one that has held its fascination for half my life, representing thirty years of enjoyable work, rather than the eight short years of my running life as a student.

Over the years of my neurological training, clinical work and research at the National Hospital and St Mary's, I have formed a great feeling of loyalty to these institutions. It was my great good fortune to find in medicine and neurology my true vocation and to be able to pursue it in these fine institutions for most of my working life. I feel such affection for the familiar buildings, the wards and all the staff. They evoke strong memories of qualifying as a doctor and then becoming a consultant. There followed friendships formed during shared projects, the satisfaction of correctly diagnosing some obscure ailments, and some unexpectedly thrilling moments when we shared new insights into the brain's miraculous complexity and power. The success of health care depends on the high aspiration of the medical and nursing staff and on their determination to advance medical knowledge and at the same time provide both compassionate and expert patient care, and so sustain the long and honourable tradition of British medicine. My colleagues, by their hard work and persistence, overcame many setbacks and constraints without losing their intellectual curiosity or their good cheer.

Chapter 16

Return to Oxford

One Sunday in 1984, we were having a celebratory lunch for Clive's twenty-sixth birthday and I had a phone call from an Oxford friend who was a doctor and himself a fellow of an Oxford college. He said, 'Would you allow your name to be considered for the mastership of Pembroke College, Oxford?' To receive the invitation was a surprise, of course. Oxford had been the foundation of my early life and is one of the world's leading universities. Its success was largely founded on a collegiate system in which I strongly believed, as it gave students a very high level of teaching and honed their skills in social responsibility. My London medical life had developed steadily over twenty-five years but most of my new satisfactions arose from my research interest in the autonomic nervous system and not from increasing administrative roles.

The Archangel Gabriel could hardly possess all of the qualities the governing body first seeks in a new Master, but, as reality prevails, the fellows may find their breadth of choice narrows. Now any head of college faces the problem of helping the college raise the funds needed to sustain the classic 'Oxford tradition' of weekly single or paired tutorials. This style is expensive, approaching £16,000 per student, more than the official fees, now at £9,000 a year.

A week later, three Pembroke dons came to visit our home in London to tell me more about what would be expected of me. Both sides had questions to ask. I passionately wanted to continue with my research in London and the dons said that it would not cause any problems if I came to London two days a week. Moyra felt in her short encounter with the dons that one of them pretty well intimated that they did not want a 'Mrs Proudie' – that bossy, interfering bishop's wife in Trollope's *Barchester Towers*.

For the final part of the selection process, Moyra and I were asked to dine at the college and stay overnight. Moyra bought a safe, discreet Jaeger outfit, I wore my Vincent's Club tie, and we set off with some disquiet. I was to be interviewed by the dons while Moyra was shown the Master's lodgings. In my interview, I was questioned for three-quarters of an hour on my views on university education and on the challenges of fundraising, including the planning of a new building. Moyra's experience was somewhat more peculiar. As she was being shown round the Master's lodgings the lights would not come on and all that could be done was to peer into the pitch-black rooms. Then Christchurch's Great Tom bell rang, reverberating through the lodgings. Moyra murmured some question about it to her guide and the fleeting look on the don's face for a brief moment disturbed her. It was almost a look of panic. We learnt later that the wife of one previous Master found the bell's reverberation through her home intolerable, and left.

Moyra joined me after my interview and together we crossed the quadrangle. Lights, coloured by the glass, shone through the windows of the hall, out across the wide lawn. It was a beautiful scene that I came to love over the years. At dinner we were seated at opposite ends of the high table, and a senior scholar then recited the college's Latin grace. Moyra then found that suddenly a huge silver platter had appeared at her elbow, piled high with whitebait, with a strange head just behind it. This so unnerved her that the whitebait she was lifting skittered across the table. The face she had seen belonged to a college servant who was an achondroplasiac dwarf, much loved by the fellows. She wondered whether her clumsiness had queered our pitch.

Since leaving Oxford in 1951 I had made a point of retaining my links with three colleges at which I had held appointments: an Amelia Jackson scholarship at Exeter, a Harmsworth senior scholarship at Merton and a Radcliffe Travelling Fellowship at University College. So I had some idea of what being a head of college involved. Though undoubtedly a position of privilege, it was no longer the sinecure it might have been half a century before. It involved hard work, including fundraising, and Pembroke was a poor college. I already knew a few of the existing heads of the thirty-two Oxford colleges. Appointing a new head of college was the moment when fellows had a sense of their power, making a decision of such great importance to their own lives and the future of the college. Though most choices were successful, occasionally some dreadful mistakes were made, usually through a misunderstanding by each side of what the post entailed. A few heads of house left the post early and abruptly. One thought his wife was badly treated; another died in office, probably harried to his grave by a don of such a bizarre and contrary nature that he blighted the whole governing body. Another, who had held prestigious posts in the outside world, found the college's atmosphere 'suffocating' and the administrative support too meagre. If the candidate had been an ambassador or Permanent Secretary with a large staff, it tended to be a rude shock when they realised the slow grinding procedures which sometimes must be tolerated before change can be brought about in the college or the university.

Through all my hospital and sports council work, I had striven to give my all and it would be fair to say I worked as hard for Pembroke as I have ever done. As an undergraduate many years before I had been oblivious of all the necessary obligations needed to keep a college on an even keel, let alone the links with a huge university. I had to learn at speed the college's inner workings. First came the governing body, which made all the decisions. I quickly realised that subcommittees tackling any problems and ironing out any wrinkles were much more likely to win the day than if it was left to the meeting itself. This has led some heads of house to describe their role as having responsibility without power. He or she is the public face of the college through any crisis. I rapidly learnt that ordering the agenda was almost as important as choosing its content, and there was no substitute for the careful preparation of all issues. The vicegerent was second in command, only acting if the Master was ill or abroad. The dean was the disciplinary head for undergraduates; the senior tutor, the academic adviser; and the bursar of the college, in addition to the financial control, was in charge of the staff, numbering about 100. The Master was expected to deal with any disagreements between fellows. My tasks as Master were many and varied – some easy but some, like the creation of change, difficult.

It was the start of eight complicated, ever interesting but taxing years there, living in a house built by Cardinal Wolsey, which had existed for some 300 years as an almshouse for the deserving soldiers and sailors, rather similar to the Chelsea Pensioners. The grandest room had once been a soup kitchen with steps leading up to it at the city's south gate. As Americans might say, 'It reeked history!'.

At an Oxford college, the only person higher in authority is known as the Visitor – a role set up in each college's original statutes. Several colleges have the Archbishop of Canterbury as the Visitor, some the Queen and some, including Pembroke, the university's chancellor. In my time this was Harold Macmillan, by then Lord Stockton. My inauguration as head of house by the Visitor, to which I invited my children, took place in Broadgates Hall, the seventeenth-century heart of the college. I had to promise in Latin with the words '*Do Fidem*' that I would do what was right and proper to uphold the honour of the office of Master of Pembroke and Lord Stockton then assigned to me the powers of that office. The vow was then repeated before all of the fellows in the college chapel. Such ceremonies may seem old-fashioned, but adapting the words of Edmund Burke on society, a college is a partnership not only between those who are present, but between those who have gone before and those who are yet to come.

Harold Macmillan at that point was in his eighties, frail and almost blind, but had developed a deliberate style in speeches in which initial hesitancy as he warmed up was followed by wit and elegance. As someone whose own family life had not been happy, he had turned to Oxford as a place where as an undergraduate he had been successful. But he did tell me he could not bear to return to Oxford for twenty years after he left because of the memories of so many of his contemporaries at Balliol who had been killed in the First World War. In 1914, young men in Oxford immediately volunteered and were put in Guards and infantry regiments and were decimated. He said German snipers picked them out by officers' cap badges before they were issued with steel helmets. The years had eased his pain and he now came back to Oxford with relish. He was a great encouragement to us and clearly gloried in being chancellor. I could not know what the future held on that day, but I was full of optimism.

Our most famous student was Samuel Johnson, whose Reynolds portrait adorned the hall of our lodgings. He looked down at us, that sad, brilliant, anguished man. He was holding up a book to his myopic eyes. There were plenty of other great names we could explore. George Whitfield, a friend of the Wesleys, who was so eloquent that it was said 'he could move the crowd so vastly, that had he asked them to tear the eyes from their heads, they would have done so.' As time went on we learnt about a nineteenth-century Master, Francis Jeune, a young clergyman of exceeding brilliance. He was commissioned in the mid-nineteenth century when he was vice chancellor to reform the then unbelievably lax situation into which both the dons and the students had sunk. His reforms included the introduction of final examinations for all students. Not surprisingly he was fiercely opposed, as innovations and reforms can be even today in Oxford, and some astonishing counterarguments were raised. However, he was persistent and in the end he triumphed. For his pains, Jeune was shunned, according to his wife's diaries, by his fellow heads of house and their wives.

Lord Stockton, as Visitor, came to the college about twice a year for some special event. He seemed to glory in his contact with the college and its fellows. Probably as most of his own contemporaries had now died, he also felt lonely. Sometimes he would stay the night in our lodgings. After dinner, he would regale our fellows with anecdotes. After each had spent twenty minutes or so with him, they felt exhausted, and I would replace one with another. At about two o'clock, Lord Stockton showed no sign of fatigue, but when at last he came back to the lodgings, I was worried lest he sleepwalk in a strange place, so barricaded his open door with big armchairs. I listened as he fell asleep, but worried as his breathing became irregular. Then, to my alarm, his breathing stopped all together. I visualised what would happen if he died in the lodgings and my mind turned to a bulletin. 'The former Prime Minister's life drew peacefully to a close in the university he thought of as his home...' Just then, with an enormous gasp, his breathing started again. Next morning, he was as alert as ever and went on his way. Politics needs stamina and courage, and Lord Stockton had both in spades.

The Oxford of the 1920s and Evelyn Waugh was totally left behind. Most obviously, the admissions process, which in the 1920s was more often a cup of tea with the Master to decide whether the applicant was the 'right sort of chap'. By the time I became Master, the admissions process was complex, but very fair. Independent schools still had the edge over the state school applicants and captured 50 per cent of the places, though only constituting less than 10 per cent of the school sector. This is of course totally disproportionate, but for many years this imbalance has continued, as Oxford colleges refuse to lower their demands for excellence and are deaf to any government bullying, intent on social engineering. Instead, colleges have begun to send out fellows and students to speak at state schools, to encourage pupils to apply and to come to open days. Today, those admitted who do not keep up with their work are unlikely to survive for long.

Though I was sixteen when I took the entrance exams for both Oxford and Cambridge, today most apply at aged eighteen and many take a gap year so that, when they arrive in Oxford, they are more mature. I welcomed the fact that many students had a gap year, gaining experience of the world, whether teaching in Uganda or any other overseas experience which contributed to their maturity. Ninety per cent of my own Oxford contemporaries had been in the war, which gave them a different sort of maturity. The greatest change at Pembroke had been the admission of women in equal numbers as men since 1980. It is shameful to record that on the first night they came in to the hall there was much thumping on the tables, more in disapproval than approbation. During my time, there was a happy collaboration in the club activities, including sport, and the women were an unchallenged positive for the college.

There was so much to be done and I had been charged with attempting to raise funds for the new building which cost £5 million. At that time, Pembroke was one of the poorer colleges. A site had already been found by the Thames, once occupied by Oxford's gasworks until North Sea gas was found and the redundant gasworks were demolished. The ground was contaminated and the council deemed it unfit for ordinary housing, but was not averse to its use by undergraduates, who were not likely to grow cabbages! The new building was on stilts in order to reduce the toxicity. Around £2 million had already been raised, but the college had not yet even bought the land. Therefore my first steps were to complete its purchase for £400,000 and, after an architectural competition, to commission full plans. I was handed some papers purporting to show funds from Middle Eastern friends promised to my predecessor, but sadly these resources were never forthcoming.

At a governing body meeting, the fellows chose the design they most preferred, which despite severe financial constraints had to satisfy a large number of aims. There were to be 100 student rooms, three fellows' sets and a wing for student meetings in term-time and conferences during the vacations. The design introduced rooms and features not present in the main college, including a gym, a computer room, a sound-insulated music room and facilities for the disabled. As the building was bordered by the river's public tow-path, it had to be secure, and looked broadly like a castle. The chosen form of two quadrangles fitted this need very well. Finally, there was to be a planting scheme to soften the outlines and create a peaceful atmosphere.

To help with the more detailed design stages and enlist the students' enthusiasm for the project, we sent them a questionnaire. Among the things they asked for, which I thought extremely sensible, was that there should be a lot of daylight in the rooms, in contrast to the artificial lighting of many of the ancient Oxford libraries in which they worked. As far as possible we incorporated this and their other requests into the final design. Some proffered a dreamy or wishful hope that there might be a swimming pool included.

And so in 1987 the two-year building programme got under way. The governing body approved our appointment of a fundraiser; I believe the first employed by any Oxford college. There had been several crises during the building, in one of which some walls had to be rebuilt. Our fundraising was at a time when there had been one of the periodic 'busts' in the country's economy and so accumulating money went more slowly than we had anticipated. A meeting of the fellows was held at one point to consider whether we should put up only half the building for the time being. But the governing body, in full possession of the financial situation, decided to go ahead. At that stage we were helped by a scheme whereby sums of money could be borrowed free of interest and repaid over a moderate period of time (business enterprise schemes). We made maximum use of these schemes, which represented a separate way of financing that was adopted by most colleges, who by then nearly all also had development offices to increase the efficiency of their fundraising.

In June 1989, in the presence of the then Visitor, Lord Jenkins, and our distinguished foreign living alumnus, US Senator Fulbright, the new building was opened. It met the aims the governing body had set out and was both aesthetically pleasing and popular with undergraduates. We held a celebratory luncheon under large marquees in the new quadrangle. The opening coincided with both the start of Eights Week, at which Pembroke's men and women's first crews were set fair to distinguish themselves, and the arrival of a good number of our American alumni, who had been very generous to the college, though the major part of the money was British.

Few seem to know where the new building is. If you walk up the south side of the river from Folly Bridge, it is where the row of houses ends. It is surrounded by fields on two sides and the river on the third side. The new buildings mark out Pembroke College's two new quadrangles. It took four years to plan and build and was the largest Pembroke project since the hall was built in 1850. I felt my main service to the college was now completed. But fundraising still continued for new fellowships. To strengthen our links with former members of the college, I set up committees for each profession, for example committees of lawyers and doctors. In this way they could share their current professional concerns with each other and with the students. The lawyers banded together and helped to pay for the annual cost of the college's law fellow, otherwise a burden on the general endowment. We also set up a 'London committee', composed of former members who had become senior executives, civil servants or politicians, like Lord Heseltine, who could not easily come up to Oxford.

Life had to be breathed into the American alumni organisa-tion and the first person I contacted was Dr Jim Hester, a former Marine, Rhodes Scholar and then president emeritus of New York University, who became a close friend. He sponsored the hiring of a professional fundraiser who travelled around the States to find out about the Pembroke alumni and their views of the college. The campaign was formally launched with a dinner at the British Embassy in Washington, DC, attended by Senator Dick Lugar and Senator Fulbright, both chairmen of the Senate committee on Foreign Relations for many years, who had both sought the avoidance of nuclear conflict and the moderation of US aggression throughout the Cold War.

I often travelled to America in support of this fundraising effort. Usually I had been invited to give lectures at several medi-cal schools on the autonomic nervous system, and then stayed on to do my fundraising. Often at the American universities I had to experience breakfast conferences. To an Englishman, breakfast is rather early in the day to construct the thoughtful answers to difficult medical questions, especially if one is jet-lagged before the meeting. Of course I saluted America's energy in all its aspects, and in general we were overwhelmed by the hospitality of our hosts. But occasionally some event left us shocked, such as being told in Boston that when driving, if there seemed to be an accident and or victim by the roadside, we should never stop, which would have been an automatic response at that time in England. Apparently, often these hold-ups were staged by gangs to mug or hijack the good Samaritan.

I remember one particular trip to Alabama, where we stayed with an alumnus Earl Mason McGowin, one of the four McGowin brothers who had funded the building of the new library at Pembroke in 1972. This library houses all the books published by our most famous alumnus, Samuel Johnson, including his celebrated *Dictionary*. There are also other items of intriguing historical importance such as letters from Nelson as well as Dr Johnson's teapot. He was a prodigious tea drinker who praised tea as 'the cup which cheers but not inebriates'. The heat of the American summer was trying. The instinct as we felt frizzled was to open a window which provoked a violent response in our hosts, as it threw their air conditioning awry. The McGowins' wealth had come from the sale of their woodland estates, which had once been the largest lumber producing estates east of the Mississippi. 'We just like to keep a bit of forest surrounding our own house now,' he explained. I asked him what he meant by 'a little forest' and he said, 'Oh just ten thousand acres'!

In the 1920s, Earl Mason McGowin's father had acquired his own railway engine and was transported across America in a family carriage pulled by it – the equivalent of the modern private jet. The engine was now stuck, in a small clearing on railway tracks, looking very out of place with its towering smoke stack and cattle fender. Mason's younger brother, who lived next door, had his own private aerodrome and a hangar filled with a specimen of each American fighter since the start of the Second World War. We were also shown letters from members of his family describing the heartrending conditions of the American Civil War, in which four of six brothers had been killed.

Another strange event occurred in the South when a bishop, an alumnus of Pembroke, had arranged for his local black church choir to sing songs for us after dinner.

I had Moyra for company on many of these trips, just as when I had travelled with ICSPE. Looking back we were much enriched by the experience, not least as our son Thurstan was able to join us in New York, where he works in banking. His passion for all things artistic helped us to revel not only in the great Metropolitan Museum, which seemed to have added a new section each time we visited, but in all its lesser collections. That great city continued to hold our imagination for over twenty-five years. We took pleasure in the huge upturn that took hold of New York, with the lessening of crime and the planting of trees making the whole atmosphere more pleasant. Responsible for many of these changes was Mayor Bloomberg, who had introduced cycling lanes in the early mornings and at weekends. Some of these are innovations which Mayor Boris Johnson has introduced in London.

In working with the fellows as Master, my principal object was to be even-handed. Of course I wished to give greater weight to the opinions of the dons who had some special knowledge or experience of a given issue, but at no time would I allow there to be a feeling that a clique existed of those who were especially linked to me or had my ear. That was important because there were – then indeed as there are now – colleges with feuding factions; their disputes tend to come to the boil when a new head of house has been appointed. Also, the group whose favoured candidate is unsuccessful may see itself as defeated and the college may lose much of their goodwill.

The governing body is a democratic one, each fellow having an equal vote. This means that difficult decisions which need to be taken necessarily go through a long discussion period. Some senior industrialists and civil servants who have become heads of houses have been startled to find how slowly Oxford's wheels grind. There have been many attempts to reform both the colleges and the university.

The financial endowments of colleges vary drastically, so

that the richest college had an endowment many hundred times greater than Pembroke's. John Roberts, former warden of Merton, remarked that the Norrington Table rating each college's success in final examinations, where Merton recently has always appeared near the top, reflects the colleges' relative wealth. Richer colleges can afford more fellows, and more generous benefits and allowances for those fellows, and so have a higher ratio of dons to undergraduates. No system of equalising the benefits for fellows within the colleges has been devised.

Apart from the new building project, another step I took was to encourage sport and particularly rowing at the college. Pembroke had last gone head of the river in 1872. It seemed to me that the performance of the Pembroke crews, both men and women, could be radically improved. Doing so I believed would have the advantage of improving students' good feelings about the college and also enabling women, only admitted eight years before, to share fully with the men in the college's sporting life. Rowing gave Pembrokians something in which to take pride. Each year after Torpids and Eights Week, it was a college tradition that the crews chalked up records of their exploits on the Cotswold limestone walls in the main quadrangle and year by year the list grew longer.

Fortunately we had a number of wealthy benefactors and in time they turned to me to guide their giving. One, a former Pembroke rower, was very much on my side and happy to provide the expensive equipment rowing requires. So we started off by getting new boats and then new oars and then professional coaching, and over the time I was there, the Pembroke crews steadily 'moved up the river'. Rowing is a complex sport – there is a lot of training and equipment – and so it lends itself to a systematic approach to improving performance. Whereas many other sports rely on the innate talents of a few individuals, success in college rowing is a team effort, and each crew member has to be disciplined, fit and strong. This planning had its effects. The men's crew did in fact go head of the river in 1995, two years after I retired. In 2003, Pembroke became the first college in which men's and women's crews were simultaneously head of the river. In 2012, the men's boat, stroked by a woman, went head of the river again.

On many a dank afternoon in Hilary term (between Christmas and Easter) Moyra and I would walk down the path beside Christ Church Meadow to encourage the Pembroke crews. Visits to the river were altogether easier during the summer as we approached the intense drama of Eights Week. On the first day of that week, to set the crews up for the trials ahead, the college laid on a splendid breakfast for them which I always joined. Our great rival was Oriel, which had enjoyed almost a thirty-year domination of rowing at Oxford, in part by attracting muscular Australians and other foreign oarsmen. For my last two years as Master, we had been runners-up to Oriel in Eights Week.

The Master's lodgings at Pembroke became our home all year round. Moyra was delighted with it from the outset and had it repainted in colours she chose and decorated with our own pictures and antiques. There were two main floors, each with large, high-ceilinged rooms, which provided plenty of space for all our social events and our children, Clive, Thurstan and Charlotte, would come up and stay. Erin was of course already living in Oxford, as her husband was the Professor of Immunology at Oxford.

From our lodgings, a door led out to a charming private garden that was carefully tended by the college's prize-winning gardener. Here we set up a swing and a croquet set for our grandchildren.

There were roses all over the place. On the advice of an expert we planted some eucalyptus trees which I now see are enormous and spill over the old city wall and are a cheerful green all year round.

The dining room had large windows overlooking the garden. During term-time we hosted two drinks parties a week, starting at six o'clock, for groups of students, but any don was most welcome. The lodgings had a very pleasant atmosphere, which we hoped contributed to happy relationships with the students, dons and the former members of the college who all often returned for social events.

Our closest friends were other heads of houses. They were mainly academics and former senior diplomats or civil servants, but also some eminent scientists. Several were new, as the typical term for holding office had become shorter. I was closest to those who had arrived about the same time as we did: Sir Claus Moser at Wadham (now Lord Moser); Barry Blumberg, a Nobel Prize winner, at Balliol; and Lord Briggs at Worcester, formerly vice chancellor of Sussex University, who had, with his wife, been friends for many years.

The other groups I came to know well were the teaching fellows at Pembroke, of which there were forty, ranging in age from twenty-five to the retirement age of sixty-seven. Among the honorary fellows were Rocco (son of Lord) Forte, Win Rockefeller and Sir Michael Heseltine (now Lord Heseltine). The number of students in Oxford had swelled considerably since I had first come up as an undergraduate, forty years before, when there were around ten fellows in many colleges. One of our more amusing fellows was the tutor in Latin and ancient Greek who had been recruited as a code breaker at Bletchley during the war, as so many young linguists were. He was Oxford's public orator for a decade and had teased us by asking our opinion on how he could describe a 'jumbo jet' in Latin, which he needed for his annual Encaenia speech.

As there was a yearly intake of 120 students, it was impossible to know all of them well. I had weekly meetings with the president and officers of the junior common room. These students were clever, politically quite astute and fought vigorously for their perceived rights, sometimes aggressively but often with good humour and at times with an impressive idealism. The head of a college has to be ready to receive their petitions. Handling them is often a matter of fine judgement. Some of their demands were impossible to provide. One of the most extreme was a scheme in 1986 to save money to arm the rebels in Nicaragua. They were welcome to do so, but of course could not involve the college or university in any way. It was a delicate balance, trying to be sympathetic to their enthusiasms but at the same time introducing them to an element of reality and the bounds of what was possible.

My links were closer to the junior deans, who were graduate students whose duty it was to be the first line of call in disciplinary matters. They could issue summary fines of £5 for minor offences such as littering, but if the offence was considered more serious, the student would be sent to the dean or even to me if the offence was particularly heinous.

There were a few isolated incidents that give the lie to the notion that being a head of house is just a glorified party. It requires vigilant contact with dons and students to pick up the first signs of trouble and respond to it. We did not find drug-taking to be a serious problem, though I had some worries about alcohol. One incident illustrating the relationship between students and the college authorities arose shortly after my arrival. The bar had come under the management of undergraduates and high-strength beer was being sold. We discovered that freshmen were being plied with excessive amounts of alcohol. It then transpired that the junior common room were in arrears in payment of VAT, to the tune of £20,000. We agreed to pay off the debt, but in return required that we should employ a professional barman, and he was to exercise a supervisory role in deciding whether a student had overstepped civilised bounds.

On the whole, student behaviour was good and sometimes they surprised me by their decisions. In a time of revolution in the late 1960s they had voted not to wear gowns in hall and my predecessors had accepted this. But then during my term as Master the students held another vote and returned to wearing gowns in hall. That is not to say that the traditions of hall were always respected. It was the procedure in the hall for one of the senior scholars to recite the Latin grace before dinner and I noticed the students began to gabble it more and more quickly. I discovered that there was a sweepstake on how short a time they could make it last! The next time a student started to gabble I reached out from my standing position next to him and, almost without thinking, I tapped him on the shoulder and said, 'Please start again and take it slowly.' He did and there were no more problems.

It was not just the students for whose safety and care we were responsible, but also our many guests. In one year I calculated that more than a thousand people had crossed the threshold into our lodgings. Some guests caused more disruption than others. We once had to provide extensive protection services for an honorary fellow who had spent time as a High Court judge in Northern Ireland, sentencing IRA criminals without a jury. In preparation for his daughter's wedding, dogs sniffed through our lodgings and sharpshooters were strategically placed on the chapel roof. We invited the bride's parents to coffee in our garden, where Moyra innocently asked, 'What are your interests?' The judge quietly answered, 'We loved playing golf – but we can't do that now.' The whole day brought home to us the personal price that had to be paid by so many in Northern Ireland.

I never anticipated when I started serving as Master of Pembroke that its administration would be plain sailing, but my previous experience in charge of the Sports Council, with its staff of five hundred and its high-profile and complex operations were a good preparation. I had not been responsible for an organisation for a while, or ever one in which the balance of power was so diffused as in the college governing body. The tasks at hand were highly unpredictable. Each morning I knew there were going to be surprises but had little idea of the direction from which they would come.

In another incident, my secretary phoned me one day from her office below my study in extreme agitation and told me in shock that outside her window there was a woman screaming, 'He's killing me!' I rushed down and discovered that no one had informed her that an episode of *Inspector Morse* was being filmed in the lodging's cellars, directly below her office, and the screams were part of a lurid crime that was being perpetrated. The filming of *Inspector Morse* was a minor source of income for a number of Oxford colleges. Soon after my arrival we rented part of the college for a remake of the film *Gaudy Night*. Our lodgings had one of the biggest coal cellars in Oxford. To create a convincing set they poured large quantities of coal into the now empty cellar. After they left getting them to remove the coal was no easy matter, particularly now that coal fires are illegal.

Moyra and I were delighted that by living in the lodgings in Pembroke we had the chance to see so much of our children and grandchildren. Erin's husband, Alain, was a junior research fellow at New College when we arrived and Charlotte came a few years later during her theological training. Hardly a day passed without Erin and her children dropping by, at least for a cup of tea. Though I was in and out of meetings in college much of the time, I could still watch the children read and play games indoors and out in our garden and prosper from Erin's creative and good-humoured nurturing. Moyra greatly enjoyed lending a hand, often by painting and doing crafts with them.

Every Christmas was a particular joy because the lodgings were big enough to include our extended family. We were sorry that we were not able to emulate what the wife of the famous Master, Jeune, had done each Christmas. She recorded in her diary how she brought blankets for deserving soldiers and sailors who had been sheltered in the Pembroke almshouse. A lasting memory is of those Christmases spent in the lodgings, specially decorated, with the college quiet, and work cares in abeyance and the family gathered, Clive up from London, Thurstan back from America and the grandchildren running down the hall, bursting with excitement about their still-wrapped presents.

Throughout the year, Erin and Charlotte generously invited us often to their homes to meet their young friends. Often we would have vigorous discussions on the topics of the day. This jolted us to see the world in another light. As an added bonus, the wide-eyed take on life given to us by our grandchildren was so refreshing. So many afternoons we strolled down that great Christ Church avenue of trees to see the river, ever vigilant that they did not fall in, so eager were they to feed the ducks. It opened an aspect of life in Oxford that was not entirely university-centred and it helped to show us an aspect of Oxford that otherwise might have been closed to us.

There is nothing to match the beauty of a college at night in winter surrounded by deep snow, when the windows of the college hall are reflected on the white ground and with the students wearing gowns filing into hall for dinner. It is a scene that could date from centuries ago.

I chose to retire in June 1993, because I considered that by then I had completed the tasks to which I had committed myself. It's a good rule to go when a task is completed and to leave the field open to a newcomer who one hopes can bring fresh ideas. I had helped to raise funds for the new building and it had been opened. Also the number of women holding fellowships and lectureships had gone up from none to seven, so that the college was beginning to become truly mixed, at the fellows' as well as at the students' level. I did not think that I was the right person to take on the next stage of fundraising. It was better that the fellows find a successor with fresh energy and their own briefing as to what the college would need.

It was a poignant moment to say goodbye to the college and our beautiful lodgings. The college had accepted my athletics trophies for display in the gallery of the hall. This reflected my concern that they be preserved together in one place, somewhere I had worked and to which I felt strong ties of loyalty, in the hope they might interest and even inspire some future undergraduates.

Shortly after I retired, President Bill Clinton came to Oxford to receive an honorary degree (he never received his undergraduate degree as he had left early to continue his studies at Yale). He was easy company and Moyra found it amusing to overhear my conversation with him discussing the benefits of having a personal trainer! As he stood in the Sheldonian Theatre and was greeted by a Latin oration, he joked, 'I've just been round Europe, and did at least think I would come to England and understand the language.' Little did he know that what he took to be hostile chanting against him by the students in the streets was nothing of the kind. They were carrying placards protesting at an increase in college charges, shouting 'Can't pay, won't pay'. My daughter Erin was at the time walking past the Sheldonian, having bought her seven-year-old son Barnaby some running shoes. By Clinton's bulletproof stretch limousine, Erin was suddenly stopped. 'What's in the box?' she was asked, brusquely.

'My son's shoes,' she replied.

The man, Clinton's security driver, softened. 'Would you like to sit in the President's car, son?'

As you can imagine, it made Barnaby's day. The same day, Clinton's entourage clashed a little with their Oxford surroundings. His smart, black-suited bodyguards, whose bulging pockets left no question as to their contents, cut imposing figures, but not imposing enough to put off a vigilant college gardener. He warned off a bodyguard from walking on a college lawn, who later remarked, 'What's this thing about Oxford and its grass?'

This was not the first time Moyra and I had shared the company of American 'royalty'. Of all the vivid times we can remember since we married, perhaps the most unusual was the inauguration of President Kennedy, to which we were invited as guests of Per Jacobsson, Moyra's father, then chairman of the International Monetary Fund in Washington, DC. On the evening of 20 January 1961, a snowstorm had brought Washington almost to a halt and the army was called in to clear the streets. From near the White House, we watched on TV as this hopeful, idealistic young President made the now famous 'Ask not what your country can do for you…' speech. At the inaugural ball that night we watched Jackie Kennedy come out to dance and the simple elegance of her ball gown outshone all others.

At another party we met Lyndon B. Johnson, a large, powerful man who almost crunched our hands as he shook them and, with that true politician's training, looked us straight in the face. Later that year, after the inauguration, Moyra and her mother were invited by Jackie Kennedy to tea at the White House, with wives of Treasury officials. As it turned out, Jackie never came but sent her mother-in-law and Lady Bird Johnson to be hostesses in her place.

I am very optimistic about Pembroke and Oxford's future and their standing in the academic world. Students coming to Oxford have the chance of a lifetime to try out different roles which might help guide them towards better choices in life. On the purely academic side, students are now selected by a very fair competitive process. In tutorials they will be trained in thinking by someone who cares about their future, in a way that exists in few other universities in the world. This, together with the weekly essay demanded, is of a high order of challenge. Another quite rigorous aspect of Oxford is the final examination process. This requires the student to take papers on all aspects of their course in about two weeks under strictly invigilated conditions. They require not only a global knowledge of a subject, accumulated from a three- or four-year course, but also, if the student hopes to be awarded a First, a spark of originality. This means the capacity to diverge from an accepted line of reasoning and to give original arguments to sustain a different point of view. The blistering criticism one of my dons gave to a student at Collections, the regular review at the end of term, was, 'He mistakes obscurity for profundity.'

One final project was sparked by Moyra seeing a 'for sale' sign on a garage in Brewer Street on the southern edge of the college. I had realised that any further expansion would need the purchase of this land and here was the chance of starting the process. I immediately rang my most generous British donor and he bought it, together with two houses which are now the Bannister Graduate Centre. I even got our architect to make drawings of a bridge with a classical design to connect the two parts of the college. Little did I know that twenty years later, under the Master, Giles Henderson, this task would be completed in a brilliant way. More land was bought and a new building the same size as the Grandpont buildings by the Thames would soon be completed, with a prize-winning bridge joining it to the main college. Every undergraduate can now be accommodated in the college. This is a triumph for the Master and Pembroke.

Chapter 17

Leeds Castle

I was made a trustee in 1985 and it became a major part of our lives.

The Castle in Kent was set like a jewel in the lake where long-necked black swans drifted sedately by. The whole view was always beautiful, but in a winter's snow, magical. The battlements and turrets were vividly outlined with blobs of snow, as though a giant had splattered ice cream everywhere. Why did our hearts lift as we drove through the gates? We greatly enjoyed our visits, jokingly calling it our 'second country home'. I had been invited to be a trustee in 1985, mainly to encourage the medical conferences which were held there according to the wishes of Lady Bailey's will, and I retired in 2010. Lady Bailey had married a rich American of Whitney aircraft engine fame and, as a widow, she had fallen in love with the now forlorn Castle. She bought it in 1929 and poured Whitney money into it; first she installed central heating and then she furnished it with paintings, four-poster beds, marble bathrooms and china birds. Birds were one of her passions; we rejoiced in finding an aviary as well as greenhouses, a vineyard and gardens that provided vegetables and flowers all year round.

In the 1920s and 1930s the castle filled up with a very glamorous, not to say racy, set of people. They included Noël Coward, Cary Grant, James Stewart and other actors and film stars. There was a private swimming pool, resembling that at the Astors' house at Cliveden, and guests would motor down at the weekend and enjoy hospitality on a lavish scale.

When the war came, the castle sobered up. Lady Bailey was generous and the doors were opened to the wounded servicemen. In particular, Sir Archibald McIndoe the plastic surgeon used the castle for the convalescence of his 'guinea pigs', the term he used to refer to the servicemen with severe facial disfigurement as a result of burns. The pre-war aura of parties vanished, just as the English queens, whose summer palace it had once been, had vanished without trace.

The Sunday lunches for trustees and their wives were often riveting. The chairman would invite ambassadors, politicians and distinguished guests from every sphere. Lord Aldington (formerly Toby Low, the Conservative politician) was followed by Lord Thomson, the Lib Dem peer, who, in turn was followed by Lord Armstrong, former Cabinet Secretary. And so it was that each of them introduced a different style to the gatherings. It was not all jollity, as on Sunday mornings the trustees would gather to keep the castle on a steady financial basis, deciding where it was possible to expand and improve where money allowed. All trustees grew to care very much about the castle and its future, and my particular contribution was organising medical conferences to tackle various problems of the National Health Service by drawing together a group of experts and then publishing their conclusions as a Leeds Castle medical conference. Moyra would often spend time painting there and delighted in all its aspects from friendships with the other trustees and their wives to an appreciation of the lovely surroundings.

Various images come to mind when I think of Leeds Castle. Araminta, Toby Aldington's wife, was a general's daughter with strong views about everything. She bred a particular variety of sheep and Lord Aldington wore a strange shaggy tweed suit made of their wool of this animal. He was engaged in a long running lawsuit, having been libelled by Nikolai Tolstoy over his role as the army officer responsible for repatriating Russian troops who had fought on Germany's side. After repatriation, many were killed by the Russians.

I remember Araminta shaking a somewhat somnolent Ted Heath to rouse him for the annual outdoor summer concert held in the open air with the castle as a backdrop. A rather grumpy and reluctant Ted Heath, and Moyra and I, sat on the back of a golf buggy and were driven through a vast picnicking crowd. Suddenly Heath was recognised and the cry went up 'good old Ted'. Plump and pink faced, he broke into a genuine beam of a smile and graciously waved as royalty might, regally turning from side to side. It was as if he were reliving the applause of a successful speech on the electoral hustings.

Only the orchestra was covered by the massive stage shelter but we were mercifully wrapped up warm in travelling blankets as the sun set and a chill mist inevitably crept up from the lake. The cannons of the Royal Artillery Regiment boomed out the finale of Tchaikovsky's *1812 Overture* before culminating like the Proms with 'Jerusalem'. There were high jinks at half-time and I once found myself waltzing with Betty Boothroyd (now Lady Boothroyd), former Speaker of the House of Commons, who had been a Tiller girl in her time. 'What fun and how improbable!' I thought to myself as we did our best not to fall on the uneven grass sward. By this time Ted Heath had cheered up, although, as the fireworks sprang to life, I heard him complain that one politically incorrect verse had been omitted from 'Rule Britannia'. It was vintage Ted of course. Back at the castle we warmed ourselves with hot soup. One year, the star of the summer concert was Pavarotti. Naturally the castle had to cede to the great man's whims. He apparently was a victim of night starvation and the director had to arrange to manipulate a sizeable refrigerator into his thirteenth-century castle bedroom!

Princess Alexandra was our patron when an intricate new garden was designed on the shore by the lake and she was invited to a grand dinner before an opening ceremony the next day. Moyra had slightly misjudged her clothing and pressed it into a small airport suitcase and realised it was not grand enough. I donned my dinner jacket quickly, as we were a touch late, having driven from Oxford. Moyra came out of the bathroom and found me sitting holding my head. 'I'm dizzy,' I said, 'you'd better tell them downstairs that I need a doctor.' In the hall, all was abuzz with that curious shimmering of a gathering expecting royalty. Moyra had to tug at the elbow of the son of a local MP who was the director of the castle and tell him, 'Roger's unwell.'

'What sort of unwell?' he asked. 'He thinks it's his heart,' Moyra replied.

A kindly local GP, who was Egyptian, came fairly quickly to our room, examined me, and immediately called for an ambulance. Moyra changed to her day clothes as we heard the sirens of an ambulance. The next embarrassment was that the ambulance got stuck at the drawbridge gatehouse and could not get up to the castle door. Mercifully, the princess had arrived by then and her two strong security officers carried me down the stone stairs and across the castle lawn to the ambulance. By then, sheets of rain soaked Moyra through as she followed. By this time the guests had gone into the dining room and the front hall was empty, so this drama could unfold in peace.

The ambulance sirens wailed all the way to the Maidstone General Hospital some six miles away. Moyra told me later the ambulance men were rather chuffed at having me on board. By the time I arrived at the hospital I really was feeling dizzy and ill and suspected I was in a state of atrial fibrillation. When the senior nurse approached, Moyra said, 'He's a doctor and he knows what's the matter. He thinks he's fibrillating.' With an ill-disguised ferocity she snapped, 'That makes no difference. He'll have to wait his turn.' I was wheeled into the only space available, a maternity cubicle, while we waited and waited. Moyra's anxiety mounted, until at last a fresh-faced doctor arrived and in a friendly way said he had heard that I was here and that he had been at school with one of Chris C's sons. At last the wheels started turning. They gave Moyra a sofa bed in the nurses' sitting room. I was indeed in atrial fibrillation and they tried various drugs to return my heart to regular beats, but they were all unsuccessful. The next day they had ominously lined up by my bedside an electric shock defibrillator pacemaker machine but just at that moment my heart spontaneously reverted to normal rhythm so this was unnecessary. A consultant cardiologist visiting the hospital confirmed that the right action had been taken. When our son Clive heard that I had been admitted to hospital he leapt into a London taxi and said, 'Drive me to Maidstone Hospital.' Never had we been more glad to see him. He had trained as a management consultant and it was not the first time or the last time he has taken charge of our situation, and it was a relief that some of what we were experiencing could rest on his broad shoulders. Our children have never let us down in a crisis. In particular, many years earlier, he took charge after our car accident until handing us over to our daughter Erin's heroic nursing. I must say, after that first unhappy encounter, the hospital staff came to the rescue superbly and compassionately and I am very grateful to them.

Chapter 18

Retirement

After retiring as Master of Pembroke in 1993, my remaining responsibilities were my links to the National Hospital and St Mary's, where I was chairman of the Development Trust, and as a trustee of Leeds Castle.

When Moyra and I left the Master's lodgings at Pembroke, we moved to north Oxford, to a flat on the ground floor of a large redbrick house in Victorian Gothic style. Our house was originally built for tradesmen or for dons, who, as the requirement for celibacy ended in 1882, were able to marry. This created the demand for large family houses, which were built on the north Oxford estate owned by St John's College. Our high-ceilinged sitting room, ideal for parties, has large south-facing windows that look out on our garden and, across the road, to the Dragon School, England's largest preparatory school. We decided to build a conservatory and Moyra has returned to her painting. The Dragon is one of four schools on our road and we both enjoy the clatter of young feet and the sound of excited voices.

Our lives are greatly enriched by having friends in all age groups, from octogenarians to young children. As our grandchildren finished at the Dragon School each day, they crossed the road to our home, where we would fill them up with food and supervise their homework, though we were baffled by modern maths, and our Latin proved to be rusty. We enjoy watching the comings and goings of parents and children and the rugby games and sports days on the school fields which border the Cherwell River. A favourite stroll is to the Cherwell boathouse, a starting point for undergraduate punting expeditions.

Our time was equally divided between Oxford and London for several years. After we sold No. 16 Edwardes Square, we bought a flat in Pembroke Court, a 1930s-built mansion block only fifty yards away from No. 16 on the south side of the square. Our children often used it as a temporary haven while they moved flats or houses. It was on the third floor and its sitting room had bay windows at each end, the north-facing one overlooking the whole square, and sitting in the window alcove one felt surrounded by trees. In a winter mist, we could see nothing but white outside, which evoked an uncanny sense of detachment from all the other buildings and indeed from London altogether. Our affection for the square continued to grow. Its gentle character, founded on its austere Georgian architecture, is even now hardly changed, though there are fewer young families than in 1964 when first we arrived. Though so close to the West End, the square is very peaceful, especially at night, the terraced houses forming a barrier to noise from the main roads nearby.

The flat was our jumping-off point in London for seeing Clive, Charlotte and their families, setting out on cultural forays, visiting friends, going to parties and attending other functions and committees. We regularly went to lectures at the Medical Society of London and the Athenaeum, and art exhibitions that excited our curiosity, being determined that in our retirement our lives should be filled with such explorations on top of all kinds of social events.

In May 1999, we suddenly felt the time was right for a real celebration. It was the year of our forty-fifth wedding anniversary, seventieth birthdays and the forty-sixth anniversary of the four-minute mile. I told Moyra that in retirement I had never been happier. There was for the first time no burden of worry about responsibility for institutions or committees in which often I had been at the mercy of forces or people beyond my control. Despite Moyra's pleading with me not to worry about these things, saying they would turn out all right in the end, it was part of my character to do so nonetheless. It was also a great relief to stop making major public or college speeches. Another element was finally having the time to enjoy leisurely social talk, to remember friends, to follow my children's careers and families, and no longer feel compelled to curtail a visit or dinner to return to my desk.

The time also marked six years since we left Pembroke, and where better than Oxford, we thought, to gather our friends and family with whom we wished to celebrate. We invited 120 people for a sit-down lunch in Pembroke on 9 May. All four of our children attended, along with our three eldest grandchildren.

The sun shone as we greeted our guests to the cheerful sound of the jazz band of our son-in-law, Professor Alain Townsend, FRS. We held the reception in Broadgates Hall, the most ancient part of the college. It was a slight squash but ensured that everyone had to chat to their neighbour. It was in this room with stained glass windows and oak panelling, containing Dr Johnson's desk, where fifteen years previously I had taken the oath of office as Master of Pembroke.

Our guests came from the different spheres of our lives. My great friends from athletics were there: Chris Brasher and Chris Chataway, Norris McWhirter, whom I had first met fifty-two years before, and Ronnie Williams, a fellow miler on the 1949 Oxford and Cambridge American tour. John Disley from the Sports Council, then Asa and Susan Briggs, Claus and Mary Moser and other heads of houses from Oxford. There were friends from Lyminster in Sussex, where we had our country cottage, as well as those from my time at St Mary's Hospital and the National Hospital, Queen Square, the colleagues with whom I worked, including some of my senior colleagues.

Our route from Broadgate's to the hall was through our back quadrangle and up the steps, where every guest signed our decorated visitors' book, the third since our wedding. What delight it gives us to look back on these pages and indeed the myriad photographs. There were so many people gathered in that great hall who had hugely enhanced our lives, with past Masters including me looking down benignly from the portraits on the panelled walls and the twinkling of silver. Following family tradition, the men all moved two places clockwise round their tables before the dessert, causing much hilarious confusion. It was forty-six years after the first four-minute mile and a huge cake topped with marzipan figures of Chris C, Chris B and me. It was cut by all three of us holding a Finnish ceremonial sword, which had been given to me with an honorary degree.

The proceedings ended with three speeches. Norris McWhirter, one of my oldest comrades and a stalwart help in my running days, in his speech recalled my parents and their passion for education and the way my mother had feared that my athletics would interfere with my medical studies. We would later grieve at his death in 2004. I often had sharp disagreements with his political views but he always took it in good part and never failed in his generosity, keeping me up to date with athletics and world affairs.

I had felt faint at the start of the party, suspecting that I had a second attack of an atrial arrhythmia (shortly afterwards it was found that I had intermittent atrial fibrillation). I had warned Moyra that she should tell my doctor friends who were present in case I started to feel worse and also I suggested she should speak instead of me. Our son Clive had arranged that the whole party should be filmed from the gallery so there is a record of Moyra's excellent speech. It came from the heart, thanking all of our friends and our children. Clive, as the older son, then wrapped it up in his usual buoyant way and presented us with a silver tray engraved with the names of all our guests.

At the turn of the millennium we sold the Pembroke Court flat and have since spent most of our time in Oxford. In retirement, heeding Churchill's advice that a man should do something with his hands, his brain and his body, I joined a wood-carving class, evolving from the easiest animal, a hedgehog, through to a leaping dolphin, a cat and finally an elephant. All of these now sit proudly on our mantelpiece, though pose no threat to endanger my wife's artistic career, which is busier than ever. As my early studies of philosophy as a medical student were unsuccessful, I have pursued my interest through the Oxford University Department of Continuing Education and the University of the Third Age. But I still find puzzling the lack of curiosity of former Greats graduates about modern neurophysiology.

In that same year, 2000, I started a book club which still flourishes to this day. Many express surprise that it should be a continuing success, but the members have become close friends. Each in turn chooses a monthly book and the meeting is in the form of a tea party at their home. The number of books now exceeds 100 and extends from the rather heavy Burke's *Reflection on the French Revolution* to cheery tales like Ben Macintyre's *Agent Zigzag*, encompassing poetry, history and novels in between.

And, rounding out the trinity of hands, brain and body, I started a walking club in the same year. There was already a women's walking club in Oxford, of which the leading light was Jill Butler, wife of Robin (now Lord) Butler, former Master of University College. So we felt that a men-only walking group would be appropriate. We once had a joint walk at Stowe with Jill's group, but they complained that we walked too slowly and never invited us to join them again. Another problem was that they brought their own sandwiches, which we regarded as a totally inadequate substitute for a pub lunch and a pint of beer. We have twelve members and meet every month; one member plans the walk and notifies us of the meeting place. This is usually in the car park of the pub he has chosen for lunch afterwards. At first we walked about six miles, but in ten years the length of the walk has become shorter and some of us are now lunch-only members.

Of our children, Erin, besides being a professional painter who has had three solo exhibitions in London, the latest in Cork Street, is the proud mother of five children. By curious coincidence, our other three children have all married Americans. Clive, now chairman of an insurance group and of the London Museum, married Marjorie, a talented entrepreneur who had invented Wax Lyrical, which eventually spread to fifty-two candle shops. They have three sons. Thurstan, also in the financial world, lives in New York and has two children and his consuming hobby is cycling immense distances with friends. Charlotte and William Parker, a fund manager, have four sons. Charlotte, an Anglican priest, has held parish, college and university posts. She has worked for thirty years in emerging countries and now chairs a pan-African youth charity. These grandchildren, whose ages range from eleven to thirty-two, keep us well in touch with the younger generation.

Chapter 19

The Modern Olympic Movement and London 2012

When the Belgian Dr Jacques Rogge succeeded Juan Antonio Samaranch as president of the IOC in 2005, he said in a speech that the Olympic movement was in crisis. In truth, the modern Olympics have suffered many crises, starting with its hijacking by the Nazis at the 1936 Berlin Olympics.

The worst one that I recall was in the 1968 Mexico Games, when 260 protesting students were killed and a further 1,200 injured after clashes with armed forces just ten days before the Games were due to start. These Games also saw the famous 'Black Power' protest by the American runners Tommie Smith and John Carlos, who raised their black-gloved fists on the victory podium as the Stars and Stripes was played to celebrate their medals. The Olympics had become too tempting a platform for protest.

This was followed by the tragedy of Munich in 1972, when eight members of the Palestinian 'Black September' movement seized and held eleven Israeli athletes hostage, all of whom eventually died along with five terrorists in a bungled attempt by the German police to rescue them. Avery Brundage, then president of the IOC, stopped the Games for twenty-four hours out of respect for the dead Israelis. The Israeli Prime Minister Golda Meir then privately ordered a systematic hunt by Mossad and over the next few years all the Palestinians involved were killed.

The Olympics are still a symbol to many of Western culture and in the build-up to the Beijing Olympics there were worries about the safety of the Games after Islamic terrorist activity had previously targeted the West. Concerns also arose about possible violent protests over China's poor human rights record and their continued suppression of Tibet.

The argument for allowing China to host the Olympics was that the nation had been excluded from international sport for over twenty years after withdrawing from the Olympics following the Games in 1952. Now, with a fifth of the world population, China could no longer be ignored by the Olympic movement. When I was chairman of the Sports Council I remember well at Heathrow in 1973 meeting the first Chinese team to compete in Britain. I greeted them beside their plane with some phrases in Chinese I had asked the Foreign Office to prepare for me. Throughout 2008, Rogge had to walk on eggshells trying both to preserve the Olympic movement's ideals and at the same time to remind China of the private agreement to respect 'human rights' that his predecessor had included as part of the deal to allow China to be the host nation.

The other crisis cited by Dr Rogge in 2008 was doping. Many of us still have memories of the scandal of East Germany in the 1970s achieving, per capita, more than ten times as many Olympic medals as the United States, supposedly proving the effectiveness and the superiority of the Communist regime. In fact, though suspicions abounded throughout, proof was only clear after the Berlin Wall fell and the Stasi records showed

30,000 East German athletes were given anabolic steroids which fuelled their extraordinary performances. Often the drugs given to the athletes were described as 'vitamins'. Excessive doses resulted in the masculinisation of some women. With the fall of Communism, several German athletes have successfully sued the state and some of the administrators of the system have been indicted and served suspended prison sentences.

Rogge's predecessor, Samaranch, had neglected to face the extent of athletes' drug abuse. He appeared to feel that recognition of its pernicious and widely pervasive influence would be bad news for spectators and sponsors, who would never know whether the victories they saw were triumphs of individuals or drugs. In essence, he swept the issue under the carpet. After all, Ben Johnson was the first high-profile Olympic athlete caught, at the Seoul Olympics in 1988, and fifteen years later there was still no organised scheme for random testing.

In the build-up to London 2012, the same issues, performance-enhancing drugs and violent social protest, were still a threat. I have never thought or said that sport and politics in the modern world can be separated. London is a more obvious target for Muslim extremist terror attacks than Beijing: the city is seen as a great symbol of Western culture and power and the organisers did not have the luxury of their Beijing counterparts of calling on the Chinese government's more extensive security forces. The worldwide media and internet coverage drawn by the Olympics creates a potentially explosive mix which no president of the IOC has the capacity to prevent. The multiple bombing inflicted on central London the day after it was announced as host city was said to have been a day late by mistake, originally aimed at catching the jubilant masses who had packed into central London to hear the announcement. Sebastian Coe told me that from the start of the torch relay to the last day of the Paralympics, his greatest source of concern was a terrorist attack.

Nor was the problem of doping resolved. There was a continuing dispute over the participation of British athletes who had previously tested positive for performance-enhancing drugs. Lord Moynihan, president of the British Olympic Association (BOA), wanted a stricter rule than the IOC, banning from the Olympics for life those athletes who had been caught doping (the IOC rule only banned athletes from the next Olympics). The proposed rule by the BOA was overturned by the Court for Arbitration for Sports in Lausanne, with the result that sprinter Dwain Chambers and cyclist David Millar could compete. From a British perspective, there were worries that this showed a tendency by the IOC towards lax treatment of athletes caught doping and a failure to face up to the extent of damage it caused to honest athletes, not to mention the credibility of the Olympic Games.

A different problem that became more apparent after Beijing, in the build-up to London 2012, is the cost and size of the task that confronts any Olympic host nation. The Athens Games in 2004 have been cited as one of the triggers that led to Greece's financial crisis several years later. Financial clouds lowered over the London Olympics all too soon. The £9.4 billion budget seemed very high at the time, notwithstanding the long-term value of transforming toxic and derelict sites in the East End into a permanent park. It is to the organisers' credit that costs were kept under control. The naysayers saw the Olympics as a useless festival of sport just adding to the nation's sorry debts. Besides, they said, the capital's ageing infrastructure would never cope with the influx of Olympic tourists and the city was bound to grind to a stop. Some London residents almost boasted that they were going to let their homes and go abroad, proud not to watch a single event. When given the opportunity, I optimistically assured doubters of the Games' intrinsic worth, of the lasting benefits both for sport and for the restoration of this barren, uninviting patch of London's East End, criss-crossed by fifty-seven electricity pylons, polluted canals and scarred by derelict factories.

The arguments about the cost continue. China spent $40 billion on their Games, Britain £9.4 billion. It was also reported that China, now suffering from a relative downturn in its economy, in a recently organised championship, presented their winners not with expensive gold, silver and bronze medals, but bunches of artificial flowers!

One potential solution might be to prune the Games back to their bare minimum to reduce the host city's burden. At present, the Olympics are required to accommodate twenty-six sports, 10,000 competitors from 204 countries, 10,000 or more journalists and cameramen, and crowds of hundreds of thousands. Only half a dozen countries in the world are now wealthy enough to host them. Perhaps surprisingly, Brazil and Rio de Janeiro have agreed to host 2016. This will be the first visit of the Games to South America but violent social protest has already occurred over whether the Rio Games are affordable. My view is that, despite their manifest success in London, the IOC's requirements for infrastructure and venues may well have to be scaled down if attractive cities are to bid to host future Games.

Should we reconsider the scale of the torch relays or prune some of the events and the opening and closing ceremonies? Certainly Rogge's opening shot when he became president was to resist applications to include more sports by saying that no new sport could be included without the demise of an existing one.

In spite of all the apprehension about the 2012 Olympics, what springs to mind are images of unbridled celebration. I particularly remember the crowds jumping for joy in Trafalgar Square in 2005 when they heard the one word from the president of the IOC in Singapore – London!

In 2010, Sebastian Coe invited Moyra and me to tour the Olympic site. It was a fascinating experience. Canals had been dredged and broadened, soon to be navigable again by barges and pleasure-boats. The power lines had been laid underground and vast tons of polluted soil had been detoxified.

That same morning, television crews surrounded me and I praised the huge improvements, citing the great promise it held for the future. This was a heartfelt belief I maintained throughout all the television interviews and to friends and acquaintances.

The expectancy had built up to a crescendo over the preceding months, starting with the Queen's Diamond Jubilee in June. In a mood of patriotism, everyone bought Union Jacks and bunting until the shops sold out, and toasted the Queen at their street parties. Staunch British reserve had started to break down. In Oxford, the heavens opened and we were forced to adjourn the party to the Dragon School's hall. 'This,' I said, 'is the only time I have ever opened a street party indoors.' In London, millions turned out to watch the Queen's flotilla process down the Thames. (The only unfortunate outcome was that Prince Philip came down with a brief illness after his brave exposure to the wind, rain and cold while aboard the royal barge.)

Three weeks later the flags were brought out again as 8,000 Olympic torch relay runners, selected for their services to the community, were, to my pleasant surprise, greeted again by enthusiastic, waving crowds, who cheered them all the way around the British Isles. The Olympic torch came through Oxford just a few days before the opening of the Games. At 7 a.m. on the chilliest of mornings, at the Bannister track, the gallant chancellor, Lord Patten, handed me the torch, watched by Sebastian Coe and my family. Despite the cold I managed to light it and I carried it all of ten yards before handing it over to the official university runner who would take it on its way to London. What a change it all was from the misery of the Beijing Olympics torch relay which had to be accompanied by soldiers protecting the flame from angry civil rights protesters, sometimes even if it meant running through towns in America at four in the morning. My torch is now glinting from the wall of the sitting room, to the general delight of the family.

After the opening ceremony, hitherto strangers, now unashamedly enthusiastic, were talking to one another, finding common ground to chat on buses and trains and joining the atmosphere of celebration.

A few critics continued to cast doubt upon the enterprise, being particularly outraged that the army had mounted heat-seeking missiles on flat roofs near the site in case of a terrorist attack from the air, though it was unclear what the strategy would be if such an attack occurred. The collapse of the company organising security guards incited the media to further criticism about poor organisation.

What then happened? Servicemen and women were drafted in to fill the gap and this proved to be one of the great success stories of the Games. After the most rain-drenched summer ever recorded, the sun came out and everyone was guided to their venue by cheerful squaddies as well as uniformed volunteers – the Games Makers – whose helpful attitude was faultless.

We had been invited to the Guildhall on the afternoon of the opening day, to a reception mostly for foreign delegates but also for MPs and ministers. The room at the Guildhall is ranged about with emblems of Britain's glorious past. Moyra had her drawing block as usual and quietly sketched a statue of Nelson with an improbable Neptune at his feet. George Osborne made a warm businesslike speech welcoming all the foreign delegates. Boris Johnson, as Mayor of the host city, could not let the moment go by and gave a disjointed but hilarious oration. I don't think that the Bulgarian delegate standing beside me understood a word of either speech.

After the reception, several buses sped us through London down the Mile End Road, which still desperately needs a facelift, to the venue at Stratford. As we passed security, Moyra and I were helped by volunteers onto the back of a modified golf buggy. As we whirred our way through the crowds towards the stadium we heard George Osborne, walking alongside us, say to Christine Lagarde, head of the International Monetary Fund, at his side, 'There's the man who broke the four-minute mile.' Whether this meant anything to her, I cannot be sure.

Though some journalists had expressed doubts as to our ability to stage a good opening ceremony, the show received universal praise. I have now attended nine Olympic Games and it was far and away the most humorous and imaginative opening ceremony I have seen. Everyone gasped as a double of the Queen fluttered down from the helicopter and momentarily disappeared before cameras then showed the Queen in the VIP box, shortly to declare the Games open. I did wonder how they had persuaded Her Majesty to take part in this scene. Meanwhile the kaleidoscope of villagers playing cricket watched by milkmaids under a windmill was replaced by the chimneys of the satanic mills of the industrial revolution. Danny Boyle, the impresario, gave us a waltz through Britain's socio-economic history. It was all delightful, with glimpses of Mary Poppins figures floating down, while we heard the voice of Sir Kenneth Branagh, dressed as Isambard Kingdom Brunel, delivering Shakespeare's lines from *The Tempest*: 'Be not afeared; the isle is full of noises / Sounds and sweet airs that give delight and hurt not'. Foreign visitors may have been a little puzzled by our celebration of the National Health Service but everyone laughed at Rowan Atkinson's 'Mr Bean' mocking parody of the opening sequence from *Chariots of Fire* when the teams run along the beach.

The ancient Olympic Games which survived for more than 500 years started as a religious festival, winners being regarded by the spectators as favoured by their gods. In the London Olympics the preordained hero was Usain Bolt, whose muscular elegance carried him nonchalantly to a new 100m Olympic and world record of 9.63 seconds. He even had time to look round at the finish line as if to ask, 'Where are all the other competitors?' To the delight of the 80,000 spectators he then mimed shooting an arrow into the sky. I suppose for many, Usain Bolt was enacting their own dreams, however improbable. Those who were there will surely relate this moment to their grandchildren. I felt it was a celebration not just of Usain Bolt or of sprinting, but of humanity itself.

As the Ancient Greeks knew, this union of body and mind, of straining for physical perfection, is also a form of cultural expression. For me it was a transforming experience, renewing my belief in the ideals of fair competition standing above the tawdry aspects of sport, such as drug abuse.

True to his promise, Dr Rogge, the president of the IOC, introduced the most comprehensive ever drugs-testing programme for the competitors. The former director of the notorious BALCO labs, Victor Conte, who specialised in synthesising anabolic steroids which he claimed could evade detection, came to London to 'work with' American sprinter Ryan Bailey. He claimed in an interview that six out of ten top sprinters had been taking prohibited performance-enhancing drugs at some stage in their training. I doubt that he is right, though I accept that some competitors are still trying illegally to boost their performance. In any case, all the 5,000 or so samples taken during the Olympics will be kept and can be analysed in the future for any drug for which at present there is no effective test. If positives are found then athletes can be retrospectively stripped of their medals and are likely to be given a life ban.

Without question the outstanding British men's athletic champion was Mohamed ('Mo') Farah, who announced proudly to the press, 'I'm British even though I was born in Somalia.' Until these Games his athletic career had been a troubled one – always the bridesmaid, never the bride. Often he would set the pace and perhaps try to sprint away from the rest of the field two laps from the tape, but his competitors always seemed to catch up with him on the last lap and out-sprint him. Then in 2005 Farah put himself in the hands of Alberto Salazar, the Cuban-born three-time New York City marathon winner. Since then his performances have been transformed. He ran with supreme confidence in the World Outdoor Championships in 2011, taking the 10,000m from the Ethiopian team with a blistering last lap of 53.4 seconds, which would have done credit to the last lap of a 1,500m race. In 2012, after Mo won the 5,000m he was given a Union Jack and did a lap of honour. Then, memorably, his eight-year-old daughter ran onto the track and he swept her up in his arms and gave her the flag. By winning both the 5,000m and 10,000m he performed a rare double for these exhausting races, only a week apart. He has now joined the list of great distance runners, alongside Paavo Nurmi of Finland and the Czech Emil Zátopek.

The outstanding British women's athletic performance of the games was indisputably Jessica Ennis's. At only five feet five inches tall, she is less than ideally suited to several of the events in the heptathlon. In London she achieved her personal best in three out of the seven disciplines and, despite not being as well suited to middle distances as she is to sprinting, she won the final exhausting 800m with yards to spare.

I watched the men's 1,500m (only 120 yards short of a mile) together with Sebastian Coe. This was the race at which he was double Olympic champion at the Moscow Olympics in 1980 and the Los Angeles Games in 1984. The pace was slow for three laps and there was much jockeying for position, each runner trying to remain unblocked for the final sprint. The eventual winner was Moroccan Taoufik Makhloufi, who had been controversially disqualified for 'not trying' in his 800m heat. The disqualification was revoked by the force of a doctor's note, which stated he had a knee problem, though one which apparently didn't prevent him from taking the gold medal in the 1,500m!

We reflected on the natural advantages of being born and living at altitude. It gives East African middle-distance runners the great advantage of being able to transfer oxygen more efficiently than athletes born at sea level. They also tend to have a high percentage of the 'slow-twitch' muscle fibres which can contract repeatedly and efficiently and so require less oxygen. Sadly, the days of British and European supremacy of the middle-distance races, which lasted nearly 100 years, therefore seem to be over. For the athlete born at sea level, even the remedy of sleeping in a low-pressure chamber, as Paula Radcliffe did, cannot always make up for other natural advantages the East African runners possess.

There was one track gold medal that was insufficiently heralded at the time. I have never seen a middle-distance runner in an Olympic event lead from start to finish, showing perfect pace judgement and breaking the world record. A 23-year-old Kenyan, David Rudisha, achieved this in the 800m final. He finished in a remarkable world record time of 1 minute 40.91 seconds. The reason world records are rarely achieved in middle-distance races in the Olympic Games is that the fields are so crowded that there is too much jostling for position. To protect themselves from becoming boxed in and hence unable to escape when the field takes off in the last lap, runners are forced to run wide and so end up running extra distance. Running just one lane out adds around 5m per lap. Rudisha is still young; with his astonishing speed and tactical maturity, I believe he could become one of the greatest track runners of all time.

Credit for crossing a sporting class social divide went to Charlotte Dujardin, a truly gifted equestrian Olympic champion. She was born to a family of modest means in Enfield, brought up in Bedford and received a comprehensive-school education. She was in no position to be able to afford an international competition-standard horse, which can cost upwards of £100,000, to correspond to her talent. Her perseverance and ability drew attention to her need and a horse was eventually lent to her. On Valegro, she won individual and team gold in the dressage.

Credit for courage of a special kind should go to the Saudi Arabian Sarah Attar, the first woman from her country ever to compete in the Olympic Games. She forced her selection in the face of religious and political prejudice and, not surprisingly, came last in her heat of the 800m but received as much applause as any winner. This marked a turning point in the Olympics in that there are no longer any countries that do not allow women to represent them at the Games, irrespective of other laws which may repress them.

A week later, the next wonder which astonished the world was the unprecedented support of the spectators who came to cheer the Paralympics. There were more Paralympian competitors than ever before. Previously, spectators' inhibitions seemed to restrict their popularity and they drew only a few viewers. It was as if spectators found it difficult to confront disability. But in London, crowds of up to 80,000 gathered. Dr Guttmann, the founder of the Paralympics, had always hoped they would eventually take an equal place alongside the able-bodied Olympic Games, and in London the margin was narrowed further than ever.

It is possible that the London 2012 Paralympics have changed the attitude of the whole country to disability. It is so much more important to concentrate on what the disabled can achieve rather than what they cannot achieve. In a country with more than one million chronically disabled citizens unable to work, we must hope that some, inspired by what they saw during the Paralympics, may feel empowered to return to some work within their capacity and that many more of us may be inspired to help them do so.

The triumph of the Paralympics was unbounded and brought to mind past stories of athletes triumphing over disabilities and handicaps in the Olympic Games long before the Paralympics were launched. Harold Connolly, the US hammer thrower, won a gold medal in Melbourne despite having a very weak left arm

from a birth injury. Karoly Tabaks from Hungary, in 1936, won
a gold medal in shooting at the Berlin Olympics. The next year,
after an accident, Tabaks's right arm had to be amputated at the
wrist. He still won gold medals in 1948 and 1952 having learnt to
shoot with his left hand. Liz Hartell of Denmark, aged twenty-
three, had an attack of polio which left her with such weak legs
that she had to use crutches when standing and walking. She
won Olympic equestrian gold medals in 1952 and 1956. These
disabled athletes competing years before the Paralympics existed
had to develop different neurological patterns. To do so required
powerful motivation and sustained perseverance. These are just
a few examples that expose the fallacy that such severe disability
should have made them abandon sport. They changed their own
destiny by making defiant and heroic decisions to continue.

The most memorable performance of the 2012 Paralympics
was that of Ellie Simmonds. She is an achondroplasiac dwarf,
four feet six inches tall with a perpetual smile. She first won
spectators' hearts at the Beijing Paralympics when she won gold
medals aged seventeen. In London she won two gold medals in
the freestyle 400m swimming and set a new world record for her
category of disability.

※

It is far too soon to judge the overall legacy of the London
Olympics. One thing is certain, however: in terms of Olympic
medal count Britain is undisputedly the third most successful athletics sporting nation in the world after America and
China. When account is taken of the size of Britain's population by comparison with those of China and the United States,
the achievement is even more remarkable. The final total of

Britain's Olympic and Paralympic medals was 185, sixty-three of them gold.

Young people watching these feats of skill, endurance and sometimes heroism can now say to themselves, 'If Jessica Ennis and if Mo Farah can do it then I can do it too.' One of my granddaughters worked for the Teach First movement in Tower Hamlets, a deprived London borough near the Olympic site. In 2005 the school was under 'special measures' – it was in danger of closure because it was underachieving. A large percentage of the children are on free meals, one of the measures of poverty. In the build-up to the Olympics, she took a group of children and started a sports programme at the local sports centre. This programme has been linked with an improvement in the academic performance of the children involved so that the school is now deemed outstanding. Moyra and I went to their first ever sports day, held for Comic Relief, to watch the valiant runners of the mile. One little boy seemed to want to go on running for ever, and had to be persuaded that the race was over. This initiative inspired very many parents to come, some of whom had not visited the school before.

Not sufficiently recognised is the part played by the wise use of government and lottery funding in our Olympic success in 2012. Over the past fifty years, official funding has provided sound coaching and administration for some eighty amateur sports, including all twenty-six Olympic sports. Giving grants to athletes with real talent means that they do not have the distraction of having to earn a living for the few vital years while they are at their sporting peak. The rigid amateurism was finally abandoned by the IOC in 1986, and the effects as far as the West is concerned are there for all to see. Our best athletes are now full-time professionals, following the earlier example of Russia and Eastern Europe, but without the use of drugs. After years of taking a critical attitude towards these Eastern countries, we have recognised the need for compensation and full-time training. There is a simple equation: access to the right facilities, plus financial support, plus a large pool of ability, plus coaching and much hard work by the athletes themselves, brings medals. Australia proved this before the Sydney Olympics, but then abandoned financial provision and has since relapsed, finishing in London 2012 without a single gold medal in track and field, and with just seven overall, dropping from fourth to tenth in the medal table. Medals are not everything, but they are the easiest indicator of a country's standing in sport.

Luck of course plays a part in sporting success. It was that great golfer Gary Player who, when congratulated on his luck, replied, 'Yes, but you know, I've found that the harder I practise the luckier I get.' Generous funding for sport makes luck more likely to happen.

There seems to be minimal time given to specialist training for competitive sport, particularly in state schools. With the overwhelming workload to get through, this is understandable, though unfortunate. Most worryingly, the way PE is taught generally seems to put so many children off participating in sport at all. The origin of this problem lies back in the 1950s, when several specialist physical education training colleges were closed down. This was coupled with a theory that sporting competition was in some way undesirable and this inevitably led to its downgrading. Now few primary schools have a specialist PE teacher. A prejudice against competitive sport was linked to the idea that competition was 'bad for character'. My own impression is that children find a variety of organised competitive sports exciting and, except for a few, take the ups and downs of success and failure well.

In the last two decades there has been a burgeoning interest in sports medicine, led by the British Association of Sport and Exercise Medicine (BASEM), of which I was the patron for many years. This field had been the Cinderella of clinical medicine and surgery because it covers so many specialties, including cardiology (for instance, sudden cardiac death in sport) and the multitude of orthopaedic and soft tissue injuries. It took some years to win over the UK government, as it is reluctant to see the introduction of new specialties, fearing increased claims for special funding. In 2008 the government finally consented to create a new Faculty of Sports Medicine within the NHS. The Royal Colleges of the United Kingdom have laid down training procedures, recognised training appointments and the first consultants have been appointed. This brings the UK up to the level at which this specialty is recognised in other countries, particularly in the USA and Germany. A telling argument used to promote this specialty has been the generally poor treatment at present of trauma in sportsmen and women by consultants. Telling an athlete with a muscle injury to rest for six weeks is unacceptable. The prospect is that this new specialty will spread expertise and indirectly improve the treatment of traumatic lesions for people in general, allowing them to return to work sooner, which could result in greater cost savings for government.

If Britain can organise such a successful Olympics, can it not capitalise on this success and use the support of the volunteers who came forward so willingly to become Games Makers and then made up for the deficiency in the official security services? Could they help run competitive sports programmes both in schools and outside school at weekends? What is needed is enough school activity to spot high natural talent and then direct the young athlete towards a local sports club that offers skilled coaching. It is very good news that Lord Coe has been made a special sports adviser to 10 Downing Street. No one could be better qualified to supervise the planning of the legacy of the London Olympics and Paralympics.

Chapter 20

The Future of Sport

The legendary manager of Liverpool Football Club Bill Shankly said: 'Some people believe football is a matter of life and death … I can assure you, it is much more important than that.' Of course, he is wrong, but sport does at times require a temporary cessation of disbelief – for example, when we watch Usain Bolt sprinting.

My fascination with sport has grown steadily over time. My own involvement was first as a competitor, swept up in the rich pattern of success and failure, those twin imposters. Then, for a time, I was a part-time journalist and I have had the chance to watch nine Olympic Games first-hand. In the 1970s I saw sport through the eyes of an administrator, as chairman of the first independent sports council, through which government money and later the National Lottery money was passed on to elite athletes. Through all of this, I have seen men and women achieving fulfilment, though like all human activity, sport is beset with human failings that can never be entirely eliminated. Life is full of ups and downs, as the whole world knows.

Organised sport only became a mass interest in the last century. Britain's love affair with sport has reached a recent crescendo since the triumph of the London Olympics in 2012, followed by successes of the Lions rugby team, Murray at Wimbledon and the Ashes team in 2013. The British team at the World Championships was led by Mo Farah and Christine Ohuruogu. The future looks bright as well, because Britain took first place in the European youth championships in Italy in 2013. Could we be on the threshold of a new golden age of athletic sport?

Speculation is running high about whether in 2015 Mo Farah can run a marathon in less than two hours. Farah has proved himself currently the best in the world over 5km and 10km out of a pool of perhaps 10 million aspiring runners worldwide. He has run a really fast 1,500m, beating the world record set up by Steve Cram in 1983, but he remains an unproven force at the marathon distance and I'm afraid it may be outside his range.

The world's current best marathon performance (there is no official world record because the courses are all different) is 2 hours, 3 minutes and 23 seconds, by Wilson Kipsang of Kenya. To achieve the sub-two-hour marathon would require running more than twenty-six miles, with each being on average at a 4-minute 35-second mile pace. This would represent a 2 per cent improvement over the current record, a lower margin than the ones by which several other world records have been broken in the past. (Probably the greatest margin post-war was 6 per cent, achieved by Bob Beamon in the long jump at the 1968 Mexico City Olympics.) I believe the 2 per cent improvement needed for a sub-two-hour marathon is physiologically possible, but it will require the conditions to be just right.

In my view it is very unlikely such a marathon will be achieved in an Olympic race. Record-breaking requires special conditions which the Olympics do not provide. In any case, I believe that by the Olympics of Rio de Janeiro in 2016 the barrier will already have been broken, if not by Mo Farah then by someone else. Indeed, Farah has created a particular difficulty for himself in Rio. He has declared that he will attempt the triple gold medals of the marathon, 10,000m and 5,000m, only previously achieved by Emil Zátopek of Czechoslovakia. My concern is that he will be exhausted by the heats and finals of the shorter races by the time he steps onto the marathon start line on the last day of the Games.

I predict the first sub-two-hour marathon will be achieved on a course without hills, on a warm but not too hot day, somewhere around 18–23°C, without wind. Wind slows the runner more than it helps on a circular course, but on a straight course, such as that of the 1908 London Olympics from Windsor to White City, a prevailing west wind would be an advantage. The aspiring record-breaker would be greatly helped by pacemakers so that the anxiety of achieving even-pace running was lifted from him. Once the two-hour marathon barrier is broken I would think that many others will also achieve the feat within the next few years; the psychological barrier will have been snapped.

❧

The distinction between amateur and professional in sport disappeared when it had outlived its usefulness, rather like Mr Bunbury in *The Importance of Being Earnest*. Though it had a complex history, by the 1960s the distinction between amateur and professional was honoured more in the breach than in the observance. Perhaps the most objectionable phase was the class

distinction between 'gentlemen' and 'players' at cricket. Dr W.
G. Grace, though qualified as a doctor, was in all senses a full-
time cricketer, functioning as a professional. His presence in a
match might attract thousands more paying spectators. One day
when he was bowled out first ball and the umpire held up his
index finger signifying that Grace was 'out', Grace walked over
menacingly to the umpire and said, pointing to the crowd, 'You
see all these people, they came here to see me bat not to see
you umpire.' The umpire changed his verdict to 'not out' and
Grace then returned to the crease and resumed his innings.

The cause célèbre in the 1920s was when Grace Kelly's father
was designated as an 'artisan'. He was in fact a millionaire
builder but was therefore considered a professional and ineligible
for the Henley Royal Regatta. When his daughter Grace Kelly
became a Monaco princess by marriage, the absurdity of this
class distinction seemed obvious to all.

During the Second World War, in athletics, brilliant mile world
records were set up by Arne Andersson, Lennart Strand and
Gunder Hägg. However, they were eventually declared professional for receiving payment of more than the maximum value
of trophies, which was then about $20. Finland had a reputa-
tion for 'shamateurism' and even of trapping foreign runners,
something of which I had to be particularly careful. Finland,
dare I say it, would not have been troubled by the removal of a
Bannister from international competition!

The respected US writer Paul Gallico, when he retired in the
late 1930s after fifteen years as a top sports journalist, wrote in
his book *Farewell to Sport*, 'Amateurs, there ain't none.' On retirement from sport he wrote the famous children's story *The Snow
Goose*. He was wrong in that the millions who play sport at a
lower level for sheer enjoyment are truly *amateurs*. It is only when

sportsmen are so gifted that people will pay to watch them that the situation changes. The sports promoters naturally want to persuade the talented sportsman to grace their 'meet', for which they are the impresario. At the same time, the athlete knows that his presence will increase the 'gate', perhaps by $20,000. The athlete and impresario are likely to seek mutual advantage and find some illicit way round the strict amateur rules.

In America, in 1951, I won and was presented with a cup worth about $5,000, which I handed back for it to be replaced by a tiny copy worth $20. The biggest and most valuable trophy some sponsors of an event wanted to persuade me to accept was a Lincoln Convertible worth around $15,000. Imagine me turning up at St Mary's Hospital as a medical student in a Lincoln! Later, after Vancouver, US promoters offered me unimaginable sums to run in various meets around America as a professional.

The president of the IOC who tried to hold the amateur line was Avery Brundage, known also as 'Slavery Avery', a reference to his effort to keep athletes as 'slaves' to amateurism. He was also, because of his short fuse, known as 'Umbrage Brundage'. He handed the presidency to Lord Killanin, a man of the world who had worked for Shell International. Killanin was more relaxed about the rules. In the 1970s, athletes could finally receive high sums if they declared them and placed them in a trust fund from which they could withdraw money, provided it was broadly used for legitimate expenses connected with their sport. This interpretation was sufficiently liberal for them to include, for example, car ownership and even property rent.

An early sign that the amateur/professional line could not be held came as early as 1947. We received visits from athletes and teams from Iron Curtain countries' teams who were all nominally amateurs, serving in the army or the post office, but who were in fact full-time state-owned athletes, a little like the gladiators in Rome, when the romance of the Ancient Greek Games had faded. A Soviet Dynamos soccer team toured Britain as early as 1947 and trounced the First Division Sheffield by ten goals to nil. At the time, most English soccer players were part-time professionals, often earning a minimum wage of £20 a week. It irked the country to see the British team beaten by full-time athletes. The eventual changes to the rules levelled the playing field and our athletes could compete, as it were, without one hand tied behind their backs.

The next battle to be fought was over drugs. Record-breaking was absurdly unfair for a period of twenty years, thanks to drug-taking in certain events. The Iron Curtain countries continued to cheat until the fall of the Berlin Wall in 1989 by evading the drugs ban. East Germany created a series of world records, some of which may never be equalled by drug-free athletes. There is a case for all such records to be accompanied in the record book with the statement 'achieved before random drug testing and therefore suspect'.

The question continually arises about elite athletes – is their success the result of their genes or of hard work? The answer is obviously both, but the balance of views on their relative importance has swung either way among experts over the last few years. Sporting genes have now been discovered, and certainly play an important part in an athlete's success, but this is counterbalanced by the effect on fitness and skill of thousands of hours training. Genes and hard work may also be intertwined: for example, a gene for perseverance helping an athlete put in the hours needed.

Take Tiger Woods. At first he appeared to be a golfing genius due to his genes, having a father who was a professional golfer. However, this was thrown into question when it emerged that his father first put a miniature golf club in his hands when he was aged two and his practice time before the age of fourteen exceeded Malcolm Gladwell's magic 10,000 hours, the supposed requirement for sculpting a 'prodigy' from any clay. When studied, many so-called prodigies from the musical world turned out not to be due to genes but part of the hard-work school; on average they had also spent 10,000 hours practising throughout childhood. Examples like this led to the 'Tiger Mother' syndrome, the pressures of which have sometimes had terrible consequences for the mental well-being of children.

Many personality traits, including perfectionism, obsessiveness and ambition, may be inherited and are elements in top athletes' ruthless determination. Neurologists have become interested in how much repeated activity can actually change the nature of the brain. It was a surprise to researchers when brain scans of London cab-drivers showed in each an enlarged hippocampus, the part of the brain concerned with orientation. This was not present in a control group of drivers who were not cabbies. (A further control test, studying relatives of the taxi drivers, has not yet been completed.) The question is whether the adult brain can still learn to make corresponding changes in the brain's trillions of nerve endings, reflecting complex learnt tasks.

In 1996, an American neurologist wrote a book entitled *Why Michael Couldn't Hit*. Michael Jordan had been the best basketball player in America for more than ten years, and one day, bored by his success, thought he might try his hand at another sport and chose baseball, which he had played as a child. However, his performance with a bat proved dismal, implying that his brain had adapted to one sport in a way that would not be carried over to another. My hunch is that the brain's formative years for developing excellent skills in a sport are between twelve and twenty. Jessica Ennis recommends children should not specialise but instead experiment with various events and sports. As they grow to maturity it will be obvious to them and their coaches which event suits their physique and skill and gives them the greatest pleasure.

Sometimes I am asked, 'Was your own running career based on your genes or hard work?' In a way, this is unanswerable, as both factors were involved. Starting with the genetic side, it certainly helped to be more than six foot tall and with long legs relative to my torso. Also, my father was a strong runner. To my knowledge, he only ran in one race in his life – the mile competition at Colne Secondary School in 1905, which he won. He was a very modest man and never told me of this athletic success until, aged eleven, I pestered him to see what was written on the medallion he wore on his watch chain. It simply said, 'Winner: R. Bannister, Colne Secondary School, one mile.' This medallion is one of the most prized exhibits in my collection of medals and trophies. On the other hand, any natural advantages would have been all for nought without rigorous training, in my case based on intensity rather than long hours.

My impression is that a large percentage of our population never approaches the sporting potential of which it is capable. Sport for All is a great idea and exposes many to the health benefits and the enjoyment to be had from sport. But the talent and training needed for an Olympic final is a step too far for almost everyone. The factor most needed is a sense of ambition, and who knows how this is triggered? (The late Chris B was fond of quoting the Browning line 'A man's reach should exceed his grasp. Or what's a heaven for?') Children may be taken by their parents, as I was, to watch some great sportsmen in action. Some return from the stadium filled with dreams of glory but never quite turn these thoughts into action. Let me list the steps they might choose to take instead.

First, you need friends to make the hard work of training if not enjoyable then at least tolerable. Second, you need to find a good coach by joining a specialist sports club.

Then, before making a choice of sport, you should follow Jessica Ennis's advice to 'try everything'. You should be judicious in selecting your event, taking into account your physique, time available and access to local sports clubs.

If you choose to be a runner, I believe you have to learn to harness a certain primeval aggression inherited from our earliest ancestors which persists though we no longer hunt wild animals. The 'fight or flight' adrenalin system helps us to excel, though it has to be kept under firm control.

The remaining steps follow the usual principles of living: collaborate with others whenever you can; share acquired learning and experience; and learn from failure. Use the trial-and-error method to make decisions about how you should train under the advice of your coach. Your coach should be neither authoritarian nor mysterious. Choose one who can set alight fires of ambition and perseverance within you.

Sometimes I am asked what I would do differently if I was starting my career today. The world has moved on and only certain athletic events would be open to me today. The training demands on international athletes have risen exponentially since the 1950s. The demands placed on medical students have also increased, so, sadly, if I were starting out today, and placing my medical career first, I would probably choose to compete at club rather than international level.

It would of course be very unfair to burden my grandchildren with any expectation of athletic success. Each has a set of special qualities and I am very proud of them all. It so happens that two of the fourteen have achieved particular sporting distinction, although all of them have absorbed from their early training some interest in and love of some sport and exercise. One grandson is on the British team for paramotoring, a form of powered gliding, and won a bronze medal in an international event. Another has already represented Britain in the GB under-18 rowing squad, winning a bronze medal at an international event. He will doubtless in time decide the level to which he may pursue his rowing.

❦

The sad truth about drugs in sport, as with other human activities, is that cheating has always been a temptation in one way or another and some have succumbed. The difficulty, as with banking in the city, is in rooting out the cheats. Even the ancient Olympic Games in Greece were not immune from cheating. When judges discovered it, the athlete was expelled from the Games and had an effigy of his head put on a plinth, recording his offence, and the names of his family and the city he had disgraced. The series of these effigies lined the route to the Olympic stadium.

My own attitude to the use of drugs stems from my training as a doctor to protect individuals from harm. I succeeded the neurologist Lord Brain on the Committee of the Department of Health and Home Office on Drug Abuse in the 1960s. We were then concerned particularly with the recreational use of cannabis and though I voted against it, the majority of the committee voted for the reduction of penalties for using cannabis.

One early piece of research convinced me of the extraordinary drug risks athletes are prepared to take in pursuit of their ambitions. In the 1960s an experiment took place in California. A group of student-athletes was asked, 'If there was a drug which significantly enhanced your athletic performance, but the medical side effects of the drug would cause your death in two to five years, would you take it?' The majority of the sample said 'yes'. The researchers were surprised and asked why. The reason most of the sample said they would take the risk was because they felt they could rely on subsequent advances in medicine to prevent any fatality. The research implied that if penalties for taking banned drugs were lifted, young athletes would themselves experiment and unwittingly run various dangers of self-administration.

Realisation of the widespread drug abuse in sport came to me when I was the chairman of the Sports Council. So I arranged for a chemist at a London hospital to devise a radioimmunoassay urinary test which detected anabolic steroids to less than one part in a million. I confess that it is one of my most disappointing failures that it took fifteen years before random testing was introduced and nearly twenty years before the first positive result. In 1988, Olympic sprint champion Ben Johnson, a Caribbean-born Canadian, was stripped of his Olympic gold medal at the Seoul Olympics after testing positive for the anabolic steroid Stanozolol. Why did it take twenty years? The president of the IOC at the time was Juan Antonio Samaranch, who felt that positive drug tests in the Olympics would deter spectators. When I was asked to lecture at the IOC headquarters in Geneva on drug abuse, Samaranch introduced me. I suppose he had been told that I would be critical of the IOC and would support strongly the idea that compulsory, rigorous and repeated out-of-season testing was the only way forward. But Samaranch evidently did not want to hear me as, after his introduction, he left, so I understood, to go to a football match! I took this as a snub. Fortunately, Samaranch's successor took the opposite view. When Dr Rogge assumed the presidency of the IOC in 2005, he announced that detecting drug abusers would be one of his highest priorities. True to his word, we have seen a much more effective attack on the problem since he took office, but the difficulties are very great.

There will always be a battle against the use of performance-enhancing drugs at the Olympics or in other international competition. Drugs are taken in training as well as in competition, hence the vital importance of out-of-season testing. This is despite large sums of money having been expended to detect and punish offenders. Testing centres are now under the supervision of the World Anti-Doping Agency (WADA). Sadly, the chemists are still ahead of the testers.

The choice of drugs varies between sports. In high physical performance sports like cycling, where sustained muscular effort is at a premium, erythropoietin (EPO) is used to increase the numbers of the red cells in the blood which carry oxygen. Cycling has had a bad reputation for many years; sometimes whole teams were caught during the Tour de France, either taking EPO or giving themselves transfusions of blood, either their own or that of other riders, extracted after training at altitude or taking drugs. Lance Armstrong, winner of seven consecutive Tour de France races, has now ceased to deny the allegation that he used drugs for the whole of his career. Sir Dave Brailsford, the current manager of the British cycling team which includes Chris Hoy,

Chris Froome and Bradley Wiggins, has made every effort to ensure that it is clean.

Since the 1980s, the use of human growth hormone (HGH) became well established in the US body building communities. Dan Duchaine's *Underground Steroid Handbook* stated in 1982 that people who use it can be expected to gain '30–40 pounds of muscle in ten weeks'. As had happened before, the athletes got there before the scientists. HGH was used by US high school male students who wanted to improve their physiques. An early problem was that HGH was prepared from cadaver pituitary glands and carried the risk of transmitting the ultimately fatal prion-induced Creutzfeldt-Jakob brain disease, also a rare complication of operations on the eye and the use of contaminated instruments in neurosurgery. Pituitary-derived cadaver HGH is still available today on the black market. A case of caveat emptor, if there ever was one! A prominent early supplier of the safer synthesised HGH was Victor Conte, owner of the Bay Area Laboratory Cooperative (BALCO). In 2006 he supplied the American Olympic sprinters Tim Montgomery and Marion Jones with HGH, as well as anabolic steroids. Both received bans and Marion Jones a six-month jail sentence for falsely denying administering herself performance-enhancing substances. Conte was imprisoned for four months for his role. On our own shores Dwain Chambers was banned but his confession, including the use of HGH, was an attempt to overturn a lifetime Olympic ban. This was successful and he returned to competition in the London Olympics. An official enquiry into doping in baseball in 2007 concluded reasonably that HGH abuse was so widespread because it was still undetectable.

Peter Sonksen, a biochemist from the University of Southampton, has devoted the past twenty years to perfecting tests for HGH. There is no problem with blood testing for drugs and he has a test which detects HGH within a fourteen-day window from the last dose. He has collaborated with WADA, established in 1989, and the IOC Medical Commission's Sub-Commission on Doping and Biochemistry in Sport. Below these bodies are the testing laboratories of different countries, which are subject to regular scrutiny, and then the international and national governing bodies of each sport designate which tests are to be undertaken on which athletes. Unfortunately, Professor Sonksen was not able to receive the necessary further funding for his research, for reasons that were never made clear to him, and so his apparently successful test was not used at the Sydney Olympics in 2000 or any subsequent games until the London Games in 2012 when two Russian Paralympians were caught using HGH. This failure of funding took place around the time of the change in the IOC presidency from Samaranch to Rogge. Meanwhile, the IOC and WADA have been working in conjunction with Italian and American colleagues on a different method of HGH testing.

Several new aspects of testing give the testers a welcome advantage. The first is the right to save all specimens and subject them to further retrospective testing when a new drug is 'discovered'. This is a very powerful tool in the hands of the testers and helps determine the length of ban. The women's world-record holder and Olympic champion Belarusian shot-putter, Nadzeya Ostapchuk, tested positive in London in 2012. A retrospective test on a specimen from 2004 was retested and proved positive. She received a one-year ban after her coach admitted to spiking her coffee. The frequently used claim by the drug offender is that it is a first offence. Retesting of earlier specimens shows this is often not the case.

The second aspect of progress is the rule that evidence of any tampering with a specimen by an athlete or someone influenced by him automatically results in that specimen being counted as positive (i.e. containing evidence of drugs). The third is the strict liabilities rule. This means that any athlete is responsible for any banned substance in their body fluid. The fourth improvement is the use of passports in which the athlete's hormone profile is established.

A note of caution is merited on the banning of athletes convicted of a drug offence if the positive result is borderline. This is especially the case for hormones such as testosterone because the normal range can be wide. What is normal for one subject may be high for another, so careful judgement is needed before banning the athlete. This is the reason why it is now necessary for top athletes to have a 'passport' in which the profile of the individual's hormones is established.

The true incidence of drug-taking is difficult to establish. In the last Olympics in London, there were 6,000 tests on athletes, of which nine were positive. We must hope that fewer elite athletes are now prepared to take the increasing risks of being caught. Some athletes might well take the view that they prefer to forgo a gold medal and to have the distinction of being, say, an Olympic finalist, rather than be disgraced as a cheat in front of their family, friends and fans for the rest of their lives.

In deciding the length of ban after committing an offence, a distinction can be made between two types of offender. The first is the mature competitor who is taking anabolic steroids and deliberately trying to cheat the testers. The second is the young or naive athlete who has perhaps been advised by a coach or fellow athlete to take a nutritional supplement that later proves to be contaminated by a stimulant.

Other thorny questions arise. Should not the doctors or coaches who administer drugs to their charges have to pay a price for aiding and abetting the offence? So far no method has been devised to do this. If an athlete has won $1 million on the Grand Prix circuit and is then convicted for drug use, should he not repay his winnings to aid the high expense of drug detection programmes? Runners who have been pushed into second place in the Grand Prix circuit would also have a valid claim to the cheating athletes 'purse'. There are of course no direct financial gains for Olympic winners but many later indirect benefits accrue.

Eternal vigilance is the price that will have to be paid for success in the war against drugs. This includes employing the best chemists to outwit the cheats and their coaches and chemists. Attempts to cheat using drugs must be expected to continue. Life is never perfect. But, as testing becomes ever more rigorous, more cheats are being taught the lesson that the odds of being caught are getting higher all the time, and so going down the drug route is not worth the candle, especially given the lifelong stigma for the athlete, having betrayed the trust and faith of his family, friends and young supporters around the world.

Chapter 21

Final Words

Sport and medicine have a vital and expanding role in improving the lives of individuals across the world. These are the twin tracks that have run through my life. I feel very grateful to have been given the chance to make some contributions in both these fields.

Sport, aside from bringing me some great friendships, has enabled me to play a part in a kind of revolution, of far larger numbers of people running or taking part in other types of recreation throughout their lives. It lifts my heart to see, all over Britain, a surge of people of all ages running half- and full marathons. The London Marathon and Great North Run have in fact become the biggest foot races in the world.

Our children are taught a lot about the wars of the twentieth century and will learn more during the centenaries of the terrible battles of 1914. But we should perhaps also remind them that many more lives have been saved by medical advances than were lost in all these wars, through better treatments and drugs, including penicillin, the first of the antibiotics. Now not a month goes by without some new medical discovery being made to help mankind.

I am proud of having become a doctor and of the two London hospitals at which I worked: St Mary's, a great teaching hospital, and the National Hospital, a pioneer in my chosen field of neurology. One of the most fulfilling aspects of my life has been to work at these hospitals with so many kind, gifted and dedicated colleagues.

As I sit in my living room in Oxford, looking out often at the same blustery weather as almost beset my efforts on 6 May 1954, I reflect on the multitude of things for which I am so grateful that have occurred in the sixty years since that day, and in the twenty-five leading up to it. Aside from those in sport and medicine, the ones that come most to mind are the experience of living in this free and civilised country, the company of friends and being part of a loving family. My great hope is for progress and continuity in this quite English way of life, so as many individuals as possible are afforded similar opportunities for happiness and fulfilment.

Acknowledgements

My sincere thanks to my editors, Sam Carter and Olivia Beattie; to my literary agent, Peter Bennett-Jones; to Jamie Ptaszynski; and to those who helped me so cheerfully with typing, notably Lil Jackson and Catherine Huckstep. It is a pleasure to acknowledge my thanks to our son Thurstan, who assembled an unpublished *Letters to My Grandchildren*, which gave impetus to *Twin Tracks*. Lastly, to my dear wife Moyra, my stalwart companion through testing times.

Index